STANDING UP TO BIG NICKEL

Standing Up to Big Nickel

The Story of the Mine, Mill and
Smelter Workers' Strike, 1958

ELIZABETH QUINLAN

McGill-Queen's University Press
Montreal & Kingston • London • Chicago

© McGill-Queen's University Press 2025

ISBN 978-0-2280-2480-4 (paper)
ISBN 978-0-2280-2493-4 (ePDF)
ISBN 978-0-2280-2494-1 (ePUB)

Legal deposit second quarter 2025
Bibliothèque et Archives nationales du Québec

Printed in Canada on acid-free paper that is 100% ancient forest free
(100% post-consumer recycled), processed chlorine free

This book has been published with the help of a grant from the Federation for
the Humanities and Social Sciences, through the Awards to Scholarly Publications
Program, using funds provided by the Social Sciences and Humanities Research
Council of Canada.

Funded by the Government of Canada   Financé par le gouvernement du Canada | Canada   Canada Council for the Arts   Conseil des arts du Canada

We acknowledge the support of the Canada Council for the Arts.
Nous remercions le Conseil des arts du Canada de son soutien.

McGill-Queen's University Press in Montreal is on land which long served
as a site of meeting and exchange amongst Indigenous Peoples, including the
Haudenosaunee and Anishinabeg nations. In Kingston it is situated on the territory
of the Haudenosaunee and Anishinaabek. We acknowledge and thank the diverse
Indigenous Peoples whose footsteps have marked these territories on which peoples
of the world now gather.

Library and Archives Canada Cataloguing in Publication

Title: Standing up to big nickel : the story of the Mine, Mill and Smelter Workers'
strike, 1958 / Elizabeth Quinlan.
Names: Quinlan, Elizabeth (Assistant professor), author
Description: Includes bibliographical references and index.
Identifiers: Canadiana (print) 20250130025 | Canadiana (ebook) 20250130122
| ISBN 9780228024804 (paper) | ISBN 9780228024941 (ePUB) | ISBN
9780228024934 (ePDF)
Subjects: LCSH: Strikes and lockouts—Miners—Ontario—Sudbury—History—20th
century. | LCSH: International Nickel Company—History—20th century. | LCSH:
International Union of Mine, Mill and Smelter Workers—History—20th century.
| LCSH: Nickel mines and mining—Ontario—Sudbury—History—20th century. |
LCSH: Working class—Ontario—Sudbury—History—20th century.
Classification: LCC HD5329.N532 1958 Q56 2025 | DDC 331.892/8697332—dc23

This book was designed and typeset by Sayre Street Books in 10.5/13 Sabon.
Copyediting by Louise Piper.

McGill-Queen's University Press
Suite 1720, 1010 Sherbrooke St West, Montreal, QC, H3A 2R7

Authorized safety representative in the EU: Mare Nostrum Group bv, Mauritskade
21D, 1091 GC Amsterdam, the Netherlands, gpsr@mare-nostrum.co.uk

Contents

Figures

Preface

In a shy corner of Canada that doesn't often clamour for attention, more than half a century ago, fourteen thousand miners and smeltermen downed their tools and walked off the job. Newspaper headlines flashed across the country, catapulting these members of the Mine, Mill and Smelter Workers (MMSW) union in Sudbury into the spotlight. Their strike against the International Nickel Company (Inco) occurred just prior to the 1960s, the era of rebel community politics, anti-colonial struggles, and the women's, civil rights, and anti-war movements that saw young people in particular experiment with new radical political practices capable of democratizing both the state and the economy. But the miners and smeltermen who struck against the giant Inco in 1958 had no such political and social currents to buoy them up in their struggle. Furthermore, they faced a cornucopia of conditions that made their struggle daunting. For one thing, the country was in the grip of an economic recession and the government of the day was intent on kick-starting the economy by urging employers to refuse workers' demands for wage increases. For another, the ubiquitous Cold War politics sent left-led unions like MMSW running for cover at the same time that corporate Canada was intent on pushing back workers' gains made during the war. And perhaps most significantly of all, there was a stockpile of nickel accumulated by Inco. A fundamental knowledge passed down to every miner and smelterman then, as now, was that striking against a stockpile was pure folly.

Over the course of my decade-long research of the 1958 strike I combed through thousands of archival documents, collected accounts from over 150 participants, and made a thorough study of the relevant literature. Guiding my endeavours were these questions:

1 Who were the thousands of miners and smeltermen who struck
   against Inco and why did they take such drastic action under
   conditions that couldn't be any more likely to lead to failure?
2 In the highly charged Cold War atmosphere, the MMSW union
   leaders were branded as subversives and enemy agents. But
   when the historical record is reviewed and the veil of the
   Cold War rhetoric lifted, what kind of men are the union
   leaders revealed to be and what were the principles driving
   their actions?
3 How did they manage to stay sensitive to their union's historical commitment to working class struggle and simultaneously
   conform to the postwar capital-labour accord that legally
   required union leaders to dampen d,;own dissent amongst their
   memberships?

This work explores these questions from the standpoint of the
strikers and their families, firm in their sense of self-worth, daring to
shut down the world's largest nickel producers for more than three
months against such improbable odds.

––––––––––

As a very young child, I was fascinated by the trinkets, buttons,
pins, and small mementos in the top drawer of my father's dresser.
Playing with dolls was less interesting to me than exploring the
contents. Precariously perched on a stool, my eyes, then my hands,
rolled over each item in succession. The MMSW button was especially captivating. Its small, embossed images of a hammer, pen,
and bar from the hand-drill once used by miners representing
labour, education, and industry. I would pluck the button from
its place in the drawer, climb down from the stool, and begin my
parade throughout the house. Clutching the button firmly in my
fist, I would bellow, "I'm a Mine Mill and Smelter Worker; I'm a
Mine Mill and Smelter Worker," each stomp of my feet coordinated
with the next syllable of the chant. Not around, but up and over
my parents' bed, I went. Through every room, up and down the
stairs of our split-level bungalow, my vocal cords echoed the tone of
that militant call for dignity, justice, and a living wage. At the age
of three, I was enchanted by the cadence of the repeating phrases,

the magic of babble that precedes meaning. I was too young to know exactly what was at stake for the Inco workers but I would have heard the animated discussions that preoccupied my parents. In tense, anxious tones, the problem of how the household finances would withstand the cut in my father's paycheque was turned round and round. I had not yet grasped that my father was not one of those Inco workers, yet the sacrifices the strikers were making were somehow the same sacrifices my family was making and their fight was our fight. Later I would learn that because my father was on the staff of the union, his wage was cut in half during the strike. As I took to my parade through the house at the time, my older brother would report to our mother, "she must think she's six feet tall and hairy all over." Winning a strike would be as much a triumph for my family as for the miners and smeltermen, a struggle that would require each one of us to declare our willingness to forgo comforts, perhaps even necessities.

The story of the 1958 strike stretches back beyond my amorphous memories of that time. With few exceptions, I did not meet the Inco workers and their family members. Yet the events that shaped their lives also shaped mine.

The Gouzenko revelations kicked off the Cold War in Canada in September 1945. No sooner had the World War II vets returned to Canada to begin preparing for the future than this other war with far-reaching destructive influences commenced. The Soviet Union, an ally in World War II, suddenly became the enemy, and continued to be so until its collapse forty-four years later. In Canada, Igor Gouzenko, a cipher clerk in the Soviet embassy in Ottawa, presented the RCMP with thirteen names of alleged Soviet spies in early September 1945 just days after the end of World War II. Sporting his trademark protective mask, a cross between an executioner's mask and KKK-styled headgear, Gouzenko found fame on radio and television with his accusations. The scandal led to a royal commission and the use of draconian police powers to arrest and put to trial those who were implicated in Gouzenko's allegations, which included Fred Rose, Sam Carr, and other members of the Communist Party of Canada. Based on Gouzenko's testimony, a royal commission warned the Canadian public of Canadian communist operatives who were receiving political directives from Moscow to infiltrate every aspect of Canada's social fabric by seizing control of organizations such as labour unions.[1]

The paranoia and fear of the Cold War were infectious and bred plentiful ersatz criteria for spotting subversives. Participation in any one of hundreds of popular causes supported by the communists became an easy way to finger firebrands. The inferences became inescapable, so anyone too closely aligned with loosely defined communist causes was unpatriotic, a traitor to be added to the public blacklist of militants. A whisper out of the night or a name similar to another suspect could ruin a career, a life.

Over the years, my curiosity about the consequences of the Cold War on people's lives led me back to my parents' lives. The story of the Inco strike began as a personal pilgrimage to understand the lives of individuals like my parents who made sacrifices in order to hold fast to their principles of justice, equality, and peace at a time when those principles were considered subversive. I was eager to find out what motivated them to challenge the taken-for-granted assumptions about the world, what it had to offer, and what we owe each other. How did they have the courage to question those seemingly immutable assumptions? And furthermore, how did they sustain their motivation to find the small cracks in our social institutions that might be made into spaces where people could flourish? By the time I began the study of the strike, both my parents had departed and I regret not asking enough questions when they could still answer.

Existing accounts of the Inco 1958 strike tend to privilege the sensational aspects of its aftermath: the jurisdictional battles between MMSW and a rival union, the United Steelworkers of America (USWA) that came to a head in the first years following the strike. But at the pivotal time of the strike, Inco workers confronted harsh realities and difficult choices. There would be much to learn, I felt, by taking the standpoint of these workers and their union in a sequel that represented the way events unfolded where the outcome was not known, a fundamental condition of the very act of striking. In most accounts of the strike, it is defined as a failure and during the interviews I conducted many participants spoke of the settlement as "only pennies." However, I came to the study of the strike as social-historical recovery and a sense of wonder about what it could reveal in the aftermath of the entrenched positions of the Cold War. At a personal level, it is a kind of origins story for me of seeking to understand loss and sacrifice, the revelation of roads not traveled, and the swell of courage needed for adversity.

When my mother, Ruth Robinson (née Cotter), contracted the Spanish flu at age one, the attending physician told her parents to have a photo taken of their beautiful baby because she was not likely to survive. To everyone's surprise, she recovered. Her triumph over the illness was a foreshadowing of the many other times in her life that she would defy the prevailing wisdom.

With the outbreak of the war in September of 1939, my mother set aside her plans to pursue graduate studies in social work at the University of Toronto, where she had graduated with a bachelor of arts the previous spring and took a job with the newly created Wartime Prices and Trade Board in Ottawa. My father, Lukin Robinson, also demonstrated his willingness to make sacrifices early in his life: as a member of the Canadian ski team, he refused to compete in the 1936 Olympics held in Germany because of the gathering dark clouds of fascism.

My parents met in Ottawa while they both worked for the federal government and were married in November 1941. Both were active in the Civil Servants' Association of Ottawa and progressive social movements during the 1940s. Subsequently, they moved to New York for my father's job in the Population Division of the United Nations (UN). His employment there was cut short in 1952 when he was fired for his activities in organizing the UN staff. Representing himself before the UN Administrative Tribunal, he challenged the dismissal. The resulting judgment in the *Robinson v. The United Nations* case included an award of $6,990 in compensation, but more importantly, the tribunal acknowledged a key element of Lukin's defence – by firing him, the United Nations was guilty of violating the Declaration of Human Rights, which the UN itself was solemnly and fundamentally pledged to uphold. My parents then moved their young family to Sudbury in the fall of 1952 when he became the first research director for the Mine Mill and Smelter Workers' Union. There my mother joined the union's women's auxiliary, a group considered important enough to be infiltrated by the RCMP, as the Mounties would admit only forty years later. When that news story of the RCMP's surveillance broke in the early 1990s, I asked my mother how the informants maintained their cover within the auxiliary. "Did you not notice the informants as you were baking off the muffins or sewing the costumes for the next performance of the union's theatre troupe?" Her answer came with her usual pronounced practical wisdom: "Yes, there were a few suspicious characters hanging around, but if we had confronted them and revealed their identity, they probably would have been replaced by others who wouldn't have been so easy to recognize."

Trained as an economist, my father readily took to the job of the union's research director. He regularly produced economic reports and market analyses for the union's oral presentations, written briefs, and submissions to government bodies. His briefs advanced the union's recommendations for strengthening Canada's economy through unrestricted international trade, improved purchasing power for workers, and expanded public works for full employment. His reports sounded the alarm about the growing US economic penetration, a trend particularly acute in the mining industry; and he called attention to Canada's unfavourable balance of trade (the excess of imports over exports) as being contrary to the country's national interests. As part of his job as research director, he also taught shop stewards at the union's annual steward schools in Ontario and BC, prepared materials for conciliation hearings, wrote articles in the union's newspapers, gave radio broadcasts in both French and English, and delivered presentations to arbitration hearings. During the strike, his economic analyses were used by the union leaders for their decision-making on matters of timing, strategy, and potential outcomes of the strike.

The book is an account of real people and events, shaped by both oral and written primary sources. The 150 plus interviews, email messages, and letters I accumulated capture first- and second-hand accounts of lived experiences of the 1958 strike. The participants included retired Inco workers, their wives, small business owners, union organizers, and the adult children, grandchildren and other relatives of the strikers, as well as union staff and church officials. The contextual factors that shaped the lives of the participants are drawn from my extensive dive into the rich array of archival sources held at Archives Ontario, National Archives in Ottawa, UBC Archives, and the Laurentian University Archives. Over a decade of archival research, I collected news stories, Inco's annual reports, negotiation transcriptions, meeting minutes, company and union conciliation briefs, arbitration reports, press releases, newspaper and broadcasting reports, union constitutions, and briefs submitted by both company and union to royal commissions, inquiries, and government agencies. In the archives I also had access to taped interviews conducted with union leaders, activists, and members by other researchers. The process was one of excavation through layers of memories, long-defended stories, and enduring narratives in order to position the diversity of my participants' voices in relation to each other, and to anchor them in the larger social and economic forces of the times.

The majority of the interviews, emails, and letters were collected during the COVID-19 pandemic when travel was restricted and people were isolating in their homes. We did not have the benefit of face-to-face interactions, nor could we share photographs, maps, and other visual cues to enhance reminiscence, such as descriptions of routes taken from home to work and the interiors of Inco's plants long gone. Without the penetrating looks and knowing nods that in-person encounters facilitate, I often wondered how to interpret the silences and hesitations. Could they be a means of avoiding my question, or censoring what might otherwise be a first response, or even signal a breakdown of the rapport so necessary to the co-creation of meaning on the sensitive topics of the strike?

There are other possibilities where the silences were concerned, for instance I wondered if they were part of a struggle to retrieve memories of lives lived long ago and filtered across generations. In conversation, I let the narratives unravel in their own time and the inevitable "ahh, let's see …," and, "oh, what was the name of that?" assume their space. Some participants shared their memories with full confidence that they did not need any explanation. For my part, precise dates and other details were retrieved by linking to other important events in their lives, a process that filled many blanks in my accumulated archival records.

The COVID-19 pandemic has been a time when the usual pace of life slowed, offering the rare opportunity for reflection and review of past experiences. For many of my participants, our conversations were an opportunity to make sense of the past in the context of the present. Often they toggled back and forth in time, reconstructing their experience in the sudden collapse of years, and in the next moment asserting their views of current events: the technological advances in mining, the status of labour unions, the enduring environmental degradation from decades of industrial extraction of the earth's minerals. In emotionally laden disclosures, some of the first-generation participants articulated the anguish of being the last standing soldier of the strike; for others, a profound sense of relief arising from the honest discussions with their adult children

in preparation for the interview with me when they unburdened
the guilt carried for decades related to the sacrifices the strike had
imposed on their growing children.

For some adult children of the strikers, the hand-me-down yarns
remained hazy, but for others who freely admitted difficulties with
short-term memory, I could still draw on their longer-term memories,
an element, perhaps, of the desire for life review associated with phases
of older adulthood. Sometimes, stinging memories would rise up as
though they had inadvertently trodden on a sleepy hive of hornets.

In the telephone interviews, hand-written letters, and email
exchanges, the voices of my participants were resonant. Most were
well-wishing, intelligent, and pleased to be sharing their remembrances with someone who was keenly interested in all they had
to say. Not all are referred to in the book but every one of them
was important to its development. In our email exchanges, memories opened up like accordions, initiated by my first round of questions, followed by further reflections in solitude that generated more
elaborate details and further questions. Vivid memories grounded in
sensory detail would often emerge spontaneously in the telephone
interviews, for instance a sixty-something woman who described
the feeling of hugging her father as a young girl, his smell, his plaid
shirt. A former smelterman, his kinetic memory keenly engaged,
delivered a detailed description of his job in Inco's sintering plant
with the same urgency that would have been required for his tasks
sixty years before. An anecdote offered by a former mechanic going
down the mine shaft for the first time catapulted him back to the
scene: the sense of depth, changes in light, smells, sense of disori-
entation and dulled navigational skills. Another quoted verbatim
a union leader's words with the inflection from more than half a
century ago intact.

In our interactions, I was an "outsider-within"[2] exploring what
was neither unfamiliar nor fully familiar. Betwixt-and-between, at
times I was an insider, at other times an outsider. The academic
nature of the study carried an authoritative punch, signalling my
recognition of the value of participants' recollections and view-
points as essential to the co-production of historical knowledge. But
my professional identity also raised a challenge for participants to
make minute-by-minute decisions on what to say to someone who
knew little about their work, their lives, or their history. Instead of
answering my question, I would often be asked, "How well do you

know Sudbury? Ever been in a mine or a smelter?" To that prompt, I would freely admit my ignorance and then share something relevant from my own history while continuing to welcome theirs. Although my revelation of a personal connection to the subject matter did occasionally foreclose the conversation, more often it would soften the boundary between us as the interview transitioned to exchange. Together, we would gather the frail wisps of inspiration, memory, and longing that marked the search for meaning in our converging histories. Our cooperative rambles through our inner worlds were at times uplifting, and at others, emotionally draining, but often closed with mutual assurances to maintain the connection sealed by the overlap in our pasts.

The book, with its sequence of chapters moving forward in time (sometimes more slowly while other times more rapidly), is written from the standpoint of more than fourteen thousand members of MMSW's Sudbury Local 598 and their families. In gathering their stories, as a sociologist I was guided by the principle of confidentiality. The protection of interviewees' identity is a firmly established norm for data collection in my academic discipline of sociology. For this study, which was approved by the University of Saskatchewan Research Ethics Board, assurances of confidentiality were especially important because of the enduring vestiges of Cold War tensions within the community. Following the strike, suspicions and distrust hung over the community, fueled by widespread fear of communist subversion with the RCMP amassing hundreds of thousands of secret files on its surveillance of Canadians. The tensions continued to simmer for years, even decades later. The impact of those highly charged times made it difficult for some of my informants to speak with me. It was with the understanding of confidentiality that the interviewees spoke as freely as they did and I honour the promise of confidentiality by using pseudonyms and codes that correspond to their relation to the strike in the manuscript (E = Inco employee; WE = wife of employee; AC = adult child of employee; USWA = USWA member; S = sundry). For those already named in the public domain – the union's leaders, Inco's senior managers, collective bargaining negotiators, and the like – I use their surname as they appear in the public record except for the initial occurrence where both first and surname are given.

By the time this work was undertaken, the pioneers of our Canadian labour movement had long since passed. Over many decades prior, cadres of men and women persevered in a relentless struggle for democratic rights and economic justice for all Canadian workers. The unions they built were towering achievements that formed a bulwark against the injustices and inequities of capitalism and brought dignity along with social and material well-being for Canadian workers. Mike Solski is one such pioneer who deserves a special thanks for his collection of historical materials. He dedicated enormous time and energy to ordering, cataloguing, and document- ing in with the explicit hope that "someday the historical record is examined in an atmosphere of some calm and not for propaganda purposes."[3] This work attempts to fulfill Solski's wish and, at the same time, invoke the essence of these trailblazers so they can con- tinue to inform those who remain in service to the labouring people of Canada, for confronting the formidable challenges that lay ahead will be made easier if we are armed with accounts of the past.

Acknowledgments

All creative endeavours are social processes. Writing is one such process that requires many hands working cooperatively towards a common purpose. Accordingly, there are numerous people whom I wish to acknowledge and thank for their assistance, support, and inspiration. Without them, the story of the 1958 strike at the International Nickel Company would not have been brought to this page.

My thanks are due first to the many interviewees who so generously shared their remembrances in conversation with me and registered their confidence in my judgment to honour their history. Also contributing were the many friends and colleagues with whom I had informal conversations about the mining and smelting processes, the evolution of the Canadian labour movement, and the zeitgeist of early postwar Canadian society.

I would like to gratefully acknowledge the financial support, in the form of research grant, from the Social Sciences and Humanities Research Council. I am also grateful to the library and archival staff at Laurentian University Archives (Sudbury); Rare Books & Special Collections, University of British Columbia (Vancouver); Archives Ontario (Toronto); Library and Archives Canada (Ottawa), Greater Sudbury Public Library (Sudbury); University of Colorado Boulder Libraries; Pennsylvania State University Archive (Philadelphia); L.R. Wilson Heritage Archive (Port Colborne); Trail City Archives (Trail, BC); Dance Collection Danse (Toronto); McMaster University Library Archives (Hamilton), Saskatchewan Archives (Saskatoon), Selkirk College Library (Castlegar, BC), Clara Thomas Archives and Special Collections, York University (Toronto). To be thanked as well are the other researchers who had previously filed access-to-information requests regarding RCMP surveillance activities, resulting in documents made available for subsequent researchers to access at Library and Archives Canada.

I am deeply indebted to Gail Taylor, editor and writing coach par excellence. Without her, the project would have been overwhelmingly bewildering, lonely, and frightening. To the work, Gail brought a special mix of expert technical skills, well-honed from her many years of editing experience, along with a sophisticated knowledge about the narrative form of writing and a sustaining belief in the value of the project. She laboured numerous hours over the myriads of chapter drafts and in the course of our conversations, she offered gentle prompts to elicit greater depth and clarity, from which emerged potential resolutions to the dilemmas that inevitably arise in the course of the writing process. From beginning to end of the project, Gail was much more than an editor – she was a confidant, comrade, and cherished friend.

My thanks, too, go to Jennifer Wynne Webber who applied her exceptional sleuthing skills to track down many sources used in the analysis, including potential interviewees, archival documents, and other sources buried deep in the recesses of the internet. Additionally, she coordinated creative work-arounds to in-person visits to the various archives so the project could continue during the pandemic.

It is my good fortune to publish with McGill-Queen's University Press. Jonathan Crago, editor in chief, and Michaela Jacques, acquisitions editor, have been wise and gracious guides in the publishing process. More special thanks are owed to the anonymous peer reviewers who made the work stronger through their comments on the drafts.

Finally, I want to thank my daughter, Andrea Quinlan, and my partner, Michael Rohatynsky. They encouraged me to write this book and helped me every step along the way. Initially envisioned as an article, the story of the strike only became a book from a lengthy conversation I had with Andrea while we walked together along the South Saskatchewan river. As first editor and attentive critic, Michael proofread multiple drafts and kept the home fires burning during the months and years I was tethered to the computer screen. Both Michael and Andrea bolstered me during the setbacks and celebrated the victories. Their enduring love and support in all respects made this book possible.

———————

At the time of the 1958 strike my father, Lukin Robinson, was the research director of Mine, Mill and Smelter Workers. It is to his memory that this work is dedicated.

STANDING UP TO BIG NICKEL

A Mining Industry on the Rise

In Northern Ontario, under the slag heaps and the Canadian Shield rock scored by retreating glaciers, lies the world's richest supply of nickel. By common account, roughly 1.8 billion years ago a meteorite slammed into the earth creating the geological wonder of the Sudbury Basin region with its bountiful nickel deposits and other precious metals. First thought to be a useless ore, nickel was separated from the highly valued copper and discarded. When the nickel-steel alloys were found to be the best material for armour plate, the nickel deposits began to wield tremendous strategic global importance, particularly for their crucial role in the manufacturing of tanks, jeeps, guns, and other armaments. In the build-up to World War I, the region's smelter stacks billowed smoke so putrid it scorched the surrounds, decimated garden vegetables, and stripped the paint from cars. And, during World War II, the blare of a loud horn announcing imminent blasting underground would send miners' wives rushing to their living room shelves to steady knick-knacks and glassware. The formerly pristine lands with its rugged forests and its deep, clear-blue lakes had been home to the Ojibwe, Algonquin, and Odawa Nations. European colonization and exploitation of natural resources banished the Indigenous peoples to the outer perimeter of the 45-mile radius of the mining operations, to what became the Whitefish Lake and Wanapitei First Nations.

Settler accounts that feature white adventurers and rugged prospectors unlocking the hidden wealth underground have obscured the role of First Peoples in the region's history, including the activity of extracting minerals from the ground. The settlement of Northern Ontario associated with the mining industry was founded on the flawed justification that Indigenous land could be taken over because the original people were not making advantageous use of it. In fact, for thousands of years, the Ojibwa in the northern Great Lakes region were mining copper and there was a complex silver mining trade conducted by the Algonquin and Ojibwa in Cobalt-Temiskaming area.[1]

The systematic extraction of the Sudbury region's metals based on the theft of Indigenous land began with the discovery of ore deposits by work crews blasting a route through Northern Ontario for the Canadian Pacific Railway (CPR) in the 1880s on the tracks of land granted by the Crown to both the CPR and the Catholic Church.[2] By the early 1900s, Jesuit missions punctuated the CPR mainline on the north shore of Ramsey Lake and there were over forty mines in the region.

An industry was establishing itself around boom-and-bust cycles that drew workers in, only to throw them out later. With their existence made increasingly difficult from the reduced hunting and gathering, the First Peoples were forced to exchange lives of stewardship with the natural world that provided for their community's present and future needs, for sporadic employment in the mines and smelters.

A gold rush did not befall the area as it did in the Yukon and British Columbia in the later 1800s. Instead, the stage for the mining industry in Northern Ontario was set by the silver boom in the Temiskaming region in the first decade of the twentieth century, sponsored by capital from the United States and supported by a legal and political environment that granted prospectors exclusive rights to stake and work upon designated Crown lands. The bust quickly followed the silver boom and mining companies moved their activities further north-west to the Porcupine region and many of the then-unemployed miners followed behind. With the transfer, methods and technologies were applied to the gold deposits in Timmins and Kirkland Lake, among the richest camps in the world, to quickly occupy a position of real importance in the industry.[3] The characteristics of the industry, established during the silver rush of the early 1900s in Cobalt, were replicated subsequently in the Porcupine area and other northern mining camps: foreign capital control, mine deaths and injuries, inadequate social services, and contractual violations of the mining companies resulting in ever-greater high levels of toxicity in the surrounding environments.[4] Huge profits from the extraction of base and precious metals yielded the capital for investments in the mechanization underground, and automation above ground, which gradually transformed the exploration, extraction, and refining processes. New drills and drilling techniques gave way to ever-deeper shafts and horizontal tunnels for access to previously elusive veins of high-grade ore. On the surface, new milling and smelting processes transformed low-grade waste rock into useable ore. Mining, initially done at the end of a shovel, began to be powered by slushers and scoop tramps to reduce the industry's dependence on labour and thereby dampen the militancy of miners, historically among the most militant of workers.[5]

In the Sudbury Basin, haphazardly strewn around each mine were bunk-houses, other company-owned housing, and company stores with their "deficit purchasing" that shackled the men to their next pay-packet as they dug out the ore deep beneath the surface.[6] Eventually, the mining camps that dotted the Sudbury Basin grew into town sites such as Copper Cliff, Coniston, Creighton, Lively, Garson, and Levack. Their ethnically diverse populations provided a plentiful supply of labour for the expanding mines.

> We were only 3,500 people in Coniston. But it was very divided, very, very divided. My best friends were always Italian, from "Little Italy," like my best girlfriends. But, there was no inter-mixing, marriage-wise, definitely not. I remember my grand-mother saying, you don't marry outside your [laughing], yeah, which I turned around and did [laughing]. She was the driving force of the family. She was Ukrainian and we spoke Ukrainian when I was growing up, not Polish.[7]

By the end of the 1930s, Sudbury proper had developed into a city with similar ethnic enclaves and hierarchies, a radio station, the YMCA, and movie theatres.[8]

Over the decades, successive waves of Ukrainians, Poles, Finns, Germans, and Italians added to the established francophone population drawn from Quebec by jobs on the railway crews. The newcomers from the "old countries" brought distinct cultural and religious practices, stories about the adversity of war, failed crops, and insufficient land to support large families. Following the pattern typical of North American one-resource towns, initial waves of a newcomer group established an ethnic beachhead where village and kin ties were re-established with others from the homeland who followed.[9]

Like in so many mining and smelting towns, the newcomers created a variety of community institutions – churches, halls, sports teams – that laid a foundation for cooperation that shaped the character of the working-class town. Although the mines and smelters employed primarily men, women contributed their unpaid labour to build civic cohesion by providing temporary shelter for the newly arrived, caring for neighbours' children, or baking for church raffles.[10]

Arriving in the Sudbury area, the newcomers found jobs in the mines and smelters, carrying their aspirations for a good life to a land where traditional social hierarchies were not yet firmly anchored. Overlapping class and ethnic divisions soon became evident: the Anglo-Saxon and northern Europeans controlling town councils and occupying managerial positions in the mining operations while the most dangerous, dirtiest jobs were allocated to the other ethnic groups. Many dreamed of returning to their beloved families with accumulated earnings from their jobs that paid up to three times more than what they could earn in rural Europe, but gradually adjusted to the new realities. Those working underground whether they be miners, muckers, carmen, timbermen, or mechanics, faced deplorable and dangerous conditions. And the dirty, dusty, loud environments of the smelters and refining plants rendered other torments for those working above ground.

Others came from across Canada, also drawn by the prospect of employment. Verne, for example, left his home in New Brunswick in a carload of friends at age twenty with only the $25 his mother had tucked into his pocket. When they arrived in Sudbury they were hired immediately. During the early postwar years, new recruits like Verne and his chums needed no previous experience. In the expanding economy of the postwar boom, selection in the mining companies' hiring halls was nearly guaranteed for those who met the minimum physical requirements, particularly chest size. The ease of securing employment was offset by the difficulty of finding lodgings in the midst of the nationwide postwar housing shortage. Verne pawned his watch to pay for his lodgings until he cashed his first paycheque; he considered himself lucky to have found a boarding house with openings during his first two weeks on the job in the mines, a job he would continue to hold for the next forty years.[11] Workers like Verne accepted the risks of their jobs, not because they were ignorant of adverse consequences to their own health but because such risks were deemed intrinsic to the rugged, masculine nature of their work and because they had few alternatives.

Working below the surface in a thick darkness that numbed the senses, miners drilled holes into the unrelenting rock. With the long working hours, they did little else in their waking hours but dig their own graves in the mines, lungs filling with the deadly dust from pneumatic drills nick-named "the widow maker."[12] Going ever deeper, the loud bangs and ominous groans underfoot from the pressure of the increasing tons of earth over top would rattle even the most coolheaded. Each time they stepped off the cage, having descended into the labyrinth of underground workings, they faced the worst of any working conditions: temperatures up to forty degrees Celsius, dust from the drilling and blasting, and poisonous gases of explosives, slowly rotting timbers and carbonated ground waters. "Falls of ground," the term used by Ontario Ministry of Mines, were among the leading causes of death among hard rock miners.[13] Fires that consumed all the oxygen in the stope, failures in the ventilation system, and arsenic, cadmium, lead, and other carcinogens were other life-threatening hazards.

Above ground as smeltermen, they sweated over the open fires, day after day, in conditions so savage very few had any more than eight years of seniority.[14] And, the dirty, dusty environments of the refining plants had their own forms of misery: hair turned green for the refinery workers and the reek of the garlic body odour of those assigned to the selenium plant was obnoxious and inextinguishable.[15]

From the early days, American capital interests dominated the metals industry, enabled by policies of the Canadian government that promoted Canada as a supplier of raw materials in response to the economic, political, and strategic demands of the US.[16] Over the first two decades of the twentieth century, the International Nickel Company of Canada (Inco) became a worldwide nickel mining monopoly with large-scale operations in the Sudbury Basin.[17] After World War I, the demand for nickel tumbled and the new conditions forced the nickel mining companies to expand their research functions in order to create new markets. By the middle of the 1920s, the demand for nickel plating by the auto industry, and the adoption of new chrome-nickel-iron alloys for use in kitchens, cables, and telephone and radio communication devices, all combined to encourage production from the mines in the region.[18] By the end of the 1920s, Inco was in the formidable position of holding 90 per cent of the world nickel market.

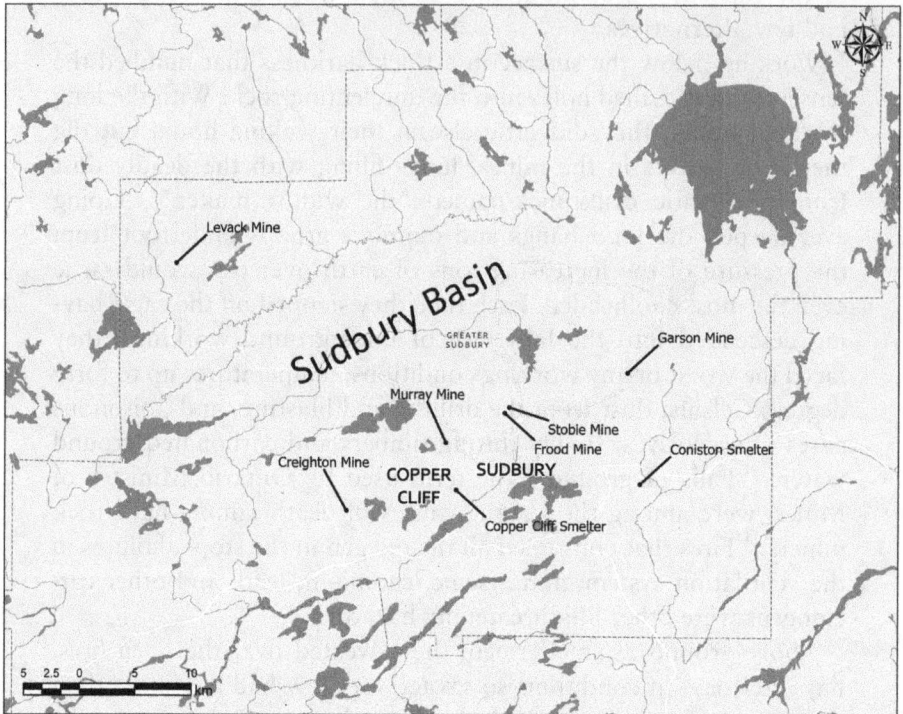

Figure 1.1 | Inco's operations in the Sudbury Basin.

As a creature of the Morgan-Rockefeller financial empires, Inco's control of the world's supply of nickel enabled the company to set prices, block the growth of competitors, and withstand the perpetual boom-and-bust cycles that characterized the mining industry, while endowing it with the power to shape the economic and social development of the Sudbury region for most of the middle fifty years of the century. Inco's headquarters were located at 67 Wall Street, New York. Although the company had established a Canadian identity and offices where executives enjoyed the view of the Toronto shoreline by the time of the 1958 strike, Inco remained a US-financed empire with president and chairman hailing from America and a minority of Canadians on its twenty-five-member board of directors.

In the years approaching World War II, Inco was the chief nickel supplier to both sides of the hostilities for production of armaments. The men strained to meet the increased production quotas. In the

Figures 1.2, 1.3 | Inco smelter stacks.

smelters, the high-grade copper had to be separated from the nickel matte in slabs that were 6-feet square. "If they were poured about 4 inches thick, you were lucky. If they happened to be any thicker, they were next to impossible to break. Five or six of us men with sledgehammers pounding the matte all day long. It was loaded into barrels and shipped to Rotterdam. A few years later during World War II, they were shooting it back at us."[19] At the end of the war, the returning soldiers gazed upon the Sudbury landscape so stripped of topsoil that it resembled the battlefields they had just left overseas.[20] Inco's assets at the time were valued at US$135 million with a net income of US$30 million.[21]

The non-ferrous metal mining industry in Canada[22] grew faster than the economy as a whole in the early postwar years. In those years of boom, Inco continued to expand its Sudbury operations. The demand for nickel was assured by the Korean War and the new applications of the metal in stainless steel, home appliances, cars, jet engines, and other consumer goods. By the time of the 1958 strike, the monthly production of processed nickel coming out of Inco's Sudbury operations averaged 32 million pounds.[23] In comparison, Falconbridge, another Sudbury mining company and Inco's main competitor, produced less than one-sixth of Inco's output.[24]

Inco's profits steadily increased in each of the years of the early postwar period, beginning in 1946 with $29,681K, climbing to $96,296K in 1956, an increase of over 300 per cent.[25] Wage increases of Inco workers lagged far behind the enormous profit increases over the same period. Neither the weapons of war nor the new consumer products of peacetime could be made without their labour, yet increasingly Inco workers were being paid smaller proportions of the value generated from their work, wage increases notwithstanding.[26] Once World War II was over, workers at Inco along with other Canadians turned to basic questions of their economic well-being: they wanted a fair share of the country's fabulous wealth being generated from their labour.

The associated arms race of the Cold War had proven extremely profitable for Inco,[27] but this turned around in 1957 when an economic recession reached its peak and the company's main customer, the United States Department of State (DOS), discontinued its stockpiling, leaving Inco with a huge surplus of nickel. By early 1958, Inco's president Henry Wingate and board chairman John Thompson warned the shareholders that the company was stockpiling its product.[28]

At different times in the early decades of the twentieth century, the Sudbury miners threw down their tools in protest of the exhaustingly long working hours, dangerous conditions, and tyrannical supervisors. Living together in the isolated mining camps and working shoulder to shoulder in life-threatening conditions contributed to the development of strong bonds between miners. They found strength in the developing labour movement amongst miners elsewhere. Already in the early 1860s, the industrialization of deep mining of the Comstock Lode in Nevada prompted the first miners' union.[29] Over the next three decades, miners' unions sprang up, on the metals-mining frontier in the West, particularly in Colorado, Idaho, and Montana. The frontier, stretching from the Mexican border up to Alaska, was very fluid. When an area's ore deposits played out, the miners moved on to new mining sites. Those who participated in labour conflicts in one locality were likely to be present and actively engaged in similar conflicts at later sites. As miners drifted from camp to camp, they carried the union idea with them.[30] These early miners' unions confronted effective employer resistance to unionism through the use of spies, blacklists, strikebreakers, citizens' committees that acted as "protective bands," local law enforcement agencies, state militia, federal troops, and the power of the courts.

In 1893, fifteen miners' unions from Idaho, South Dakota, Utah, Colorado, and other Montana mining camps came to Butte, Montana in response to the call for a unified organization. There, the major North American union in the nonferrous metals industry, the Western Federation of Miners (WFM) was born. Two years later, the first Canadian WFM local was established in Rossland, BC. Like the nickel in the Sudbury Basin, the copper-gold deposits in the Kootenay mountains of southwestern BC had attracted capital interests seeking to exploit what lay beneath the ground.

WFM's Local 38 in Rossland fought to establish a miner's wage of $3.50/day. The Kootenay miners quickly learned the value of political influencing in the face of intense, well-organized resistance from the mine owners.[31] Through persuasive lobbying in both the provincial and federal parliaments, they won the statutory eight-hour day for hard rock miners in February 1899, two years before similar action was taken in Montana.[32] During its first few years, the WFM focused on immediate issues of wages and working conditions. Gradually, after the strike in the Slocan silver mines in BC, and other battles in Coeur d'Alenes, Leadville, and Cripple Creek south of the border, the WFM leaders found that radicalism was the route to strength and success. The more radical the WFM became, the more it grew.[33] In just a few years since its inception, the WFM grew to more than two hundred locals to become the most militant champion of industrial unionism, thirteen of the two hundred locals being in BC.

The union leaders were most responsible for WFM's radicalism, yet the rank and file must not have held opposing views since the democratic structure of the organization would have encouraged the members to replace officials found to be unpalatable.[34]

In 1906, as the WFM south of the border was contending with its troubled relations with the Industrial Workers of the World (IWW), the miners' union was making inroads into Northern Ontario.[35] The silver miners in Cobalt established themselves as WFM Local 146 and struck the following year for a wage of $3.50/day and an eight-hour day. Other WFM locals soon developed in the mining camps of Gowganda, Porcupine, Silver Centre, Kirkland Lake, and Boston Creek, to form District 8 of WFM with approximately seven thousand members. The Sudbury mine owners, nervous about the growing radicalism in the region, went to great lengths to ensure WFM leaders, initially dispatched to Sudbury to serve sentences in the district's jail for instigating strikes, were relocated to North Bay to prevent unionization in Sudbury's copper mines.[36] Like their counterparts in BC, and in the US, the Sudbury mining companies responded to unionizing attempts and job actions by firing the agitators, contracting Pinkerton spies, and ransacking union offices. Added to such tactics of intimidation were the consequential shutdowns of several mining operations in the early 1920s and then the Depression, all of which dampened the efforts of miners and smeltermen to establish their elemental rights and dignity in the workplace. Without the legal right to organize themselves into unions, they were subject to the mining companies' absolute rule that ravaged both human bodies and landscapes in the course of extracting the earth's minerals from below the surface.

The workers would have to wait for World War II to win the legal right to unionize and thereby endow them with formalized mechanisms to collectively challenge the absolute rule of their big company bosses. To ensure that industrial unrest did not disrupt wartime production, government and capital begrudgingly granted Canadian workers the right for unions of their choice to bargain on their behalf. This concession, intended to last only for the length of the war, was the first major advance in policy governing labour relations since the first decade of the century. The hard-won right to unionize was bestowed on Canadian workers by miners in Northern Ontario when they walked out in November 1941 to confront the gold mine owners during one of the most bitterly cold winters on record.

Union Advances in the Mining Camps of Northern Ontario

The winter of 1941–42 in Northern Ontario was bitingly cold, but the gold miners were on fire. Thirty-eight hundred discarded their tools, clambered out of their dark, damp dungeons and struck against the powerful gold barons in Kirkland Lake. The mine owners had defied the recommendations of the federal government conciliation board to bargain with their union, International Union of Mine, Mill and Smelter Workers (IUMMSW, or fondly, Mine Mill). So the miners were confronted with the choice of giving up the idea of having a union to represent them, or to strike. They chose to strike.

The *Wagner Act* had been introduced in the United States in 1935, which provided for compulsory collective bargaining. On the basis of a majority vote of the workers in a given workplace, unions could establish their right to represent the workers in collective bargaining with employers. Kirkland Lake became the battleground for similar legislation in Canada.

In the decade of the Great Depression when jobs were scarce, miners like Ray Stevenson had criss-crossed the country, courtesy of CPR's boxcars, in search of work, occasionally resorting to relief camps where a day of physical labour yielded a bed and three scant meals.[1] Only under the gathering clouds of World War II towards the end of the decade did employment opportunities open up in preparation for the industrial production needed to prosecute a war. In droves, unemployed men like Ray found their way to the gold mines in Northern Ontario, the hardships of their rag-and-bone existence in the "Dirty Thirties" fresh in their memories. The mountain of human misery during the massive economic collapse of the Depression had made a mockery of their lifetime dreams. Their burgeoning radicalism grew out of their direct experience of the ineptitude of the capitalist system. Stevenson, like so many Prairie farm boys, had been pushed off his farm, buckling under the weight of excessive compound interest payments on their mortgaged land and the dust storms that swept through for weeks on end carrying away both soil and crop. Because he was an accomplished baseball player, Ray was hired in the summer of 1941 by Macassa Mine, one of the gold mines in Kirkland Lake with its own ball team. Along with the other players on the mining company's payroll, Ray put down his shovel in the afternoons to play baseball for the company team, proudly displaying his Mine Mill Local 240 button on his ball cap to the consternation of the mine managers.[2] Along with so many others, Ray was determined to have a union that would fight for better working and living conditions.

The conflict between the miners and the mine owners was never far from the surface. Most hard rock miners were imbued with a strong spirit of independence of thought and action. They were hard-working men, rugged as the ore they extracted, with strapping statures both lean and large, who conformed to the standards of virility of the time: they had little regard for the mine owners in their herring-bone jackets and polished shoes. But the arrogance, malice, and inhumanity of the gold mine owners during the late 1930s and early 1940s generated a degree of defiance among even those few miners who didn't ordinarily question the legitimacy of the owners' control. And so it was with the Kirkland Lake miners who were provoked by ill treatment into militancy. Few were members of the Communist Party and even fewer cared that several of the union leaders were party members; rather their militancy was generated by the longstanding solidarity required by exceptionally danger-ous work. For them, the idiom, "you watch my back and I'll watch yours" was not a philosophical abstraction but a matter of utmost practical importance for workers who risked life and limb every day as they entered the dark subterranean passageways to excavate pre-cious metals from the guts of the earth. For workers whose every-day survival depended on such close collaboration, joining a union would have seemed like a natural of solidarity.

When Ottawa refused to send in the RCMP during the strike, pre-mier Mitchell Hepburn's alternative was the self-styled police force known as Hepburn's Hussars, or Sons of Mitches. They arrived in Kirkland Lake one week after the strike began and marched down the town's main street every morning in a flagrant show of force. The federal government adopted a no-interference position that indirectly supported the owners, despite the need for labour's cooperation for the war effort. Prime Minister Mackenzie King refused to meet with the union representatives and waffled on the issue of whether gold was an essential war commodity, a designation that would have given the miners a degree of job security. The mine barons lobbied for public support by filling the print media with anti-union propaganda. Conveniently for them, The *Globe and Mail* was controlled by one of their own.[3] The nation watched with bated breath as the struggle unfolded. Workers and business owners alike recognized that a victory by a brazen mining union could spell subsequent victories by unions in other industries, for a breakthrough that legitimized the power of a militant union in the mining camps of Northern Ontario would inspire workers for whom collective bargaining had appeared hopeless.

As the strike dragged on through one of Canada's coldest winters, public support for the strikers was fuelled by the blatant refusal of MacKenzie King's government to enforce its own laws, or intervene, as well as the spectacle of the self-styled provincial police force backing the mine owners. Across the country, there was a growing sense that workers were deserving of rights and dignity, especially in the face of the sacrifices required by production speed-ups, food rationing, and lives lost to the war. The historic refusal of the government and the capitalist class to grant concessions to labouring people and their unions was about to be vanquished. The industrial unions forming in the United States under the banner of the Congress of Industrial Organizations (CIO) were gaining a foothold into Canada, fuelled by the activities of the Workers' Unity League in the auto and other industrial plants of Oshawa, St Catharines, and Windsor. Having endured a long night of unfettered domination by the capitalist class, Canadian workers were ignited by the potential of the newly forming unions; word was spreading quickly of workplaces like the Kirkland Lake mines where workers were asserting their power.

The Kirkland Lake strike did not win the miners the recognition they sought for their IUMMSW union, nor did they win a wage rate or a reduction in the forty-eight-hour week.[4] Yet, the strike was victorious in precipitating the labour legislation that gave all working people the right to union representation and collective bargaining.

In February 1944, federal legislation similar to the US's *Wagner Act* introduced a new legalistic order governing labour relations in Canada. Provinces soon followed with trade union acts requiring companies to bargain with unions as legal representatives of the workers. The gold miners' strike had paved the way for the government-enforced, employer recognition of unions that forms Canada's present-day codified system of industrial relations.[5]

Perhaps more importantly, the Kirkland Lake strike bolstered the self-confidence and organizing skills of the miners and in so doing played a decisive role in the development of industrial unionism in Canada. Neither the overwhelming majority of the strikers, nor any of the union officials and strike leaders were rehired after the strike, even though this violated the anti-discrimination clauses of the Criminal Code.[6] The ensuing dispersion of unemployed miners to parts of the country where they could get work, primarily Hamilton, Sudbury, and Sarnia, resulted in the concentration of class-conscious workers in the industrial centres of Canada with newly honed organizing skills and proficiency in strike tactics. Ironically for mine owners and other Canadian capitalists, this phenomenon accelerated the growth of the industrial unions in the months and years ahead: precisely what they had wanted to avoid. The nickel mining giant Inco in Sudbury was one such target for the veterans of the Kirkland Lake strike.[7]

TURNING SOUTH TO SUDBURY

After a struggle that lasted through the cold winter for close to four months, the Kirkland Lake strike ended on 12 February 1942. Like the dawn breaking that morning, the union organizers emerged from the strike gray and half-hearted. In the few weeks that followed, they gathered in their Local 240 hall to console each other and ponder next steps. The strike had collapsed under the economic burden of providing the 3,800 strikers and their families with food, firewood, and other necessities. Could they have held out just a little longer and would it have made any difference? But soon, the strike veterans were whipped out of their contemplative intermission when news came from Sudbury that two of their fellow Mine Mill organizers had been badly beaten up.

Rapidly organized into a couple of carloads, the strike veterans sped over the two hundred miles of snow-bound roads from Kirkland

Lake to the world's nickel capital. Their journey south seemed interminably long. But, eventually, as they approached Sudbury and descended the steep hill toward the city centre along Elm Street, they were greeted by a skyline garishly lit up by the twenty-four-hour activity of Inco's massive operations. To supply the voracious demands of the war effort for nickel, the ore was being torn from the earth at record speed, hauled up to the surface and processed in the smelters and refineries by Inco workers toiling seven days a week, with only alternate Sundays off. Copious tons of nickel were needed for bombs, airplanes, tanks, anti-aircraft guns, portable bridges, and battleship engines with their many nickel alloy parts to withstand the corrosive effects of salt water for the Atlantic and Pacific campaigns as well as for refining uranium for the atomic bombs dropped on Hiroshima and Nagasaki. More nickel was extracted from the Sudbury mines during the war years than in the entire fifty-five years of their production. The push for ever greater amounts of the war-essential nickel was expedited by the intimidation, discrimination, and spontaneous firings that were the hallmarks of Inco's treatment of its workers.[8]

Upon their arrival in Sudbury in late February 1942, the Kirkland Lake fleet learned the details of the beatings that had prompted their travel to the nickel capital, and with alacrity offered to assist the organizing drive of Inco workers. Several days prior, a senior supervisor at Inco's Frood Mine had punched the timecards for a "goon squad" of several shift bosses to storm the second-floor downtown union office in broad daylight where they found Jack Whelehan and Forrest Emerson signing up union members. By the time the twelve-member squad left the office, Jack Whelehan was bleeding copiously from the deep gashes to his face, and Forrest Emerson lay crumpled on the floor with a disabling injury from the heavy office typewriter slammed down over his head.[9]

On the day of the egregious attack, it was Kay Carlin who arrived shortly after the two union organizers went to hospital. She was the wife of IUMMSW Local 240 executive member and Canadian representative on the union's international executive board, Bob Carlin, who worked alongside him in all his union activities albeit without the title or formalized role, as dictated by the gender norms of the time. A few hours after the assault, Kay climbed the stairs to the second-floor union office on Durham Street, pausing to gaze at the dresses in the window of Levine's Ladies Wear store below the office. As she took her first step on the stairs, she was horrified by the palpable evidence of the violence:

> [There was] glass all over the front stairs and big blobs that
> looked like blood. So I went up farther and turned to the right
> to go into the union office. Here was the door torn off and the
> place was in a shambles and not a person around, not a soul!
> There was nothing but chaos, everything that was in that office
> was smashed to pieces and I was just petrified. I couldn't move.
> And finally it dawned on me what happened. And I came down-
> stairs just shaking and stood outside looking into Levine's Ladies
> Wear and somebody tapped me on the shoulder and said, "Have
> they got the list, have they got the list?" It was one of our good
> union men, an Italian, and I turned and I said, "No I don't think
> they had," because it was never kept in the office, the list of the
> miners. "Every one of my people will be fired if they have that
> list, every one" and he was almost in tears ... I was scared stiff
> ... I didn't think anybody would want to kill us because we were
> trying to organize miners, it seemed incredible at the time.[10]

The union took swift action by publicizing the events, including the names of some attackers, in a union leaflet "Murder Will Out."[11] Yet no charges were ever laid and the *Sudbury Star* claimed the attack was staged by the union organizers themselves to try to gain local sympathy.

The brutal assault on Jack Whelehan and Forrest Emerson took Inco's intimidation tactics one step too far. For too many years, the company's reign of fear and suspicion had been enough to extinguish any spark of unionism, sustained as it was by a carefully cultivated bevy of informers who reported directly to Inco's Canadian vice president R.D. Parker. Now, however, Inco workers were spurred to collective action, seeing that a union would be their only recourse to address the intolerable conditions of their work.

THE FRUITS OF INTIMIDATION AND WAR: ORGANIZING INCO

The union drive at Inco was already underway by the time help came from Kirkland Lake following the gold miners' strike. In the late 1930s, a sign-up campaign had been set in motion by rank-and-file union members who managed to escape the firings aimed at rooting out union activists. Bill Santala was one such miner who found a unique strategy to sign up union members without attracting the attention of the shift-bosses. Bill was badly injured at Levack mine in 1937 during an accident in which five of his fellow workers were killed and many others injured. While they were recovering from their injuries in Inco's first aid room, "Bill had a field day signing up members for the union."[12] Even earlier, in the first part of the decade, the Workers' Unity League was active in organizing in Sudbury, and in 1936, IUMMSW had chartered a local with 150 workers signing union cards. However, Inco's intimidation techniques, coupled with the union's shortage of funds, curtailed the success of these early union organizing efforts.[13]

With the Kirkland Lake strike over in February 1942, Mine Mill's campaign to organize Inco workers experienced a boost on several fronts. First, funds from the union's international office allocated to Kirkland Lake were now redirected to Sudbury. Second, the strike veterans from Kirkland Lake added valuable experience to the organizing effort – some managing to get hired into Inco's mines by shortening or changing their names to outmaneuver the company's blackballing of union organizers. And perhaps most significantly, Prime Minister MacKenzie King assisted by declaring a job freeze in nickel and other essential war industries.[14] Now Inco workers were free of the fear of retaliatory firings for the clandestine conversations that brought vital news from the other mining camps and industrial plants across Canada where workers were revolting against capital's absolute rule. With their new-found sense of immunity, the workers began to turn their yearning for union representation into action. To signal their intentions, they elected Bob Carlin, a Kirkland Lake strike organizer and IUMMSW board member, to the provincial legislature on the Cooperative Commonwealth Federation (CCF) ticket in 1943. Carlin won with the biggest majority anyone had ever achieved, and he was re-elected in 1945.

Soon, the union organizing campaign at Inco was accomplishing what both the United Steelworkers of America and the Canadian Congress of Labour had given up on, concluding that Sudbury was "owned lock, stock, and barrel by the company."[15] By virtue of their doggedness, Inco workers kept on the long, arduous march towards dignity and rights. In small, disaggregated cells, they joined the drive to unionize. Designed to circumvent the firings of union sympathizers, each cell member only knew the other few in their own cell. Men working shoulder to shoulder, travelling up and down the cage together, and sharing lunch-bucket contents often didn't know the other had signed a union card.[16] The union being organized would bring together three groups of workers corresponding to the processes in the metal industry: the hard-rock miners working deep within the earth extracting the ore; millmen in the mills above ground breaking up and crushing the ore; and the smeltermen sweltering over the furnaces to remove the metal from the waste rock.

The organizing campaign animated men like Mike Solski. In the outlying company town of Coniston, 15 km east of Sudbury, Solski grew up under the shadow of the two smokestacks of an Inco smelter, surrounded by blackened rock stripped bare of life by the sulphur gas.[17] Like most of his fellow workers in the Coniston smelter, Solski's father came to Canada eager for work shortly before World War I from the Galicia region of the former Austro-Hungarian empire. Mike followed in his father's footsteps and at age seventeen he lied about his age and convinced the Inco doctor responsible for medical exams of prospective hires to add a few pounds to Mike's weight on the chart. He later recalled the horrendous working conditions: "The Coniston furnaces were built very badly. The flue chamber was right over the slag chute. So, if you were 6 feet tall like me, you had to bend down to about 4 ½ feet to clean the slag. When you finished the shift, you were soaked, winter and summer. I used to ask myself what did I do to deserve this kind of hell."[18]

Intermittent deliverance from the smelter's "hell" arrived in the form of Solski's participation in the Coniston's musical band, which sharpened his desire for an alternative to the shift work that caused him to miss band practices and performances. From the smelter, he made his way into the mechanical and blacksmith shops where daytime shifts were possible, though Solski was an exception. Jobs such as plate-maker who forged large pieces of metal in the shops, and the top jobs of craneman and skimmer in the smelter were reserved for Anglos first and Franco-Ontarians next. Placing "Slavs at the bottom of the line,"[19] Inco's discriminatory practices were the crucible for Solski's fiery challenge to the injustices that would persist, like his slightly accented English, for the rest of his life. Watching his father die of respiratory disease at an early age from the dust, gas, and sweat of the smelter further cemented his determination to battle against Inco's tyranny.

Solski's chance came in late 1942 when he caught a ride into Sudbury with two fellow Coniston smeltermen to attend a clandestine meeting called by Solski's brother-in-law, one of the early IUMMSW organizers. Solski was curious to know what it was all about. At the door of the rented Lisgar Street union office, they paused in trepidation of what might be inside, and worse, the consequences of entering. Each prompted the others to go in. After a few exchanges of "you go first," "no, you go first," the young twenty-four-year-old Mike Solski drew the short straw. With his 6' 3" intimidating stature and stiff but rhythmic walk, he led the way in, a harbinger of the years ahead when he would lead the seventeen thousand members of the union's largest local. At the meeting, Solski signed a union card, paid the one-dollar membership fee, and in a matter of days, he was arranging secret house meetings with the smeltermen in Coniston's "Polack Town" to encourage them to sign cards while their wives and children stood vigil for stool pigeons.[20]

WOMEN'S PARTNERSHIP IN THE DARING ACTIONS

Simultaneously, the card-signing campaign at Inco's other mines and smelters was picking up steam. Not by mass meetings, but rather by heavy slogging by foot, door-to-door contacts, and small gatherings, carried out along ethnic lines. Italian organizers recruited Italians; Slavs recruited Slavs.[21] Women, too, were active contributors to the organizing drive, including those who worked in the smelters after being hired to fill the void left from the war's drain on male workers; they signed up new members on the job. And women who were fully occupied with domestic duties did their part, too, for in addition to the traditional women's care work of feeding, clothing, and providing emotional and material support for families and neighbours, they stuffed mailboxes with union pamphlets surreptitiously in the dark hours of the night, and organized meetings with other women. The broadly-held assumption that the concerns of women were limited to the domestic sphere, and salacious gossip in this case conveniently camouflaged their activities.

Regardless of the fact that most women were not themselves Inco workers, they had high stakes in the organizing drive. For one thing, the union's mandate to improve workplace safety was a compelling impetus because every day their husbands went on shift, miners' wives rolled the dice with death.[22] They never knew if their husband would ascend back to the surface with all limbs intact or be delivered from the depths on a slab. They had to find creative ways to distract themselves, hour by hour, as the men blasted, mucked, and drilled in dirty, dank tunnels at the behest of employers who considered the price of life to be trivial. As well as the shock and grief caused by injury and fatality on the job, workplace accidents were economically devastating to the entire family in the one-industry mining towns that offered so few jobs for women.

Bringing an end to the unsolicited sexual advances made by Inco supervisors was another motivation for women to join the campaign. As one woman chided her grandson years later when he asked her why she dedicated her time and energy to establishing the union, "Erin, when the foreman comes to your home to take your wife out for dinner, do you not think we needed a union to protect both men and women from that?"[23] While a male-dominated union could not guarantee women's safety from the sexual harassment and assaults, a union willing to flex its muscle against Inco's corporate fortress was their best and indeed their only hope, given the lack of mechanisms in the judicial and political domains for redressing these kinds of violations.

Following in the footsteps of their Kirkland Lake sisters, the Sudbury women formed a women's auxiliary under the union's own slogan "a union without women is only half organized."[24] At the same time, auxiliaries were being created in other hubs of IUMMSW activity. The auxiliaries would grow into full-fledged IUMMSW-chartered locals with their own agenda of consumer action, public education, and political participation considered essential to the creation of a better political and social order. By 1945, there were over six hundred members in nine women's auxiliary locals of the union in Manitoba, Ontario, and Quebec, the provinces that constituted the union's eastern district, and locals in Trail, Kimberley, and Britannia Beach, BC were chartered in the western district. IUMMSW's constitution was among the few to give auxiliaries a voice and vote at conventions.[25] Although constrained by the gender-biased attitudes, actions, and abuses of the times, the auxiliaries' imaginative agenda, bolstered by their pragmatism and hard work, exemplified the union's values of inclusion to say nothing of the determination and resilience of the women involved.[26]

A UNION IS BORN: "DEMANDING AND GETTING DIGNITY ON THE JOB"

In the fall of 1943, close to 90 per cent of the eligible 10,500 Sudbury's Inco workers cast their ballots in the union certification vote with a resounding 79 per cent of the voting Inco workers who favoured IUMMSW. To dissuade workers from voting for IUMMSW, Inco had tried to confuse the workers by informing them that the company already had an agreement with the United Copper-Nickel Workers, popularly named the "Nickel Rash." The ploy only worked on slightly more than 10 per cent of the voting workers. The IUMMSW Local 637, representing Inco's two thousand refinery workers in Port Colborne, had similar success. The painstaking work of the early organizers had paid off.

The union's certification application was among the first to come before the newly created Ontario Labour Relations Board (OLRB) in February 1944.[27] These were early days for the legal framework regulating unionization and collective bargaining in Canada. The radical labour lawyer J.L. Cohen represented IUMMSW in the certification hearings.[28] At the time, Cohen was establishing himself as a key architect of the legal framework that was a crucial component of the postwar accord between capital and labour. Cohen's passionate commitment to civil liberties and working-class struggle ensured that trade union freedoms of association and collective bargaining were enshrined in the evolving legal industrial relations framework.

Within a month of certification, the first collective agreements with Inco were signed in March 1944. The preamble in the first agreement explicitly reflected the objective of labour peace in the emerging industrial legal system. "It is the intent and purpose of the Union and the Company to further the War Effort by promoting and fostering harmonious industrial relations between the Company and its employees."[29] For Inco workers, there was reason to hope for improvements to their waged work now that the capitalist and labouring classes shared the overarching objective of ending a world war that was costing millions of lives and unspeakable suffering. Along with many other Canadians, the end of the war brought a tremendous upsurge of determination and confidence in their ability to build a better world that would benefit working people.

The negotiations leading up to the first agreement were conducted jointly with representatives of the fourteen thousand workers at

Inco's Sudbury operations, IUMMSW Local 598, and the two thousand workers at Inco's Port Colborne refinery, IUMMSW Local 637. The two locals provided strategic bargaining strength to each other because the Port Colborne refinery was an integral extension of Inco's Sudbury operations and conversely, the refinery's production was dependent on the labour of the Sudbury miners and smeltermen. The pattern of this joint bargaining would continue for years to come, producing similar but separate collective agreements between Inco and their respective locals.

The first collective agreements between Inco and IUMMSW brought an end to the "whiskey seniority," the clandestine dispatching of brown-bagged bottles of liquor to the supervisor to preserve one's job. The agreements included seniority rights, a grievance procedure, and protection from discrimination on the basis of sex, race, creed, colour, nationality, or political opinion. For men returning from World War II service six months later, protections such as these were connected to the battle for democracy and equality they had fought overseas, perhaps even more important to them than the additional seniority Inco granted them for their wartime service.

The first collective agreement did not win the members a wage rate increase because of the wartime freeze on wages. Nonetheless, wages automatically improved for the miners in Local 598 because of the inclusion of "collar-to-collar" pay in the agreement. Whereas prior to the agreement miners were paid only from the time their shovels hit the ore, "collar-to-collar" remuneration covered them from the moment they began their descent right up until they arrived back at the surface at the end of their shift. For instance, travelling up and down in the "cage" could add a half-hour to their work time, for which they would now be paid. Importantly, the first contract also contained provision for "voluntary check-off," the union dues of $1/month deducted from the paycheque of authorizing workers, paving the way for later negotiations that would win a measure of financial security via the "automatic check-off."[30]

With the first collective agreement in March 1944, Inco's tyranny was effectively over, which meant that a range of issues from arbitrary firings to poor ventilation and production speed-ups that sacrificed safety, were soon to become a bad memory for Inco's miners and smeltermen. "We were demanding and getting dignity on the job. This meant bosses couldn't swear at you or abuse you verbally."[31] Discrimination based on race, colour, creed, or political opinion could be challenged through the newly won grievance procedure enshrined in the collective agreement.

NATURAL LEADERS EMERGE

The first grievance filed under the new collective agreement was a test for everyone. Before this, the supervisors were required to justify their actions only to their superiors. Now with the collective agreement they were to learn the power of a finely tuned grievance procedure that stipulated different lines of accountability. The responsibilities of front-line supervisors to meet the company's tonnage quotas were now combined with their accountability to thousands of miners and smeltermen. One of the very first grievances was handled by the steward at Inco's Frood mine, Nels Thibault. During his initial meeting with the griever, Thibault reassured him that the procedure was now a right of all the workers but warned him that he couldn't promise the outcome simply because the grievance procedure was still new. Only years later did Thibault learn during a casual conversation with the supervisor of the time that he, too, was anxious during the first- and second-stage grievance meetings.

Nels Thibault was well-positioned to handle the first of the grievances. He was one of the twelve union representatives who signed the Local 598 agreement, and an avid member of the organizing drive. Thibault had been one of thousands of young men whose life course was irreversibly diverted by the Depression. After traveling the roads and rails with small suitcases in hand in the early 1930s in search of work, Thibault arrived in Sudbury in 1935 where he found over three thousand men like him lined up in orderly groups of eight at Inco's hiring hall on Frood Road.[32] After two weeks of waiting in line without making it into the hall, he gave up and rejoined the myriad of other unemployed men criss-crossing the country. For the next four years with his stomach seldom filled, Thibault travelled countless miles, witnessing the rampant spread of hunger, despair, and misery. In the citrus belt of southern BC, he watched mounds of fruit being sprayed to make the food inedible. On the Ontario dairy farms, he saw vats of milk being discarded. How could this be happening when there was such widespread suffering? When he asked why, he was told it was being done to maintain the price. He could not reconcile the contradictions of a system that would destroy food when so many were hungry. Having grown up on a farm in Saskatchewan, Thibault was no stranger to long hours of grinding work. As an able-bodied man with a firm desire to work, why was he rambling about in a wonderfully rich land in search of the odd job timbering or firefighting in exchange for 15 cents an hour? Why did he often have to resort to begging to keep body and soul together, tagged as one of the "lazy bums."[33] Along with the many young men who wore out both their shoes and their hopes during the Depression, Thibault felt the sharp sting of dignity denied and his confidence in capitalism was badly shaken by the economic crisis.

On Halloween night in 1939, Thibault arrived back in Sudbury on the train from Sault Saint Marie and was hired by Inco as a labourer. The wave of employment in the burgeoning war industries brought thousands with him. Like the other new hires, the young, spirited Thibault brought his dreams of sustaining himself and perhaps earning enough money to finance a return to the formal education that had been cut short by the Depression. Disillusionment came quickly once he descended into the damp, dark mine at Levack: no ventilation system and constant pressure to muck out more ore for the war effort. Perhaps worst of all, the shift bosses never addressed him by his name. The identity of the gregarious, energetic, determined young man, as fond of crosswords as fellowship, was reduced to his employee number, 10-2-20. At the end of each shift, he fell, exhausted, into his top bunk in the nearby bunkhouse for single men, where there was no privacy and the bottom bunks were reserved for men with the most seniority. He vowed to himself, "come spring, I'll be long gone." As he reflected years later, there were "a hell of a lot of springs and I was still there." Inco favoured hiring farmers from the West for their strong work ethic and their more expansive lung capacity fostered by the dry climate. On both counts, Thibault excelled, and he soon became "a damn good miner," first at the Levack, then in Inco's Frood mine.[34] Inco recruiters also preferred to hire farmers because they believed that the independent spirit of farmers would dampen down any fomenting of a union. Reflecting back on those times, Thibault chortled, "I think I sort of fooled them on that count."[35] Shortly after being hired, Thibault threw himself into the work of the union to achieve improvements for his fellow Inco workers. Thibault's service to IUMMSW – first as a steward, then recording secretary, vice president, and president of Local 598, and later president of Canadian IUMMSW – spanned twenty-five years. His charisma, intelligence, oratorical skills, and steadfast belief in the capacity of humans to cooperate made him a natural leader.

SCORING THE ACHIEVEMENTS

IUMMSW members achieved union recognition and the first collective agreements in 1944 within the burgeoning legal framework that reflected the tacit postwar settlement between capital and labour. The settlement and its laws governing employer-worker relations brought both gains and sacrifices for the IUMMSW members as well as other union members in Canada. The legal framework gave unions much-needed recognition and the ability to negotiate wages and benefits with employers. But this came at the cost of relinquishing control over how the work was to be done. The pace of work, working conditions, job security, and health and safety were elements of the labour process that were dictated by management, captured in the "management rights" clause in collective agreements. In addition, there would now be stiff sanctions that could be leveled against workers and their unions for direct job actions such as wildcatting and organized slow-downs used by Inco workers, among others, to express resentments related to workplace problems in the past. Significantly, workers forfeited their most powerful weapon: the ability to strike spontaneously.[36] Only in the fullness of time would the implications of such a trade-off become apparent to Inco workers.

The settlement came with the implicit promise of wages and benefits that would allow workers to afford the new products and services generated in the postwar boom. The rise in the nation's productivity since the end of the war should have meant higher living standards for workers since it was their labour that was responsible for producing the country's increased wealth. The nature of Canada's economic development in the postwar years, however, did not deliver the continuous economic prosperity assumed by the accord between capital and labour. Within a very short time, the boom of the early postwar years led to economic slumps. Already by 1949 Canada was producing more goods and services than could be profitably sold, and again in 1954, the economy stumbled. By 1957, the country was in a full-scale economic recession.

Union certification and the first collective agreement in 1944 gave Inco workers reason to believe their children would have better working lives than their own. And for the fourteen years that followed the first collective agreement, substantial improvements to their day-to-day lives were achieved, including shift premiums; up to four weeks of vacation; a management clause that required demonstration of just cause to suspend, discharge, or otherwise discipline workers; and a labour rate that went up by $1.19/hour between 1944 and 1956, an increase of nearly 100 per cent.[37] The steady advances made through negotiating fourteen years of collective agreements had been accomplished without a strike.

That record would be broken in 1958 when Inco workers decided they would not be denied the continuing improvements in wages and benefits that had been the promise of the postwar boom. Because the union had delivered enriched wage and benefit packages every year since 1944, surely it could bring Inco to heel once again – even if the company was sitting on a large stockpile of nickel.

Building a Working-Class Culture and Establishing a Canadian Identity

At the beginning of each shift, as the miners descended into the bowels of the earth of the Creighton, Frood, and the other Inco mines, they would hear the sounds particular to the sub-terrestrial habitat they occupied with every shift: the steady drip of water; the rumble of the muck dropping down through the ore passes; the ominous bangs and groans of the pressure shifts; and the hissing of the air line and muted roar of a jackleg drill in some distant stope – all to be obscured when they started their own drills. Speaking to one another over the din was made even more difficult by Inco's practice of pairing Ukrainians with Germans, French-Canadians with Poles, and British with Italians for the explicit purpose of preventing workers from banding together to challenge the supervisors' frequent and grievous abuses of power.

In postwar Northern Ontario, Inco's workforce was like a little League of Nations, with many newcomers from Europe who carried pro-fascist political leanings that caused rifts with others who had fought in resistance movements. Cleavages between Red and White Finns, and similar cut lines among the Ukrainian workers, created divisions within the membership. And then there was the large population of Franco-Ontarians hived off from everybody else, many of them conservative anti-communist Catholics.

With each collective agreement negotiated after Local 598's certification in 1944, the Mine Mill members in Sudbury enjoyed material gains year by year. The union leaders with "balls of iron"[1] who dared to confront Inco from across the bargaining table had secured significant victories where wages and working conditions were concerned. Yet achieving a working-class unity among Inco workers with such diverse backgrounds was a conundrum beyond the scope of negotiating collective agreements.

The question was how to create the communal structures for union members to unite in their crusade for dignified, multi-faceted lives. How were the ethnic, political, and cultural differences of the membership to be transcended? The inherent collectivity of song, art, and athletics was the answer. In the late 1940s, Local 598 set out to develop an expansive program of cultural and recreational activities "to provide for the constructive use of leisure time for the members and their families and achieving conditions of life in the home and the community, which make for health and happiness."[2] The work of the union was now extending well beyond the bargaining table to enrich the social and cultural lives of Sudburians and surrounding communities.

Mine Mill's social unionism was part of the larger ambition shared with other left-led unions in the early postwar years to tether broader social improvements to the wartime gains of union recognition. The reasoning was that to safeguard the wartime gains would require more than negotiating improved wage packets for its members. If unions were to be a permanent fixture in Canadian society, their activities would have to go beyond the parameters of the newly won framework of industrial legalism.[3] These unions formulated progressive social and economic policy as a bulwark against prospective incursions on the rights of workers achieved during the war. MMSW's unique contribution to the project of securing wartime gains was to develop programming in the arts, culture, and sports for its members and their families.

The union's social programming filled a marked vacuum in Sudbury, for while the city had its share of movie theatres and a radio station, YMCA, church choirs, and even a few amateur acting groups, there was a paucity of recreational facilities such as swimming pools, sports arenas, and playgrounds due to the limited tax base that could be traced back to the turn of the twentieth-century legislation that made municipal taxation exempt for the buildings and machinery used by the mining companies. Though community halls were sites for the expression of rich and varied cultural legacies brought by large numbers of Italian, Finnish, Ukrainian, and other immigrant groups, they were largely eclipsed by Sudbury's goldrush atmosphere with its streets filled with transient miners flush with their bonus earnings. There was a disparity between

Sudbury's elite who could travel to Toronto for theatre and art galleries, and entertainment for those of lesser means in the form of a sports game or a night of heavy drinking in the bars with segregated "Men Only" and "Ladies and Gents" entrances.[4] Consequently, the evolution of union halls, dance school, summer camp, and sports teams spearheaded by the local over the years was the crucible for a working-class culture – a powerful unifying element for an ethnically diverse workforce and a source of both health and enrichment for workers and their families.

BUILD IT AND THEY WILL COME

Each new feature of the union's social program with associated expenditures was debated on the floor of the membership meetings through the union's long-established democratic procedures. Members first signaled their readiness for the enrichment of cultural activities by voting in favour of the construction of five union halls. Later, they endorsed other aspects of the union's social programming including the recruitment of dance instructors from Toronto, salaries for full-time French and English-speaking editors for their local's newspaper, *Local 598 News,* and a $20,000 purchase of 120 acres on the shores of Richard Lake twelve miles southeast of the city for a summer camp.

The building of the first union hall was initiated in 1949 under then-President Thibault. Resolute in his belief that Inco workers and their families were entitled to lives enriched by sports and recreation and the arts, Thibault introduced a building fund from the 50-cent increase to monthly union dues to allow for purchase of the property at 19 Regent Street in Sudbury for the first hall. The halls, eventually five in total, soon became hubs ablaze with banquets, bowling nights, community dinners, variety shows, and performances by such notable singers as The Travellers, Pete Seeger, and Paul Robeson; programming ran from the local's Boxing Club to the Saturday Morning Club entertainment for children with cartoons and movies, and covered Sunday Family Nights and the Wednesday Afternoon Club with vital baby-sitting services for mothers with pre-school age kids.

The popularity of activities offered at the union's first hall on Sudbury's Regent Street led to the construction of other halls in the outlying communities of Garson, Coniston, Creighton-Lively, and

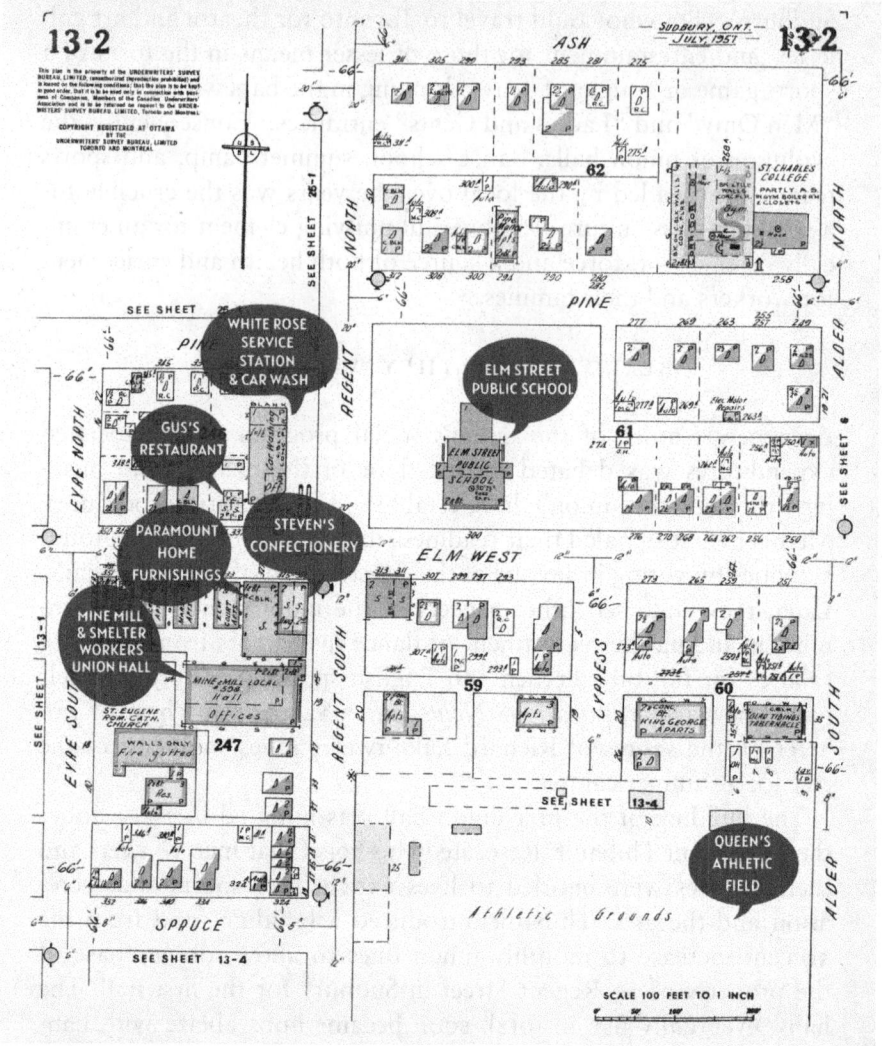

Figure 3.1 | MMSW union hall and surrounds.

Chelmsford. As late as in the early months of 1958, the year of the strike, Local 598 Executive members were contemplating the purchase of property for a union hall in the most distant of Inco's communities, Levack, and a $14,000 loan to the local in Elliot Lake to build a union hall for the uranium miners. Both proposals had to be dropped in anticipation of the hefty expenses of the impeding strike.

The Regent Street hall was designed by the prominent Sudbury architect Louis Fabbro who had received praise for his design of the Sudbury General Hospital and the Sudbury High School. The hall was conveniently located close to the bustling intersection of Regent and Elm Streets in the rapidly expanding west-end neighbourhood of Sudbury. Within a few steps from the hall were Paramount Home Furnishings, Steven's Confectionery Store, White Rose Service Station with its massive car wash, and Gus's Restaurant, a local institution that offered miners living in nearby boarding houses a lunch-pail service. At the end of their shifts, men would filter in for monster meals served on large oval plates, and on their way out leave their empty lunch pails to be packed with sandwiches, cigarettes, and chocolate bars for pick-up on the way to their next shift.

The three-storey hall at 19 Regent Street readily accommodated all types of activities. If the hall's bowling alleys were not occupied with league practices and tournaments, they were busy with family bowling nights. Multi-purpose rooms housed choral group practices and dance classes. The fully equipped commercial-sized kitchen was a beehive of assembly-line sandwich preparation for evening meetings, bake-offs for the next bazaar, or full meal service for the steward appreciation banquets. The hall's spacious 1,200-seat auditorium, with its sizable stage and grand piano, was regularly filled for performances of touring professional singers and dancers, as well as membership meetings. In the basement, the beverage room was a favourite destination for the miners and smeltermen coming off shift. Over a pint, they would tally up the day's production of nickel, play a game of cribbage or shuffleboard, share the latest gossip about whose wife was the latest casualty of an Inco supervisor's unwanted sexual advances, and debate the weight of the moose or size of fish from the weekend's excursions.

In their third-floor offices of the hall, the secretary and elected officials carried out the work of the union: project planning, record-keeping of membership lists and financial accounts, creating and dispatching information to the members through bulletins, notices, and the local's newspaper. The rifle tucked behind the president's office door, hopeful for a weekend hunt, seldom moved. There was simply too much to do to represent the more than fourteen thousand members, and evening and weekend meetings were routine. When they could push themselves away from the Gestetner copying machine, their typewriters, and their large wooden desks piled high with papers, the staff and members of volunteer committees enjoyed a spectators' view of the activities on the Queen's Athletic Field across the street from their office windows. A two-bedroom spacious apartment, also on the hall's third floor, was home to the recreation director and his family, hired to organize activities in the halls and manage the union's various social programs.

The Regent Street hall was built in the same style as the Western Federation Miners' 1898 hall in Rossland, BC, featuring majestic laminated arched beams that represented the union's arc of bestowal in relation to the labour movement. At the time of the gala opening of the main union hall in 1951, international union vice president Asbury Howard came to Sudbury. A Local 598 Executive member remembers: "We took him on a grand tour and as Mike Solski was showing him all this beautiful stuff, Ashbury didn't say very much. He kept looking and looking with his hands behind his back. Finally, Solski poked him, 'Well, what do you think of it?' In his southern drawl Ashbury responded 'Well, it sure is a beautiful building, I've got to say that. It's a beautiful building. I just hope it don't take your mind off the union.'"[5]

At the time of his visit, Howard had just finished a six-month sentence on a chain gang for registering Black voters in Alabama. As an African American, it was racial injustice that commanded his attention so perhaps to his way of thinking if the union was going to stray from bread-and-butter issues of serving members through negotiating and policing collective agreements, it should concentrate its efforts on the political rather than the cultural domain. As the union local was to learn in the years to come, these were one and the same, for developing a working-class culture was a profoundly political act. To the Cold War warriors of the day, a mining union that championed the notion that men who mucked, drilled, shoveled, and smelted could enjoy dignified, creative lives and bridge their differences to depend on each other in times of struggle must be marching to the tune of the Soviet influence and therefore should be brought to heel.

HAYWOOD PLAYERS: CULTIVATING WORKING-CLASS CULTURE

One of the art forms especially suited to collective experience was drama. Shortly after hiring Weir Reid, the Recreation Director in 1952, the local organized its own amateur theatre troupe. In a salute to the union's radical lineage, the Haywood Players were named after Bill Haywood, the famous labour organizer of the Western Federation of Miners and the Industrial Workers of the World in the early 1900s. Carpenters and electricians who worked for Inco by day became set designers and lighting crew in the evenings; the miners and smeltermen were the actors. Women's auxiliary members and other miners' wives sewed costumes and found themselves under the stage lights, too. A liberal allocation of budgets made it possible to supply sets and costumes for the plays performed at union events as well as provincial amateur drama festivals and competitions.

The troupe's labour-themed plays were deliberately chosen to entertain while commenting on the lives of workers and the crippling effects of the Cold War on the labour movement. Barrie Stavis's *The Man Who Never Died* dramatized the events that led to the arrest and execution of Joe Hill, the famous Industrial Workers of the World organizer. Dalton Trumbo's comedy, *The Biggest Thief in Town*, portrayed an undertaker seeking financial benefit from a dying industrialist, a Haywood Players' performance that garnered top prizes at the annual Northern Ontario Drama Festival in the year prior to the strike.

DANCE SCHOOL

The union halls were also home to the union's own dance school. Recruited by the recreation director, Toronto-based dancer Nancy Lima Dent established the union's dance school in the fall of 1955. To give an indication of the quality of teachers, Nancy Dent brought years of studio and stage experience as dancer, choreographer, and artistic director in Toronto and New York.

Ms Dent was hand-picked for the unprecedented job of launching a dance school for miners' children. Her varied dance background combined with her political views made her the perfect choice to undertake a task that some considered preposterous, for she considered dance as an expressive art form that could cultivate active citizenship when taught properly. By building confidence in students of dance, Nancy Dent believed they could better contribute to their communities in adulthood. In her pioneering dance pedagogy, she introduced her students to a variety of dance techniques intended to be tools for reducing divisiveness and inter-ethnic tensions. Her purpose was to empower students to express themselves with poise, imagination, and critical intelligence.

Nancy Dent's warm, generous spirit and infectious optimism won her the adoration of parents and children alike. In a letter to a friend, she described her reception in the communities: "We have a terrific committee of about 30 in Garson and about 80 in Sudbury. And, I have never found such a willing and cooperative group of people as here. I ask for something – it's done. Just like that. No fuss, no bother, no 'how do you do it?' no 'well, maybes.'"[6] Ms Dent's charismatic personality and cultural sophistication endeared her to a community eager for her offerings. Upon her arrival in Sudbury in the fall of 1955, she went right to work setting up classes in the union's halls in Garson and in Sudbury, having found, as she later recounted, "the local stages as barren as the landscape."[7] Classes began in November 1955 at 50 cents, a cost easily afforded by even the lowest paid worker, and considerably less than the fees charged by the other two dance schools in the area.[8] When Nancy Dent left Sudbury in the summer of 1957, the union executive was quick to seek a replacement who could continue the students' cultural enrichment. As another plum recruit, Barbara Cook brought advanced classical ballet training and accreditation. The students readily made the transition from Ms Dent's expressive dance forms to the rigorous discipline of Ms Cook's ballet classes with live piano accompaniment and Royal Academy of Dance (RAD) syllabi and examinations for the aspiring dances. Both of the MMSW dance school teachers, each in her own way, made significant contributions to the development of dance in Sudbury, their imprint felt for years to come.

THE SUMMER CAMP

The Richard Lake camp, twelve miles outside of Sudbury, first opened in 1951 as a day camp with two hundred boys and girls attending each week, bussed from the Regent Street union hall in the morning and returned each night.[9] The camp soon drew workers' children from other Mine Mill locals as far away as Buffalo and Alabama for a rich array of creative and nature-based activities during the summer months. In the following years, hundreds of overnight campers stayed on the rolling hills and quarter-mile long beach and enjoyed a wide assortment of programs in archery, drama, hiking, baseball, softball, and social dancing. Campfire sing-alongs brought together all age groups. The camp's waterfront programming included boating, canoeing, and swimming lessons, complete with Royal Life Saving Society lessons and certification managed by a full-time waterfront director and assistant director. An extensive arts and crafts program offered everything from papier-mâché and weaving to leather work, and clay sculpting. The twenty children in each of the four dormitories were supervised by two counsellors and two counsellors-in-training. The camp's majestic building contained the dining hall, large kitchen, and an open central fireplace with surrounding seating. As one regular camper remembers, the library "was filled with any and all books from *Winnie the Pooh* to Robert Heinlein's science fiction and reading was always encouraged."[10] With camp costs subsidized by the union, the $9 a week/child fee made the camp accessible to the working-class families.[11]

The Richard Lake camp also welcomed the shop stewards for regularly scheduled steward schools. To ensure the hard-won improvements achieved in the successive collective agreements negotiated with Inco, an educated, militant pool of shop stewards was needed. At the weekend-long training sessions, the three hundred plus stewards learned the principles of unionism, details of the most recent collective agreement, and how to present a grievance.

The camp's beach and picnic facilities were open to the union's members at all times and made available to community groups for outdoor social events. On hot summer weekends, throngs of union families filled the campgrounds for afternoon picnics, swimming, and nature hikes. Young children found their way to the small zoo and playground equipment; and picnic baskets could be supplemented by the concession stand offerings. A full program designed to entertain all family members included music, games, softball tournaments, tug-of-war matches, timed competitions amongst miners filling mock ore cars, and wheelbarrow races with separate children and adult divisions and shiny new silver dollars awarded to winners as prizes.[12] Each year hundreds of volunteering members made incremental improvements to the campgrounds, adding new picnic tables, planting trees, and landscaping. By the mid-1950s, the camp had attracted the attention of trade unionists throughout Canada and the US who recognized it as a jewel of the labour movement.[13]

The union's social programming took shape in the union halls, dance school, theatre troupe, and summer camp and served as a cultural incubator for resistance and solidarity. Given the vitality of the union's social programming, it wasn't surprising that it was a lightning rod for Cold War warriors. The summer camp was cast as a training ground for Soviet spies, a site for the communist brainwashing of young minds. The reputation of the camp director as an agent of communist indoctrination was the subject of legal battles that lasted close to a decade.[14] Another element of the union's social programming that fell victim to Cold War fever involved the pirouettes and pas de deux of the Royal Winnipeg Ballet (RWB). The ballet performances were abruptly cancelled when the RWB was informed that it would have to forfeit its subsequent American tour, which included a Washington performance for president Dwight Eisenhower, if it kept its commitment to perform for the union members in Sudbury. Years later, even after sober reflection, the union leaders who arranged the RWB performances reiterated their firm belief that the US State Department was involved in the cancellation as part of its Cold War crusade,[15] a conviction that has been plausibly advanced by others.[16]

The union's innovative programming reached beyond the bargaining table to enhance the everyday lives of its members and their families in continuous and concrete ways. One of the founders of the union's social programming summarized its origins in an interview several decades later, "we decided that we were going to have a little bit of socialism of our own. That's really what we were saying without knowing that we were saying that."[17] Had he used the word "socialism" to describe the impetus of the union's social program at the time, it would have fed directly into the growing misguided perceptions that Mine Mill was intent on spreading communist ideology, particularly amongst the youth. And only after the buffer of intervening decades was it safe to use such a term in its broadest, most benign sense without immediately evoking Cold War paranoia.

BLAZING A TRAIL FOR CANADIAN AUTONOMY

At the same time the culture and recreational programs were flourishing, the union was forging a path for the Canadian labour movement on another front. Mine Mill was the first international union to grant autonomy to its Canadian members with their own national officers and constitution in 1955.[18] Other Canadian workers followed in the 1960s, when they pushed against the powerful international influences in the Canadian labour movement of the American-based international unions.[19] Unlike the Mine Mill union, however, control of the Canadian locals' funds, strike calls, policies, and appointment of administrators was left with the international unions' American offices in most cases.

Unlike most other members of Canadian unions who sought similar independence in the 1960s, too, the Canadian Mine Mill members continued to identify themselves as part of the same American union, simply dropping the "International" from the name to become MMSW. Historically, miners were itinerant workers who drifted back and forth over the border between Canada and the US depending on where the work was. "One week they'd be working in Kellogg, Idaho and the next in Kimberley, BC." Miners wandered up and down the entire north-west side of North America to follow work, so "being a member of an international union made the utmost sense."[20] Although there were disagreements between the Canadian and US memberships over such things as trade tariffs and quotas, they were usually settled, albeit with some contention.[21] Formed in 1955, the Canadian MMSW was self-regulating with its own constitution in a fraternal, rather than a functional, relationship with its American counterpart that was based on shared experience, aspirations, and identities as hard rock miners – perhaps achieving the best of both worlds.[22]

Formalizing the independence of the thirty thousand Mine Mill members in Canada might have been a strategic maneuver in the face of the Cold War hysteria that threatened the survival of the IUMMSW locals south of the border.[23] Perhaps the leadership dispute over the embargo proposed by the US government that threatened jobs of Canadian members and yet was supported by American leaders, inspired the Canadians to forge their own path.[24] But a more significant factor in the independence of the Canadian MMSW was the desire of Canadian members to be authors of their own destiny. To develop and coordinate their own bargaining demands was an urge the Mine Mill leaders in the US understood well and the union's democratic structure dating back to its incarnation as the Western Federation of Miners made it easy for them to support the aspirations of the Canadians. The union remained as a federation of locals, each with the autonomy to sign collective agreements and control their own finances; neither the national nor international officers had the power to override decisions made by the locals.[25] The 1958 strike highlighted the significance of this autonomy in relation to calling a strike without the authorization of the national or international boards.

Nonetheless, the formation of a distinctly Canadian MMSW entity in 1955 with its own national officers and constitution ushered in new complexities. For one thing, the legitimacy of the Canadian MMSW's identity under provincial labour laws was now thrown into question, opening the door to the USWA. As the traditional rival of MMSW, the USWA leapt at the opportunity to mount challenges to the newly formed Canada MMSW's right to bargain on behalf of workers at Elliot Lake uranium mines, Deloro Smelting and Refining Company in Marmora, Ontario, as well as a number of other workplaces where MMSW had held the bargaining prerogative. The Canadian and Ontario Labour Relations Boards were USWA's willing partners and refused to recognize the Canadian MMSW. In their rulings, the labour boards argued that the Mine Mill union had "split at the border" and was now two separate and distinct "legal entities." As a consequence, the boards would recognize the Canadian MMSW only if a vote was held in each of the workplaces and a majority of the workers voted in favour of MMSW. Furthermore, while these votes were underway, each local would be open to raids by the USWA. The legal wrangling was finally settled when the *Ontario Labour Relations Act* was amended to introduce successor rights that clarified the legal status of Canadian breakaway unions. The amendment paved the way for other unions eager to establish a Canadian identity without risking the loss of their Canadian locals. However, in the meantime, Mine Mill lost ground in the effort to organize several Ontario mines including the newly developing uranium mines in Elliot Lake.

In 1955, with the labour boards on side, USWA quickly set up a temporary office in Coulson hotel in downtown Sudbury as it had done several times in the past. Once again, the USWA attempted to capture the signatures of Inco members so it could apply to the Board for bargaining rights of the more than fourteen thousand Mine Mill members. As one young man working at Copper Cliff smelter recalls: "One day, I guess it was the end of the shift, maybe four o'clock, 4:30, I was on my way to meet my ride home. These three guys just sidled up to me and blocked me off, I couldn't move and said, 'Are you a Mine Mill member?' I said, 'Yes.' They said, 'Well, we're recommending that people like you sign on with Steel. No ifs, buts or maybes.' [laughter] I was aware there was what was called a recruitment drive going on, but I really wasn't sure what to do. I was just intimidated. I did what these big boys, big boisterous guys told me to do."[26] USWA was unsuccessful in this as in previous raids. It would take the protracted strike of 1958 for USWA to overtake a pivotal centre of militant trade unionism in the heart of the Canadian mining industry.

In the spring of 1956 in Sudbury, as bargaining was about to begin for the next collective agreement, Inco executives refused to meet with Mike Solski and the other members of the MMSW negotiating team, citing the labour board rulings that decertified the Canadian MMSW. However, the collective agreement was in fact negotiated once Solski set the Inco team straight with the pronouncement, "The minute we are not recognized as the legal bargaining agents for your employees, not ONE pound of muck is coming out of your plants."[27]

This was not an idle threat. From the early days of being a union, the Inco workers had sought out their own leaders and in Mike Solski had found a courageous, cool-headed trade unionist able to prevail under pressure. As chief negotiator since 1952, Solski had become a tenacious defender of the MMSW members. Having grown up among these men and shared years of sweat and toil with them, he knew their aspirations and capacity, the fire running through their veins. If the Inco negotiators doubted Solski's assessment of Inco workers' temperament in the spring of 1956, they would learn how right he was a mere two years later when contract bargaining brought Inco's operations to a shuddering standstill for thirteen weeks.

4

Inco and Mine Mill Come to the Bargaining Table

The numerous negotiation meetings leading up to the 1958 strike followed much the same protocol as the previous thirteen years had established, although the outcome couldn't have been more different. Assembling first at the union hall on Sudbury's Regent Street for fellowship and last-minute discussion of the bargaining proposals, the union's negotiating team – eighteen or nineteen in number – would pile into cars for the fifteen-minute drive over to Inco's offices in Copper Cliff, lingering only long enough in front of the hall for a few snaps from a local journalist's camera for the following morning's *Sudbury Star* front page. Whatever the weather, the sky was inevitably obscured by the dark, poisonous sulfur dioxide wafting upward from the smelter stacks. On their way to Inco's office building, they had to pass the hiring hall and the snaking line of men of all ages eager for a job, dangerous and arduous as it might be. Each potential recruit was weighed, measured, and x-rayed to determine lung capacity, yet few were taken on in 1958 when Inco's recent hiring blitz was suspended because of the economic recession. Just a couple of years before when the postwar economy was booming, Inco was hiring over one hundred each day from the "cattle pool" of men gathered in front of its Copper Cliff hiring hall.[1] But, in the pivotal year of 1958, hiring slowed to a trickle. There would be many disappointed summer students who in previous years were hired to work underground as driller helpers or timberman helpers, or on the surface as slag-dump-man helpers or maintenance mechanic helpers. However high up their fathers and uncles might be in Inco's hierarchy, they wouldn't have jobs mucking out the ore in the dank mines or sweating in the steaming smelters.

Typically, when the union negotiators arrived at Inco's two-storey office building for a negotiation meeting, they would sign in at the front door before being ushered by a secretary up the flight of stairs to "Mahogany Row,"[2] the opulently furnished president and vice presidents' offices. Had they been investors or fellow industrialists instead of union men, the meetings would start with the ritualized pouring of drinks from the well-stocked, free-standing liquor cabinet occupying one corner of the room. Instead, they seated themselves without ceremony along one side of the long, imposing boardroom table across from Inco's team assembled on the opposite side with its panoramic view onto the road that led to the security gate and the buildings of the smelter complex. Union negotiators just off their afternoon or graveyard shifts might have eyed the soft leather lounge chairs lining the oak-paneled side wall of the office with longing as they settled on the stiff-backed chairs instead, for plusher chairs were reserved for friendly meetings and they understood all too well that negotiations between the union and Inco were far from amicable. With both sides seated across from each other, the cigarettes and pipes were lit, signaling the start of the meeting, and the muffled voices and ringing telephones of the outside offices receded behind the mahogany-paneled boardroom walls.

THE MEN AT THE TABLE

The union's negotiation team consisted of men working in Inco's mines, smelters, and refineries, the years of hard, physical labour worn on their lined faces. They were dedicated union activists from Mine, Mill and Smelter Workers (MMSW) Locals 637 and 598 who represented two thousand workers in Inco's refinery in Port Colborne and more than fourteen thousand workers in the Sudbury and district operations respectively. On the team were men like William Cryderman, who left his Saskatchewan family farm during the Depression to ride the rails across the country and jumped off in Sudbury when word travelled along the train cars that Inco was hiring. By the time of the negotiations in the spring of 1958, William had been with Inco for more than twenty years, working his way up to become a crane operator in their copper refinery; he was one of the most skilled surface workers. The safety of others working within the radius of the crane was entirely dependent on William's dexterity and coordination with the on-the-ground supervisor. After witnessing too many instances of shift bosses' arbitrary abuses of power, his instinctive sense of justice drew him into union activities; he eventually became chief steward of the refinery section and a member of the bargaining team. But William had no aspirations to a leadership position in the union but rather was content to be a willing combatant to right the wrongs he saw around him, showing a steadfast commitment to the union that was evident to his fellow negotiators.[3] He could be counted on to attend every meeting, every union function, the only exception being when winter approached and it was time to create a skating rink in the backyard to nurture his son's enthusiasm for hockey.

Another member of the negotiating team was Jack Quenneville, a tall, curly-haired fellow who learned the reasons for a union the hard way. His father was killed while working in a non-unionized paper mill, and because there was no compensation for fatalities, his wife was left with few means to raise the six children in the family. So in 1943 at the age of eighteen, Jack started work as a labourer in Inco's Copper Cliff smelter and when he heard the whispers of a group of workers secretly organizing for a union, he was quick to join the effort. With women working in the smelter during the war, the early organizers were men and women both. The meetings in people's basements, covert change-room conversations, and leaflets passed out under cover of nighttime added up to the union's application for certification to the Ontario Labour Court in August of that year and six months later, the union was authorized as the legal bargaining agent for both Inco and Falconbridge workers and Jack was part of this tremendous accomplishment. Apart from his World War II service, Jack remained active in the union for years to come, including his involvement in the union's cultural program. Shortly before the start of negotiations, Jack starred in the union's Haywood Players' production of Dalton Trumbo's comedy, *The Biggest Thief in Town*, to packed houses and a complimentary review in the *Sudbury Star*.[4]

Norman Jaques, a miner in the Frood open pit mine, was another negotiator intent on changing adverse conditions on the job. Unlike others on the team, Norman was one of the Local 598's fifteen-member executive who was elected by the membership. His head for figures favoured him for financial secretary, a role he fulfilled for most of his decade-long tenure.

Mike Solski, as chair of the Joint Locals 598 and 637 Bargaining Committee, was the union's spokesman in the negotiations. Solski sported a pencil-thin moustache and wore a suit and tie as often as the occasion allowed, but especially when meeting with Inco negotiators. As another union organizer recalled, Solski's 6' 3" frame and formal dress added to the impression that he was "a man you're not going to say no to." An intrepid negotiator who led Local 598 through seven previous collective agreements prior to 1958, Solski was rarely rattled, unafraid of taking the offensive or using strong language, and had a knack for calling well-timed recesses to consult with the rest of the negotiating committee.[5]

At times during contract talks when MMSW's Canadian president Nels Thibault would join in, he yielded to Solski's primacy as the negotiating team's main spokesperson. The two men had been together through many negotiations with tyrannical Inco representatives and bonded through the struggle. MMSW's constitution allowed collective agreements to be negotiated and signed without the national or international union leadership's involvement,[6] a provision dating back to the union's beginnings in remote areas in the days before telephones when communication between locals and international headquarters was difficult or impossible. So for all practical purposes, the union's structure was horizontal and the locals had a great deal of autonomy. But Thibault was uniquely motivated to join negotiations, having experienced Inco's ruthless managerial practices firsthand as he sweated out the ore at the Levack and Frood mines in the days prior to the union's presence. Thibault and Solski tightly coordinated their delivery, each one following the overall agreed-on direction but allowing the other to insert his own moves into the intricate choreography of negotiations.

With their higher levels of education and social status, Inco's negotiating team faced off with the scrappy MMSW negotiators. T.D. Delamere, a QC lawyer, led a team that included B.M. Osler, a fellow lawyer; F. Benard, assistant to the vice president; N.H. Wadge, manager of industrial relations, and B.K. Seli, an industrial relations engineer. The remaining team consisted of managers and assistant managers of the various sections of Inco's extensive operations. Delamere was a heavy-set, slightly balding man with eyes that seemed small for his spectacles.[7] His comportment and three-piece pinstriped suit loudly declared his lawyer class. To the MMSW negotiators who were World War II veterans, Delamere was a prototype of certain officers they'd met, with his air of oblivious entitlement.

They were sensitive to the pocket of insecurity just below his polished surface and attuned to the contempt he used to reinforce his
social standing.

THE FIRST SLASH AND THE FIRST TALKS

For all their similarities to previous negotiations, the 1958 meetings
started like no other contract talks in the years since the union was
certified in 1944. Before the teams even met in April, Inco fired a
shot across the bow. In mid-March the company announced layoffs
of one thousand of its Sudbury workers, with an additional 330
scheduled to be laid off in September, referring to the economic crisis
and a decline in metal markets as rationale.[8] Immediately, the union
issued press statements and wired Prime Minister Diefenbaker and
the opposition leaders. The statements outlined the union's four-
point plan for the economic correctives: an end to overtime and
contract bonus work; government-set prices for metals to balance
supply and demand in the metals industry; expansion of commer-
cial markets for Canadian nickel; more robust international trade
relations.[9] The union's response to the layoffs had little effect on
either the government or the company.

The March layoffs loomed disastrously for workers like Kesler, a
labourer at Inco's Levack mine with a wife and five-year-old daughter to support. His assumption had been for his two years at Inco
that he had achieved the security needed to be a "good provider for
his young family."[10] But Kesler had less than the minimum seniority required by the company and so he was laid off along with the
other 1,300 Inco employees on 15 March. Produce from his brother's farm in nearby Chelmsford fed his family until he was rehired at
Inco's Frood mine the following year. Others left Sudbury for jobs
in surrounding towns and northern mining camps, an exodus that
many more would undertake in the months to come.

At the first of the contract talks in April in the "Mahogany Row"
offices, the union's spokesperson Mike Solski took charge once introductions and scheduling were out of the way. Like a tennis player
with coiled energy launching the first set, he opened the negotiations: "Let's go over our proposals for clarification but not to argue
them." The union's proposals, given to Inco's team in advance of
the meeting, reflected what was developed the month before at the
union's annual convention. The 150 delegates from all MMSW locals

across the country had gathered at Winnipeg's Marlborough Hotel in February, where they followed the usual practice of caucusing to prepare for collective bargaining with their respective employers. Through discussion and debate among the delegates, basic demands were crystallized and language from previous agreements brought forward as potential models for convention delegates to take back to their locals for bargaining with their respective employers. The resolutions were broadly framed so that local unions could tailor their demands to the particular needs of their own memberships. Flexibility in bargaining demands was necessary because the terms and conditions of members' work varied widely across the country and labour legislation differed from province to province. In some locals, the members worked forty-eight hours per week (e.g., Denison Mines in Elliot Lake), while others worked 44, 42, or 40 hours, and some, like Local 480 in Trail BC, had negotiated a four-day schedule of twelve-hour shifts to accommodate members who wanted three days to get out of town and away from the smelter.

The bargaining proposals developed at the Winnipeg convention in February 1958 were intended to guide the negotiations affecting the twenty-four thousand employees of the mining giants, Consolidated Mining and Smelting in BC, and Inco and Falconbridge in Ontario, given that all their collective agreements were due to expire. The agreed-upon bargaining pillars spanned a 10 per cent wage increase, higher pensions at age sixty, a return to one-year contracts,[11] and improvements applied to annual vacations, health and welfare plans, and working conditions. The union officers proposed an emergency strike fund designed to back up "the determination of our membership to win wage increases and other benefits this year."[12] The delegates passed many additional resolutions on wide-ranging topics such as lobbying for government legislation to make joint labour-management safety committees compulsory, condemnation of union raiding, contracting out, and tariffs that restricted the free flow of base metals between Canada and the US.

Debate at the convention was heated over resolutions that anticipated the developing economic crisis.[13] Miners and smeltermen across the country were facing the first recession since they had won their right to union representation and the mining industry was one of the hardest hit. In the year prior, there were twenty shutdowns or suspensions of mining and milling operations, including Britannia Mining & Smelting copper mine in BC, one of MMSW's oldest locals.[14] The first cracks in the postwar settlement between capital and labour were becoming apparent and there were new issues to consider.

In one-industry towns such as Levack, Coniston, and Creighton-Lively, layoffs meant leaving friends and family to find work elsewhere, a common requirement in an industry as volatile as mining. However, with the hard-won unionization, the incremental gains in fringe benefits so painstakingly negotiated over previous years were also at stake. How should the collective bargaining proceed under these different conditions to ensure that previously won gains would not evaporate?

The economic crisis challenged the sacred union principle of job security based on seniority. If layoffs were based on seniority, the cohesiveness of the union's membership could be undermined by splitting along age lines. The younger cohort with less seniority but likely more militant union members would be pitted against the older workers. To prevent this potential split in the membership, the bargaining proposals developed at the Winnipeg Convention advocated for: pensions to be introduced at age sixty; secondly, all workers to go on reduced hours rather than layoffs, which would allow them to keep their negotiated health and other benefits and be eligible for government unemployment insurance for their lost days.[15] The idea of maintaining the same take-home pay for fewer hours was expected to appeal to most members, except perhaps those working in the isolated northern camps with little else but work to occupy themselves. The Sudbury negotiators left the Winnipeg convention with a plan of how to bargain in the face of the economic crisis; yet they were unprepared for what Inco's negotiators had waiting for them.

The second meeting with the company negotiators in April began with Delamere's dire economic forecast, delivered in his typically flat, authoritative voice. The lecture was a preface to announcing a 10 per cent cut in production and the further layoffs of another three hundred employees. His cupboard-is-bare speech opened by revealing that the company had a 105-million-pound stockpile of unsold nickel. While the union negotiators were catching their breath from this stunning news, Delamere rattled on about the evils of the Cuban producers who were responsible for reducing Inco's monopoly on the world nickel market from 90 per cent to 70 per cent; the disadvantageous change to the terms of Inco's contract with the United States government; the declining civilian nickel consumption; and the catastrophic drop of prices in the metal markets in general. He then casually closed the daunting lecture without fanfare: "Now you can see why we cannot meet any increase in costs. Any questions on this mass of information?"[16] Although his litany did not reference the hold-the-line wage restraint policy introduced by the freshly re-elected Diefenbaker government, it was in his quiver if he needed to further justify the lack of a wage offer. The government's fiscal policy was intended to reverse the economic recession by encouraging the business class to withhold wage increases to workers. The hold-the-line policy was introduced by Diefenbaker in February 1958 as a lead-in to the election the following month. Although wage restraint policy did little to correct the downward economic spiral, it did contribute to industrial strife.[17] The unions in construction, auto, and other key industries were determined to negotiate wage increases for their members while knowing they faced employers who had the support of the federal government in refusing those demands for increases.[18]

Delamere's announcement of the second round of layoffs momentarily left MMSW negotiators confounded. The company had given the union notice of the first set of layoffs in March prior to their public announcement, but this was a calculated, shabby move to appropriate negotiations as a platform for announcing the existence of a stockpile and make an economic case, a harbinger of the intractable negotiations to come. While layoffs were nothing new in an industry characterized by boom-and-bust cycles, endemic to a pattern of drawing workers in, only to throw them out later,[19] these layoffs in the spring of 1958 were especially damaging. Workers must now deplete their savings at the crucial time of negotiations, thereby weakening their bargaining power.

INCO'S FILIBUSTERING NON-OFFER

After another month had limped by, the negotiating teams met again on 6 May. In light of the layoffs now totaling a disastrous 1,300 workers, the MMSW negotiating team opened the meeting by arguing for maintaining the purchasing power of its members as a means of correcting the recession. The assertions were well prepared prior to the meeting with the help of the union's research director, Lukin Robinson, who spent many hours collecting and analyzing figures on the cost of living, market prices of nickel and copper, and other economic data from the Dominion Bureau of Statistics,[20] as well as perusing articles in the *Globe and Mail's* business section, Chamber of Commerce reports, and Inco's annual reports.[21] Since the company did not publish its production figures, the union's grasp of the extent of the stockpile of nickel was limited to what could be inferred from these sources and the few production figures the company negotiators shared during bargaining.

As chief spokesperson for the MMSW team, Solski proceeded by pointing out the contradictions in Delamere's lecture on economics delivered at the previous meeting: "You can't say 'buy' to Canadians and then take away their ability to do so."[22] Then, in line with the union's position developed at the Winnipeg convention, he submitted the additional demand of a reduction in working hours of 10 per cent without a corresponding reduction in take-home pay. But the savings from the cut to hours, carefully tabulated by Inco's Burrough's adding machines, was too firmly imprinted in the minds of their negotiators to consider Solski's demand. After some further debate about the theory of supply and demand, Delamere avowed, "I regret that we cannot agree with your formula on economics," to which Solski retorted, "We're interested in reaching a satisfactory agreement without theory if necessary. Shall we continue?"[23] They did continue over the next several meetings, but little was resolved.

Nels Thibault, MMSW Canadian president, was a serious, straightforward negotiator who sometimes gave into playful injections. One such occasion was during the May meetings. The deduction of union dues from workers' pay-cheques, an article in the collective agreement known as "union security," was being discussed.[24] With every worker paying monthly union dues as a condition of their employment, the union would have the certainty of financial means to represent its members. Now, because the locals intended to hold a referendum vote on a $1 increase in monthly dues from $3.50 to $4.50 as specified in the collective agreement article, it needed the company's agreement. Even such a small and simple change to the collective agreement language gave Delamere the ground to display the particular mix of malice and single-mindedness that made him Inco's pick for spokesperson in the negotiations. With obvious sarcasm he asked, "Do you contemplate setting up a strike fund?" – certain that his adversaries would recognize how preposterous it would be for a company to manage deductions for a union's strike fund. But before Solski could answer, Thibault cut in, "That's a good idea. I wasn't thinking of it."

In fact there was a strike fund, established as part of the Canadian constitution in 1955 with a 5-cent monthly contribution from each of the Canadian MMSW members out of the per capita payments. The fund was managed by MMSW's national office with monthly deposits of $1,500.[25] Although this fund was insufficient for what lay ahead,[26] it did exist. As president of the Canadian MMSW, Thibault would have been intimately acquainted with its balance but at this moment in the talks he was inclined to have some fun at the expense of Inco's spokesman. When Delamere returned to the issue by asking caustically if the union really expected the company to collect for a strike fund, Solski played off Thibault's volley: "Your deductions now might be going towards a strike fund,"[27] challenging Delamere to consider that such a distasteful practice could be occurring at Inco without his knowledge.

Much of the discussions in the May meetings focused on reclassifications. With thousands of workers at Inco, there were many instances of workers performing tasks that rightly belonged to higher paid classifications. Complaints about the correspondence between the actual work and over one thousand job titles were first brought to the attention of the union by the affected members and argued for reclassification in negotiation meetings. To justify a higher rate of pay on the basis of comparisons with closely related jobs required intimate knowledge of the job and its comparators. For each of the reclassification arguments, Solski would turn the floor over to the fellow negotiator who was familiar with the production processes in the relevant section of Inco's massive operations. In these discussions, the union negotiators' extensive hands-on knowledge of how the work was actually done directly challenged the company's managerial prerogative enshrined in the collective agreements of unionized workplaces as part of the postwar accord between labour and capital. Even though this condition most often won out in negotiations, both sides knew full well that the MMSW negotiators' expertise, rooted as it was in the direct experience of keeping the mines and smelters productive, was the more durable authority.

WORKPLACE HEALTH AND SAFETY

In addition to reclassifications and union security, the issue of safety committees was raised by the union in the May talks. Given the record, a demand for a joint union-management safety committee was not unreasonable. There had been sixty-one fatalities in the past eight years[28] and at the time of the May negotiations, close to one hundred men had been disabled in work-related accidents, some only in their thirties. The collective agreement provided the union with "the right to discuss matters related to safety at any time,"[29] but there was no obligation on the part of Inco to act on the matters brought forward by the union. MMSW had negotiated safety committees with other mining companies, including Consolidated Mining and Smelting in Trail, BC, Eldorado Mining & Refining in Saskatchewan, and Denison Mining in Elliot Lake uranium mines, securing paid time off the job for the union's committee members and regular joint union-management meetings and inspections.[30]

Despite these instances of accountability and oversight for safety in the industry, Inco remained steadfastly opposed and Delamere refused the request when it was reintroduced in the 1958 negotiations, insisting that safety was best left up to the company safety staff. "We have the means to carry out safety. Many grievances arise against enforcement of safety conditions. A committee would not be much help." Rather than arguing about the company's abysmal safety record, the union negotiators returned to the principle of co-action: "We don't under-estimate the concern of the employer but you don't convince us that greater objectives can't be attained with greater co-operative effort."[31] Without a dedicated committee, health and safety concerns often arose in collective bargaining and the May negotiations were no exception. The union reported that despite the $4 million that Inco had recently spent on increasing the air flow in the smelter, many members had recently sustained serious illness from the conditions of their work.

The conditions were especially shocking in the sintering plant within the Copper Cliff smelter complex where the nickel was cooked for the dried-up grey nickel called sinters.[32] There was no escaping the dust, gas, and intense heat in the sintering plant. Harold, a summer student who worked there, remembered "the washroom, a little toilet that was a wood frame building inside the plant. I'd have to take a shovel to find the toilet because the dust was so thick that it would be buried in silt. And, in half an hour, the whole thing would disappear again under the silt."[33] The company issued masks and stationed buckets around the smelter filled with a solution intended to neutralize the sulphuric acid circulating in the air. Workers were encouraged to dip the masks in the buckets, make use of the water fountains and salt pill dispensers, and to put orange peels inside their masks to help them smell better.[34] Because wool was relatively less flammable than other fabrics, they wore woolen undershirts in case of sparking. Some smeltermen double-masked for greater protection, which made it even more difficult to breath. One worker recalled relief from the nosebleeds and mask-wearing came only on the days of the inspectors' visits:

> The smelter ran normally with the dampers above the furnaces open and only a fraction of the gas reached the chimneys. It cost money to heat the gasses to go up the three chimneys that preceded the super stack. As a result the sulphur dioxide was emitted at quasi ground level and when the conditions were right, little wind or else damp weather, especially during the night at graveyard shift, the gas hung heavy over the whole smelter. Hence my nosebleeds even though I wore a mask constantly. Then occasionally, INCO would get the word that the inspectors from Toronto were coming to test the air quality. On that day, the dampers would be closed, the gas would be transferred to the chimneys and the natural gas fired blowers would function to send it shooting above the refinery to pollute Sudbury, Coniston and environs to the east or Copper Cliff and environs to the west, depending on the wind direction. Merciful relief at the smelter itself. It was a day or so of bliss! I could breathe. I didn't need the mask and no nosebleeds.[35]

The company-supplied masks were almost useless as later determined when Jean Gagnon, his fellow union activists, and the MPP for the Nickel Belt, Elie Martel, petitioned the Ontario government to order Inco to clean up its operations in the late 1960s.[36] The sulphuric acid was lethal not only for the smelter workers, but contaminated the air and soil in the district to render it as barren as a moonscape. Stefano, one of Inco's smeltermen who lived in the nearby community of Gatchell, started working in the sintering plant in November 1948 after arriving from South Calabria, Italy. Like others, he was determined to grow vegetable and flower gardens. When the winds blew towards their houses, they would drench the garden with water; otherwise, the produce so skillfully tended all season would be lost.[37]

Turnover rates were especially high in the sintering plant where new recruits were needed each day because so many quit even before putting in a full shift.[38] Soon after his hiring, Stefano insisted on a transfer to maintenance so he could bid on other jobs that would take him out of the sintering plant. He told his supervisor, "If you don't give me transfer, I quit. I'm not going to stay any longer here. I'm used to breathing pure air not that stuff." Homer Seguin, who started at Inco at age seventeen and eventually became a safety advocate and president of the local under USWA leadership, described the effect of the working conditions, "With every downdraft from the stack, it felt like someone was strangling you. Your throat burns and you can't breathe. ... Sometimes we'd smash a window just to breathe and the carpenter would replace that window within an hour because Inco didn't want any of the dust outside because it was so valuable. It was almost pure nickel."[39] Once a week, the sintering plant workers took their work clothes home for washing, a task that usually fell to wives and mothers. On the weekends, Claire, newly married to a sintering plant labourer, would dutifully wash the clothes in the landlady's wringer washing machine. After the laundering, the rollers of the wringer washer were midnight black from the nickel dust. To avoid the wrath of the landlady, Claire would spend another hour scrubbing the rollers with Ajax to return them to their original colour.

A CHOIR OF "NOS"

During the May talks, Inco stalled on both new and outstanding union proposals. In addition to the proposal for joint safety committees, the union's purchase of land from Inco to build a union hall in Levack was another of the union's proposals left unresolved from previous contract talks. The local had built halls in four other surrounding communities and each was a vibrant hub for cultural and recreational activities. As in previous years, no progress was made on the purchase of land during the talks in May 1958, and for years to come there would be no union hall in Levack. Other unsettled issues brought forward during the springtime negotiation talks included paid time for union officials to represent members at grievances and meetings with managers. Solski launched: "I have another item I'm getting tired of raising. It's this question of time off for committee men." After a few remarks back and forth, Delamere went for the escape hatch, "I want to check my notes, but my recollection is different." Full of fury with fingers drumming on the table,

Solski insisted, "Well, look at your notes and quit wasting time," to which Delamere snarled in a futile attempt to regain lost ground, "I intend to."[40] Solski's impatience with the lack of an offer from Inco had been growing and the pile-up of outstanding issues from previous talks only aggravated him further.

Finally, after five days of meetings, Inco presented its first offer on 23 May 1958. Apart from a few changes to job classifications, recall rights for workers returning from a layoff, and a revision to the existing benefit plan to dovetail with the soon-to-be-introduced Ontario hospital program, there was nothing. Notably, there was no wage increase over the proposed two-year contract. Inco's total cost for the offer was one-seventh of one cent/hour for each worker. A very short recess to convene the union team was all that was needed before they unanimously agreed that the company was pushing them towards conciliation, a move quite familiar to them. Back in the posh boardroom with the company negotiators, Solski affirmed, "Unless the company has something further to offer, we can see no useful purpose in continuing and so we must apply for conciliation." Delamere responded, "Apparently, we've failed to impress you with the seriousness of the situation and we've little if anything further to offer."[41] A stalemate in the talks was not out of the ordinary. Conciliation boards had been unavoidable for all but one of the past five rounds of negotiations of collective agreements[42] and the members had come very close to striking before.

In the week that followed the 23 May talks, the offer presented by Inco was firmly rejected by the MMSW members in the series of membership meetings held at the union halls. By virtue of the union's constitution, women were endowed with voice but no vote at the meetings. If they had voting privileges, many would have joined the choir of "Nos." There was nothing in Inco's offer to address workplace safety and grant greater assurance of their husbands' safety when they rode the cage into the depths of the earth at the start of each shift or took up their posts at the smelter furnaces. It would be almost two decades later before improvements in safety emerged, largely a result of the legislatively mandated joint management-union occupational health and safety committees.

The "No" vote was an opportunity for members to declare their support for their union. Rejecting Inco's offer was an endorsement of a union that had delivered year-by-year wage gains, protections against vindictive foremen, and cultural and recreational programs – all of which brought dignity and tangible improvements to their lives and their families' lives. Some members like Ivan, a raise driller in Frood mine, had become loyal supporters as far back as 1942 when two union organizers were viciously attacked and with no sanctions applied to the perpetrating Inco shift bosses, Ivan and his fellow workers had no recourse in the face of the swaggering admissions of guilt made with impunity in the lunchroom,[43] but their resolute support for the union was sealed from then on. In formulating their response to the Inco offer, the MMSW leaders could count on the loyalty of men like Ivan and their wives working behind the scenes. But, in the months ahead, even the most dedicated of MMSW members would be tested by a series of events and circumstance that augmented the treacherous maneuverings of the company as the government's covenant with the business class coincided with the Cold War rhetoric issued from the pulpits and media.

BRADLEY AND THE SOLID BRICK WALL

Following the membership's rejection of Inco's 23 May offer, the conciliation officer R.V. Bradley appointed by the Ontario Labour Relations Board convened conciliation talks. On 19 June, Inco and union teams each occupied one of Inco's conference rooms in the company's main office building in Copper Cliff. Bradley toggled back and forth between them over the course of the day-long talks.

Starting with the union contingent, Bradley went right to the point. "What is going to buy an agreement?" Without hesitation, Solski shot back with a habitual honesty, "A hell of a lot more than has been offered."[44]

The cigarette smoke began to saturate the room, and the silence stretched endless and taut. Finally, Bradley recommended to the union negotiators, "If you are going to accept what they've offered, you might as well accept now."

Solski fired back, "Shit, I'm not ready to commit suicide yet. If they're prepared to move, we are." Bradley turned on his heel to meet with Inco's negotiators. Hours later he came back shaking his head. Solski asked, "No dice?" Bradley confirmed with a head shake.

Sharing his assessment of the current stalemate, Solski remarked, "Their minds are made up not to move at this stage. We knew it from the start. They tried to scare us by laying off men but after the contract is signed, they'll hire them back."[45]

As a last-ditch effort to forge a settlement, Bradley then suggested to the union negotiators they could propose a 10-cent-an-hour increase as danger pay. "That doesn't clean the air" rebutted the union side.[46] The idea of trading safety for pay was a thorny topic for the union. On the one hand, advocating for workplace safety was in the union's DNA, stemming back to the early days of the militant Western Federation of Miners. And then, too, many more members' wives than Millie McQuaid were pressing for better, safer working conditions for their husbands and the trade-off of safety for wage increase was not viable for them despite the prospect of a new couch or chair to brighten up their lived-in living rooms.

On the other hand, there were many members earning over and above their hourly wage as drillers on Inco's bonus system and although it was often at the cost of their safety, they didn't want an end to their augmented pay cheques. But during the conciliation talks, the union didn't have to wrestle with this contradiction. Bradley didn't pursue his suggestion of redefining a wage hike as danger pay. By this time in the day, nerves were frayed and there was no point in escalating the tensions any further. He made one more effort with the company's team but eventually, the conciliator admitted there was no room to negotiate with Inco: "I'm prepared to stay today, tomorrow and the next day to get a settlement, but I'm up against a solid brick wall."[47]

Spirits had been high in Sudbury during the morning of 19 June. Summer solstice was nearing and the day's temperature was forecast to be the warmest yet, and conciliation held the promise of a settlement. But by the end of the day, Bradley's talks had failed. Inco's smelter stacks stood darkly forbidding against the late afternoon's cool grey sky, belching out the poisonous sulphuric fumes. As the miners and smeltermen trundled out of Inco's plant gates at the end of their shift, word spread. A three-member conciliation board would now have to be formed, hearings scheduled, and carefully crafted presentations delivered by their union detailing Inco's bad-faith bargaining. With their characteristic solidarity and salty language, the workers braced each other for the next faceoff with Inco.

Bargaining Breaks Down

The open skies of Monday 7 July brought an end to the drizzle and fog that socked in over the weekend. A dazzlingly bright sun was breaking through and about to warm the seedlings in Sudbury's backyard gardens. Just as promising was a favourable outcome of the conciliation hearings, now scheduled for early August. The union presentations had turned the heads of conciliation board members numerous times in the past and surely this set of hearings would be no different. Before the conciliation hearings could begin, however, Inco threw another curve ball.

An announcement came on 7 July to cut the working hours of all unionized employees from forty to thirty-two per week. Like the notification of the layoffs in March, Inco timed its announcement of the cuts to working hours to coincide with a pivotal time in the bargaining process. In its announcement, the company claimed to have chosen an across-the-board reduction in hours instead of further layoffs. The company officials claimed as many as 2,500 men would need to be laid off for an equivalent curtailment in production and because that would impose undue hardship on the community, they opted for the reduction in hours.[1] But nobody was fooled. If Inco had opted to lay off 2,500 workers, the company would run the risk of losing some of the most experienced workers, and not knowing how long the recession would last the company officials didn't want to be caught short in case markets rebounded quickly. Yet the 20 per cent cut in hours was the least cost-efficient since Inco would have to continue paying benefits to its entire workforce. So, why did the company choose this approach to the curtailment instead of the layoffs? Only much later, when the strike was in full swing, did anyone realize the full effect of the across-the-board wage cut. It fueled the workers' contempt for the company, inclining them to strike; at the same time, it left them with little to no savings to weather a lengthy strike. Both effects served Inco's interests very well.

Immediately following Inco's announcement of the cut, a press release was drafted at the Regent Street union office that warned of the danger to the country's economy of such a substantial pay cut for Inco's fourteen thousand plus workforce, making the case that a further reduction in the purchasing power of so many workers "may well drive the current recession into a full-scale depression."[2] MMSW members packed into union halls in Sudbury and the surrounding communities of Garson, Creighton-Lively, Levack, and Coniston to hear from their leaders on the recent developments. Solski cautioned against assuming that cutbacks were just a well-worn company ploy to negotiate an inferior collective agreement that once signed would return to the usual forty hours: "You can't compare past tricks used by the company in other negotiations because there is one big difference, and that is the general economic situation."[3]

Far from giving into despair, Solski would lay out an economic analysis for his audiences that quoted Inco's yearly profits and assumed a level of numerical literacy amongst the assembly to demonstrate there was more than enough in Inco's kitty to weather the present economic storm. The punch line was that since it was the labour of Inco workers that created those financial reserves, they should have a share in them so that nobody would have to endure hardship while business conditions improved. Solski would close the meetings with a call to action. Winning the fight for the revised bargaining proposals, which now included a return to the forty-hour week, would take all hands on deck. "Don't look at the union as some separate third party that can solve all problems without your participation. You *are* the union."[4] The membership took the reins. The resolution that endorsed the fight for the contract demand for forty hours pay for thirty-two hours of work was moved and seconded by two members who were otherwise inactive in union affairs.[5] It was carried unanimously by the overflowing halls.

Had Irene, the eight-year-old daughter of an Inco electrician, been there, she would have voted against the resolution because the reduction to a thirty-two-hour week was a godsend that would give her an extra day a week with her beloved father, Carl, a first-class electrician at Inco. Ordinarily the family spent their weekends at a summer camp on nearby McFarlane Lake. But then quite suddenly, as Irene remembers, "he didn't have to go back on Monday and I thought, 'This is lovely!'" Irene's memories of this time with her father were vibrant: "I had my dad to myself and he would just do camp things. He would walk me out [into the lake] and anchor the rowboat he had made, maybe 5 feet, 10 feet from the shore. He would bait my hook and I would pull up perch and sunfish and put them in a big pail of water in the boat. I wouldn't take the fish off and I wouldn't bait my hook. So, my dad would get up off that chair, walk down the slope, get in the water, pull my rod up, disconnect the whole thing, and put some more bait on. Sometimes, he'd no sooner get back up the hill and down he'd come again."[6]

FUTILE CONCILIATION HEARINGS
AND STRIKE PREPARATIONS

Inco's intransigence in the 1958 contract talks came as no surprise to union members. Most rounds of bargaining had been fractious, but the two sets of layoffs in March and April, followed by the thirty-two-hour week, signaled a strategic difference for this round. In his opening remarks at the conciliation hearings in early August, Solski offered his assessment to Judge Thomas, chairman of the Conciliation Board: "It's the first time they've said 'no' to everything, so it's hard for us to help you," adding later, "We've told them we're prepared to bargain if they make a proposal."[7] In all the years of bargaining since 1944 with Inco, despotic as the company was, the union had not encountered such implacability.

As in previous conciliation hearings, the union's research director, Lukin Robinson, had prepared a brief to be delivered to the three-member Conciliation Board over the four days of hearings in Toronto's plush Royal York Hotel. The brief proposed increasing the purchasing power of Inco workers via a 10 per cent wage demand as part of a larger economic argument. Drawing on national data, the brief affirmed that Canadian workers were more productive than ever before and therefore deserved wage increases. Further data detailed the recently stalled consumer spending of Canadians. To pull the country out the recession, wages would need to be boosted for workers' greater purchasing power. As if to quash any criticism of the brief's ideological bias, Robinson quoted an unlikely ally to support the union's prescription for a healthier economy. The

Canadian Chamber of Commerce had recently published the recommendation that, "Consumers must be persuaded to add to their consumption by about $1 billion each year."[8] Comparisons with 295 collective agreements from other industry-sector employers in the brief showed that a 10 per cent wage demand accorded with the average wage increases of the past year and a half. Inco's reported profits were reiterated to illustrate that the company was more than capable of bearing the effects of the recession without shifting the burden onto the shoulders of its less fortunate employees: "This fabulously wealthy corporation, Inco, has been able to continue its widespread operations including vast expansion in northern Manitoba, all without recourse either to bonds, lending institutions, or the stock market. All these activities have been made possible out of earnings. The company has no funded debt. The same cannot be said of its employees."[9] Further contrast between the company's position with its stockpile of nickel and the workers' position was made explicit in Solski's oral address to the three-member conciliation panel: "Workers can't stockpile the $17.60 loss [as a result of the cut of eight hours/week], but the nickel is money in reserve."[10] The already-low purchasing power of Canadian consumers was one of the major reasons for the current recession, and Inco's recent lay-offs and reduced work weeks was further contributing to the economy's free fall.

The union's presentation to the conciliation hearings drew on another unlikely source to support the union's economic analysis of the recession that was gripping the country. Ontario attorney general Kelso Roberts was no friend of unions, his sympathies were with the small businesses in the province. Yet he was disgusted by the greed of the large mining corporations and had gone public with his remedy for the economic recession: "Those leaders in the nickel industry, in the International Nickel Company, should take another look at their profits and relate that to the employment of workmen to see whether they cannot give some leadership at this time, in something other than a negative direction."[11] In his speech, Roberts pointed to improved consumer purchasing power as the remedy to the economic downturn.[12] The remedy aligned with the union's recommended approach that was well within the nation's memory, for just three years prior the increase in consumer spending, which was a direct result of the higher wages fought for and won by the labour movement, had held the 1953–54 economic downturn in check.

On the last day of the conciliation hearings, Judge Thomas tried to initiate bargaining on the basis of a 2 per cent wage increase. When this proposal was refused, Thomas admitted to the union negotiators, "It's the first time I've had a failure." Solski thanked him for his effort on behalf of the MMSW joint negotiating committee and ended with the foreboding declaration, "We will have to go back home now and do it the hard way," for the first time alluding unequivocally to a strike.[13] Retreating from the Royal York Hotel meeting rooms to their more humble accommodations at the Prince George Hotel, the union negotiators discussed the corner they found themselves in. MMSW Canadian vice president Harvey Murphy had joined them for the conciliation hearings; now he recounted details of the several strikes in his long career of union organizing dating back to the early 1930s, warning the committee of the many obstacles that would be placed in front of them and preparing them for the extent of effort that would be required to win the fight that lay ahead.[14] His words might have sounded ominous, but they were the words of hard-earned experience, and since most of the union team members hadn't lived through a strike, much less organized one, they listened up.

Following the fruitless conciliation hearings in early August, the MMSW leaders began to prepare for a strike in earnest. Some initial measures had been taken in March, for instance, when a Local 598 Executive member contacted the Unemployment Insurance Commission to inquire if benefits would be paid to applicants who were receiving union welfare payments. The commission's ruling was a disappointing no.[15] In July, Local 598 cancelled its loan of $30,000 to a sister local in Elliot Lake for the construction of a union hall. By the end of August, six committees would be formed and approved by the stewards: picket detail, public relations, welfare, transportation, publicity and finance, and recreation.[16] By early September, Weir Reid, the local's recreation director, was busy selecting films, games, and other recreational activities for the strikers and their families to be held in the union's Regent Street hall during the strike.

In anticipation of what was to come as they awaited the Conciliation Board's report, the union leaders instructed the members to tighten their belts. "Don't spend a cent that you don't absolutely have to spend. Don't tie yourself to any additional debts; don't take on any installment payment commitments."[17] For some members, the instructions were difficult to follow. Families were expanding. Ivan, a raise driller, had twins on the way; he was building a new house in the Flour Mill district for his family and his bonus pay was needed for the supplies.[18] A labourer in the baghouses at the Copper Cliff smelter, Benjamin, had just married and the four-day workweek required the couple to forego what they would have otherwise spent on a wedding in order to rent a small apartment on Whittaker Street.[19] Some members with already-expanded families were making house, furniture, and car payments, often on the costly installment plans of retailers and sales finance companies, and were in the habit of going to work even when they were sick so as not to lose pay. For them, even one day away from the job was a tremendous blow to the already-stretched family finances.

Others who had lived through the sacrifices of the Depression and war years shuddered to think they would soon again have to ration their meat consumption, substitute milk powder for fresh milk, rely on the generosity of neighbours and friends. Even in the early postwar years, the economic policy directing the national reconstruction prioritized exports and heavy industry over the availability of household goods and Canadians were encouraged to contribute to the postwar reconstruction through thrift and delayed acquisition.[20] As a consequence, Canadian families, in contrast to their American counterparts, did not plunge into mass consumption in the immediate postwar years and instead continued their tradition of "making do."[21] Only by the mid-1950s were shortages easing, regulations relaxing, and the decades of deprivation fading. Experts were beginning to give Canadians permission to spend, albeit responsibly, and popular magazines were advertising household and labour-saving appliances while advising on prudent family budgeting. The notion of a consumer culture gained strength over the ensuing decades, so that by 1958, what might have been considered a luxury at one time was beginning to be thought of as a necessity.[22] And, to participate in the emerging consumer culture, required income – something Inco's striking families were lacking.

At the same membership meetings where Solski urged economizing in anticipation of a strike, he stoked the energy of fury. Reporting on the growing unrest of other Canadian workers who were equally steadfast in their demands, Solski stormed, "Today, we find workers in all unions standing up on their hind legs and refusing to be intimidated by the boss. They are not frightened by the company propaganda of lower profits. They are demanding their just share, not only for this year, but for the years that have gone by. Our demands of Inco are highly justified and whatever battle we must put up in order to realize them is well worth it."[23] Away from the public spotlight, Solski busied himself exploring possible avenues of industrial sabotage in the event of a strike. In a letter to the union's Buffalo local, he asked Joseph Scioli, president of the local, to investigate the possibility of blocking the shipments of nickel and copper from Inco's warehouses on Clinton and Elmwood Streets in Buffalo.[24] The plan didn't come to fruition during the strike, but later, true to the historical militancy of their union, a group of strikers would travel from Sudbury to the docks in Montreal to picket tankers loaded with nickel at the height of the strike.[25]

From its end, Inco was signalling its uncompromising position to its employees. In its letter to the workers, the company stated that because of the 100 million pound stockpile, "we now have to tackle the job of finding and holding a greatly increased market for our nickel …. All this forward planning is going to require very heavy outlays of money. Consequently, the company … must avoid any increase in its production costs [i.e., wages]."[26] Finding new markets for Inco's output was indeed a problem. Inco had become reliant on its lucrative armaments' contracts with the US State Dept and put no effort into developing other markets. Nickel sales had remained relatively steady during 1957, but dropped substantially in 1958,[27] in part because of the economic recession, but also because the US State Dept had discontinued its stockpiling of nickel, which left Inco with a huge production surplus.[28] In response to the surplus, Inco deliberately slowed down its production, dropping from 331 million pounds in January 1958 to 201 million pounds in August 1958.[29]

JITTERS AND INCO'S SHUTDOWN PREPARATIONS

The Conciliation Board's report, issued on 9 September, sided with Inco and recommended no wage increase. The only concession the board made to the union was the length of the contract and recommended it be one year, not two as Inco had proposed. The union leaders immediately condemned the board's report as "making a mockery of the conciliation process [that] could very well have been written by the company itself,"[30] and turned to their memberships for direction.

Over the next thirty-two hours, the union members registered their disgust for the no-wage offer in a strike vote managed by women from the union's women's auxiliary at the eleven locations of Inco's operations, including the quarry on Manitoulin Island, eighty miles from Sudbury. Of the 90 per cent of the eligible members who cast their ballot, 82.7 per cent voted to instruct their leaders to "strike if necessary to back up the contract demands."[31] A greater proportion of miners voted for the strike in comparison to the smeltermen, in keeping with the historical trend of miners' militancy compared to their fellow smeltermen that came from the necessarily close coordination required by their dangerous work.[32] The strike vote spelled a clear yearning for a militant collective action to command Inco's attention. Clearly, the peaceful approach of the negotiators on both sides of the table had failed to deliver the security of employment and incremental improvements in working conditions and living standards promised by the postwar economic boom.

Even deeper than the members' frustration over the unfulfilled wage demands was their naked rage over Inco's persistently vindictive managerial practices. Too regularly, workers were moved to Levack, the most isolated, far-flung of Inco's mines with only a gravel road in and out. Supervisors intent on disciplining outspoken employees would say with paternalistic contempt, "While you drive out to Levack every day to put in your eight hours, think about your stupidity on your way. And you can think about your stupidity on your way home too."[33] Over the years, the venomous exercise of control by Inco supervisors in the mines and smelters had been met with defiance, even by workers who did not ordinarily question the legitimacy of managerial authority. The strike vote was another eruption of the conflict that was never too far from the surface of relations between Inco's workers and managers.

For its part, Inco was eager for a strike and even more so for an early strike, since in the warmer weather the smelter stacks didn't have to be heated and there was no worry about frozen steam and water lines. Inco's executives did not wait for the result of the conciliation to begin preparing for a shutdown. The priority was to get all the loose ore to the surface before the strike because Inco ore, high in sulphides, would catch fire if left in a pile underground. Salaried employees were given instructions on how to maintain the pumps for flood control in the mines during the anticipated strike while in the smelter they received training on how to tap the matte from the furnaces, skim the slag, and safely shut down the converters. One of these salaried employees remembers, "It was a rudimentary teaching, only enough to shut down the equipment safely. The union men didn't mind showing us how to shut down, as they realized we could never learn all their operation tasks in a short while."[34] As it turned out when the time came, the smeltermen stayed past the strike deadline to safely shut their equipment down. Although they were disgruntled and ready to strike, they had pride in their duties, and smeltermen, like miners, were not inclined to engage in sabotage for the danger of their work discouraged this kind of action.

Another key preparation Inco made well before the conciliation report was issued was to relocate its executive airplane, a four-seater Beechcraft, from a hanger close to Frood mine to the Toronto airport in the first week of September to discourage strikers who might take to vandalizing. Inco's two pilots were also relocated to a Toronto hotel, to return to Sudbury only when the executives were to be flown to meetings in Toronto, New York, or Thompson, Manitoba. For Mason, one of the pilots, the time away from Sudbury for the duration of the strike turned out to be an especially hefty sacrifice: his son was born just days before the relocation to Toronto, so he missed the first precious months of his newborn's life.[35]

While Inco's "Mahogany Row" executive offices were bustling with shutdown preparations, the MMSW negotiators were still straining for a settlement. They were hopeful that the strike vote results would sober up Inco's negotiators, as it had in the past. At the company-union meeting seven days after the conciliation report was issued, Solski opened with an offer to resume negotiations. Inco's team dismissed his overtures, fixated as they were on finding out the exact amount of notice MMSW would give the company before striking.[36] Still eager for a settlement, Solski offered his summary of how the negotiations had proceeded thus far: "We were hopeful of doing some bargaining, not with two clubs but with one, and you said you won't bargain." Delamere countered, "That's wrong; we tried to convince you of our position," to which Solski made reference to the overwhelming majority strike vote: "Your employees don't believe you." But after some wrangling he accepted Inco's request for seventy-two hours of notice before the start of the strike, although he refused to name a date.[37]

The closer the days ticked to the strike date of 24 September set by the union, the more that MMSW members were filled with fear and trepidation. They had come close to striking several times before. With solid strike votes, Inco would cave at the last minute and offer an extra few cents an hour, which was considered a fair settlement given the times.[38] They had never come this close, though; nor had most members been on strike before now. What would it be like to head out to a picket line instead of trundling off to work in the mines or smelters? It couldn't be as dangerous as the working conditions faced every day mucking out ore from the bowels of the earth or tending the blazing furnaces in the smelter. Yet, without the benefit of rehearsal – and no strike has the benefit of rehearsal – they were advancing headlong into the unknown. How long could they last on savings and whatever union support they could get? Some reassurance came with the promise from the union's international executive board in Denver for "full moral and financial support to achieve victory of the Inco workers."[39] And, their fellow Local 598 members working at Falconbridge Mines in Sudbury generously pledged one full day's wages per week towards the strike fund. But would the support from combined sources be enough to sustain them longer than the length of time the company could hold out?

THE DAM BURSTS OPEN

With every day, the anxiety of union members mixed with exasperation. The process of negotiations was taking far too long for some. If there was to be a strike, why delay further when the company made it clear it wasn't interested in negotiating? Their work in the mines taught the members how to act quickly when they had to, when their lives depended on it. The frequent cave-ins and rockfalls had miners dropping tools and rushing to the safe room at the faintest rumble in the rock, however far away the sound might be from the stope, the miners' work area. Waiting for even a split-second could spell injury or death. Smeltermen, too, knew the perils of delayed action. Just in the past couple of months, the apron of a puncher working in the smelter caught fire and burnt his right leg and both buttocks.[40] And that wasn't the only serious accident. A tapper's helper was assisting in the budding up of a furnace's skimming hole when slag splashed over the side of the chute causing his trouser leg to catch fire.[41] A labourer at the reverb furnace was tightening the cable on the car-puller hoist when the clutch slipped, causing him to fall and hit against the hoist, injuring his leg.[42]

The anger and frustration of the workers spilled over first at Garson mine. The combination of log-jammed negotiations, evidence of Inco's greed, and supervisors who lorded over them every day was too much for these miners. Cecil Ralph, an outspoken, strong-minded Garsonite, prompted others to walk off the job. Cecil had attended an earlier Local 598 Executive meeting as an observer to find out the progress of preparations for a strike. Learning how under-developed the executive's plans were, he was incensed. When he reported back to his peers at Garson, it was easy to recruit fellow mutineers especially after a few beers in the town's hotel beverage room. Cecil knew where to turn to get signs for his posse. His nearby neighbour in Garson, Archie McArthur, one of the original organizers of the union in the 1940s known to all as Fritz, could be counted on to support militant actions and Archie's son happened to be employed as a sign painter. In the McArthur's basement, he went to work to produce signs reading "On Strike" and "32-hour week" with 32 crossed out and "40" marked in its place. Archie's younger son, who would later lead Local 598 through the worst of the jurisdictional disputes with USWA the following decade, delivered the signs to Cecil's house in the dead of night.[43] The picketers placed boulders to barricade the road leading to the Garson mine gate where they stood to brandish the signs, shovels, baseball bats, and pick handles, daring anybody to walk across the line drawn in the gravel at the gate.

Word of the Garson walkout spread quickly and the workers at Levack mine, the iron ore plant, and Coniston and Copper Cliff smelters quickly followed suit.[44] The walkouts, unauthorized by union leaders, were a calculated act to proclaim that workers were fed up with what they perceived as the dillydallying by Inco as well as their own union leaders.

While the historical record is devoid of concrete evidence, there are those who believed that the walkouts were led by provocateurs with the aim of undermining the union.[45] Unelected leaders who emerge suddenly from the rank and file during an unauthorized walkout can destablize the mandate of elected union leadership to act as the official spokesmen for the members. Additionally, and significantly, the labour laws enacted as part of the postwar settlement between capital and labour required a trade-off: union leaders would police their own members from walkouts and other job actions deemed illegal in exchange for maintaining their legitimacy

Figures 5.1, 5.2 | Garson Mine wildcatters.

as representatives of the workers. Stiff penalties were imposed on unions for contravening the labour law. Consequently, there would be much to gain by encouraging walkouts prior to the official start of a strike if the aim was to undermine the union.

Whether union dissidents were behind the walkouts in September 1958 or not, the membership's history of militant action is indisputable. In the early years of the 1950s alone there were several walkouts.[46] At the smelters, men stormed out in protest of the noxious fumes and in the mines the men threw down their tools when a shift boss physically abused one of their fellow miners for refusing to speed up production. Often there was no picket line and no signs, but only a mass of men, sometimes joined by women, with watchful Inco police standing at the sidelines. At times, there were sufficient numbers participating in actions for production to be temporarily discontinued. To stay within the law, the union leadership responded to these revolts by assuring the public officials they were not sanctioned by the union.

Similarly, during the walkouts leading up to the strike, the union leaders played their part as dutiful chaperones of the members, as required by law governing labour relations. The MMSW members were cautioned by their leaders against riotous action: "From now on every move has to be carefully considered. Let no one either provoke or be provoked into any unauthorized action."[47] At every shift change, Local 598 officers, stewards, and volunteering members were dispatched to Garson and Levack mines, the iron ore plant, and to both the Coniston and Copper Cliff smelters in order to forestall an all-out wildcat strike that could jeopardize a settlement. At each of these plant gates, they tried to reason with the wildcatters so the rest of the men weren't prevented from getting to work. One of the union 'diplomats' remembers driving out to Garson at shift change late one night to talk the wildcatters back to work: "I was a pretty tough guy, weighed 212 pounds and fought in every bar and club in Sudbury, but these guys met us with pipes and pick handles, drew a line in the dirt, and shouted, 'You put one step over that line and I'll lambast you with this baseball bat.' We left with our tail between our legs."[48] The diplomats had better luck at the iron ore plant and the Levack mine, where there was a partial resumption of operations.[49]

At the same time as issuing a clarion call for cool heads in the membership meetings, Solski shared his outrage over the state of negotiations and the company's excessive greed. "For less than 1% of the company's surplus undistributed profits, 14,000 families could keep up with the standard of living they had achieved after so many years of wage struggles .... If we permit them [Inco] to impose these conditions this year, there is nothing to stop them from going even further at any time."[50] It was a very fine line for a union leader to be walking! On the one hand, to stay on the right side of the law, he needed to contain members' fury up until the strike deadline. On the other, if a strike was unavoidable, he needed the members' support. His job was to stoke the justifiable outrage of the majority while engaging the few who harbored reservations about a strike. Men like Konrad were fiercely loyal to the company since his accident that cost him an eye several years before. Without the required depth perception to continue as driller, Konrad was convinced he'd lose his job with Inco; instead, he was re-assigned to the mucking machine.[51] The discordant demands of the law on the one side and the members' wishes on the other had to be balanced. At the same time Solski recognized that preparations must begin for a strike of staggering organizational scale and complexity. The high-stakes strategic maneuvers required of the union president and the executive members would have challenged even the most seasoned of high-ranking military leaders.

At their next meeting with the company's negotiators, Solski laid the blame for the Garson members' transgressions at the feet of Inco supervisors: "We're interested in an orderly shutdown without provocation. Some of your bosses are doing a good job of it now." When the Inco negotiator pressed for the name of the reckless boss who was provoking a wildcat, Solski declined the chance to have him fired, which would have been the likely outcome for instigating a wildcat at such a volatile time of an impending strike. But hiring, firing, and disciplining were the responsibilities of supervisors and Solski wasn't going to help them do their job.[52]

The dam holding the membership in check had burst open and the union leaders needed to act quickly to prevent an all-out illegal shutdown. A press release stating "our membership has exhausted its patience" was promptly dispatched by Local 598's secretary, Stella Despot. At the same time, the ever-efficient Stella punched out a telegram to labour minister Charles Daley urging him to intervene before the strike deadline.[53] Concerned about the devastating effect a strike would have on the community, that very evening Sudbury city councilors also prevailed upon Daley to intervene. Councilors of the joint Neelson-Garson municipality went further by requesting that Daley leave the comfort of his Toronto office and come to Sudbury to sort out the mess.

Daley agreed to host mediation talks between the company and the union in Toronto on two conditions: the union must lift the

strike deadline of 24 September and agree to mediation commenc-
ing on 25 September. This was a minister of labour with an ear
turned to the captains of industry who were advising him to curtail
the rights of unions accorded by the *Ontario Labour Relations Act*.
In a series of submissions directed to the anticipated reforms to the
act in 1960, Inco and other business enterprises in Ontario had been
exerting their influence on Daley, most notably to leave the issue of
union security (the deduction of union dues from employer payrolls)
outside of the act. Lifting the strike deadline was a condition too
high to accept. Moving the strike deadline forward would further
inflame the members who had demonstrated their irritation with the
delay in the negotiations.

THE COUNTDOWN AND LAST-MINUTE EFFORTS

With a strike edging ever closer, the union's national and international executive board members made their travel arrangements
to assemble in Sudbury on Saturday, 20 September to strategize
a way out of the circumstances that were rapidly foreclosing the
possibility of a negotiated settlement. The three western board
members from Vancouver and Calgary and the two international
members from Denver converged in Toronto, facing a four-and-a-
half-hour train ride up to Sudbury before booking into the Coulson
Hotel on Larch Street. To open the emergency meeting, MMSW
Canadian president Nels Thibault brought the national and international executive members up to date. Having accompanied the
MMSW negotiators at their last meeting with Inco's team on 16
September that followed the issuing of the Conciliation Board's
report a week before, he was very familiar with the company's
obstinance. Thibault summarized the details of Inco's demands for
an orderly shutdown, freedom for contractors to cross the picket
line to carry out repairs on the smelter stacks, and a threatened
lapse in health insurance for strikers unless the union paid their
premiums. But the worst aspect of the circumstances by far was
the stockpile, for 105 million pounds of nickel in Inco's reserves
was enough to last at least six months, on top of which the US
government had a 100 million pound stockpile that meant that
Inco's sales for 1958 would be pushed ahead to the next year. As
miners and smeltermen alike, the union leaders understood the
folly of striking against a stockpile.

Once converged in the Regent Street hall boardroom, the national and international executive members agonized over the gathering storm. The discussions in the emergency meeting that Saturday morning would prove to be among the most difficult of their careers, second only to what lay almost a decade ahead when they would debate the consequential question of merging with the larger, bureaucratic international United Steelworkers of America after eighteen years of jurisdictional disputes. Exactly who said what in the Regent Street board room that day will never be known for certain, but all the evidence points to Harvey Murphy, vice president of the Canadian board arguing against the strike in his bombastic style accompanied by fist-pounding, while the others concurred with his point of view.[54] Research director Robinson, having seldom found cause to agree with Murphy, would nonetheless have bowed to the wisdom he could recognize in the views expressed by certain others. The two international representatives would likely have offered their opinions while respecting the autonomy of the Canadians to manage their own affairs. The summary of the national accounts delivered by secretary-treasurer of the Canadian board Bill Longridge, and the sorry state of the international coffers examined over bent heads were an overwhelming worry to everyone in the room.

It was clear that the union didn't have the financial resources necessary to provide for fourteen thousand strikers and their families (approximately fifty thousand people) for the six months that the nickel stockpile would likely last. However, even with these stark figures laid out before them, the executive boards had no choice but to authorize the strike ·because the autonomy built into the MMSW constitution allowed the locals to make their own decisions, which included calling a strike.[55] In 1958, that ship had sailed eight days before when the Inco members voted 82.7 per cent to walk off the job.

With significant mulling and sacrifice, the union's international office decided to donate more than $44,000 over the course of the strike for the Inco strikers and families. It cannot be overstated how severely the finances of the union south of the border were being drained by the hefty legal expenditures required to defend the union against the Cold War machinery. In the highly charged Cold War atmosphere of fear and suspicion, left-led unions such as MMSW were painted as communist on both sides of the border. The accusations flew despite the reality of a miniscule proportion of avowed communists among the MMSW's seventy-four thousand members in the US and the fifty thousand in Canada.[56] The assault on MMSW in the US and other American unions took the form of formalized, state-sanctioned actions directed against officers, members, and the unions themselves covering the gamut from FBI probes, congressional investigations, denials of security clearances, grand jury sessions, and subpoenas to the hearings of the House Un-American Activities Committee.[57] The *Taft-Hartley Act*, another component of the state's Cold War arsenal, was especially effective in crippling the ability of left-leaning unions to properly serve their members.[58] The harassments of MMSW's officials charged under Taft-Hartley wound their way through the courts for a full decade before the Supreme Court exonerated all those charged, but not before the union had spent over $500,000 on the legal costs.[59]

What was left for the national and international executive board members to do? MMSW's constitution, inherited from the Western Federation of Miners, allowed the elected representatives at the local level to call a strike without authorization by the national or international officers. But without a unified position amongst the union leaders, the strike was sure to fail. If the national or international officers were to go over the heads of the local's elected representatives to address the members directly, they would have risked a boomerang of simmering anger directed against their union leadership rather than the company.

In the smoke-filled boardroom of the Regent Street hall, as a last-ditch attempt to avert the strike, the national and international executives urged the negotiating team to accept Daley's proposal to engage in mediation the day after the strike deadline. But the negotiating team saw things differently: to them it seemed impossible to postpone the strike, given that members were intent on closing Inco down with or without their leaders. Explaining their reasoning to the national and international leaders, the negotiating team asserted their constitution-enshrined autonomy and rejected the boards' recommendation.

The Regent Street hall boardroom was not the only place where heated discussions were taking place. Feelings were running high in the entire town and surrounding communities. Sudbury's residents crowded into the Coulson Hotel bar on Larch St and the Nickel Range Hotel bar on Elm St, the usual places where they settled their disagreements. Some took to other means to express their views. In her letter to the Local 598 Executive, one Inco wife addressed the handicap of the stockpile, "It is time you realized that the workers need Inco more than Inco needs the workers."[60] In his telegram sent to Solski, Peter Zahavith of 243 Van Horne Street, a MMSW member, declared, "You are going to be crucified regardless of what decision you make so use your own honest judgement."[61] It must have been gratifying for Solski and the other negotiating team members to know there were members like Peter who recognized the tight corner the union was in with the risks of striking, and had confidence in their leadership anyway. In the next couple of days, Solski would have more than one chance to use his judgment in circumstances where significant consequences hung in the balance.

The union's next move to avert a strike was to appeal to Ontario premier Leslie Frost. The premier's agreement to his request for a meeting had Solski bolting to catch the night train to Toronto for a next day meeting with Frost to petition "the man I had never talked to in my life before," as he would muse years later. If Solski was losing his nerve at this point, he didn't show it. He considered himself to be quite conservative, not prone to taking drastic action, but he was spurred on, as he so often was in challenging circumstances, by the thought of the early days before the union. As he recalled years later, men like his father sweated over the smelter furnaces and toiled underground in grinding, perilous conditions, but because they had big families to support and there was no union, they couldn't fight back at risk of being blacklisted.[62] In tense times like the current struggle with Inco, he would ask himself, "How can we let a company that has made millions and millions out of the sweat of workers completely have its own way?"[63]

Solski's short meeting with Premier Frost on 22 September resulted in Frost's promise to arrange for mediation talks to occur before the strike deadline, pre-empting his minister of labour's previous proposal. It would give the parties only one day to settle before the strike was set to start, but it was worth a try. Word of Frost's intervention came late that day to the Sudburians gathered at the Regent Street hall – just half an hour before the night train to Toronto pulled out – and a committee of seven quickly assembled to join Solski who would wait for them in Toronto's Prince George Hotel. Union Station would be deserted when their train arrived in Toronto in the wee hours of the morning but the hotel was just across the street from the station where they could rest for a few hours before the mediation would begin the next day.

On 23 September, with just one day to the strike deadline, the parties assembled in the Department of Labour offices: Thibault, Solski, and the five others on the MMSW team; labour minister Charles Daley, deputy minister J.B. Metzler; and Harold C.F. Mockridge, Inco's spokesman and negotiator of several previous collective agreements. The ticking clock hanging over their heads in the government offices was more urgent than any other that a MMSW team had slaved under before.

During a short recess in the meeting, a phone call from Sudbury's union office informed the MMSW team of a perverse turn of events. Inco supervisors were telling the men they were finished for the day and were to take their clothes and go home. Outrage mixed with bewilderment for the team receiving the news, for when else did a company ever encourage a strike even as the union was trying to avert it? It was the union leaders who told the men to go to work, walk past the wildcatters and picketers, stay on the job; and the company that was telling them, "There's a strike here, you guys go home."[64] The world was turning inside out.

The team in Toronto promptly confronted Daley with the terms of the mediation that stipulated the status quo would continue: no walkouts, no shutdown. The feeble explanation Daley delivered was that the company had told him, "We're not running an ice cream factory, we can't shut down on a dime."[65] This was not the only context in which Inco explained its decisions and actions with the distinction between a mining operation and a confectionary factory. Inco's lawyers, appearing before government hearings and inquiries into mining accidents, would frequently justify the fatalities with the assertion, "After all, Mr Coroner, a mine is not a chocolate factory."

As the clock in Daley's office pushed 5 pm, the MMSW team caucused over sandwiches and revised their bargaining demands by dropping the wage demand from 10 per cent to 8 per cent. Having taken the revised demands to the Inco team, Daley returned a mere twenty minutes later to announce, "I regretfully inform you that the company does not think it's a serious attempt on your part to settle." He then bid the MMSW team goodbye. The room must have suddenly felt as a small as a telephone booth. All hope of a last-minute settlement was exhausted. The mediation had failed and tomorrow was the start of the strike. The negotiators bowed to the inevitable, but just for the record, Solski issued a parting shot, "No matter what proposal we made, they refused," to which Thibault

Figure 5.3 | The eve of the strike; last minute instructions are given to MMSW members.

added, "They had no offer." The team retreated to Sudbury to face a set of circumstances they had never faced before: a strike of over fourteen thousand members. With tar-like circles under their eyes, they pulled into Sudbury's Elgin Street train station to be greeted by eagerly awaiting journalists with cameras and microphones at the ready. Immediately after stepping off the train, the union's team announced the beginning of Inco's first full-fledged strike. The four-teen thousand members and their families were about to face cir-cumstances that couldn't have been any more challenging: heading into a bitterly cold Northern Ontario winter while striking against a company with a huge stockpile and a track record of bargaining in bad faith; a government intent on reversing the economic recession with its punishing hold-the-line wage restraint policy; and union coffers woefully inadequate to support that many families for the time it would take to reach a settlement.

On Strike – Respect Our Picket Line

For the first time in their lives, Sudburians woke to smokeless stacks on the morning of 24 September 1958. The periwinkle sky was free of the noxious sulfur dioxide clouds emitting from the Copper Cliff and Coniston smelters. While hanging the laundry on the outdoor clothesline, Edna, mother of eight-year-old Irene, fixed her eyes on the familiar stack of the Copper Cliff smelter, the only one of the three stacks in her direct sightline from where she stood on the small stool on the back porch to reach the line. But today was like no other day because there was no smoke billowing from the stack; the clothes drying on the line would be the first truly clean load of laundry Edna had done. As she took one last long look at the novel view, she wondered about the Inco policeman who chaperoned the children crossing the street to and from Copper Cliff Elementary School. Unsure if he would have been reassigned to patrol the picket line, she made a mental note to shuffle her already busy day so she could walk Irene to school.

At 8 am that morning, more than four hundred Mine Mill picketers with their "On Strike – Respect Our Picket Line" signs spread themselves out in an orderly fashion across twelve points in the greater Sudbury area to cover the various gates of Inco's operations: the smelters at Copper Cliff and Coniston, the Frood-Stobie mine a mile north of Sudbury, the mines in the outer-lying towns of Creighton, fourteen miles west, Levack, thirty-three miles northwest, and Garson, nine miles northwest of Sudbury. In Port Colborne, the 1,540 members of Mine Mill's Local 637 patrolled the six gates of Inco's refinery. Now that the turbulence of the previous six months of negotiations with Inco was over, and the moment of the strike had arrived, exhilaration was mixed with fear.

For the overwhelming majority of the picketers, 24 September marked their first time on strike. With the September timing of the strike, the bugs and extreme heat of the summer months were passed and the children back in school. Most of the union's members and leaders had little experience of the challenges ahead. The few veterans of the union's Kirkland Lake strike sixteen years prior were the exceptions who understood just how easy it was for a strike to fail when the strikers' basic necessities weren't provided for. Food, fuel, clothing, and other necessities would be needed very soon for close to fifty thousand citizens of Sudbury if you counted the strikers together with their families.[1] With a strike fund of barely $40,000, the union would need to garner a great deal of financial support from other unions.

As a way of marking the start of the strike, MMSW Local 598 negotiating team member Albert Routliffe announced he was growing a beard, vowing to shave it off only when the strike ended. How long his beard might be at that point was anyone's guess, considering the perilously wide gap between the company and the union when bargaining broke down. Whereas the company's most recent offer was a continuation of the existing contract without a wage increase, the union's demands included an 8 per cent wage increase, union security (raised by $1), and formalized union input on safety. The union's wage demand was in line with previous years' negotiated settlements that placed the Inco members among the most highly paid in the industry.

The Sudbury skies were slightly overcast, but by noon, when the temperatures soared to 74° F degrees and warm southerly winds picked up, shirt sleeves were rolled up and coffee thermoses replaced by cold drinks. Despite the glorious weather on the first day of the strike, the Strike Coordinating Committee was already laying plans to build shacks or supply trailers for protection from the snow and sleet that would come soon enough. Independent in spirit and isolated by geography, the Levack members didn't wait for the committee and started building a picket cabin, complete with wood stove, windows, hydro hook-up, and outdoor benches.

Several hundred spectators turned out to watch the picketers take up their duties, expecting altercations and brouhahas on the lines. They were sorely disappointed. The union executive had called the picket captains to the Regent Street union hall three days before to issue instructions on preventing violence on the line. The captains

Figure 6.1 | Picket line beginning to form.

Figure 6.2 | Crossing the picket line.

were warned of the severe penalties to the union if there were violations of the labour laws. Unnerved by the wildcatting in the days leading up to the strike, the executive wasn't taking any chances. The captains had been advised by the executive that the wildcatting "did more harm than good to the union's position."[2] As a result of the union's network of disciplined picket captains, stewards, and other union activists, the strikers' anger burned within the bounds of the law. As Local 598 president, Mike Solski, proudly reported in future interviews, the only violence on the picket lines during the 1958 strike amounted to a few punctured tires on cars driven by Inco's senior managers, a notable difference from subsequent Inco strikes.[3]

Union members registering for picket duty jammed the union halls the first day of the strike. Under the direction of Tom Paradis, a member of Local 598 Executive, the four-hour picket shifts were assigned via telephone; only men over sixty were exempt. The arrangement of the picket assignments ensured the squads at each gate remained small as a precaution against violence on the line, but at a moment's notice, hundreds of picketers were available for any emergency that might arise.[4]

Picket duty was deliverance from the dirty, dangerous jobs in Inco's mines and smelters and relief from the chafing yoke of Inco's tyrannical management practices. Picket duty also provided a temporary reprieve from the rotating shifts of day-afternoon-graveyard that changed every week and breached the workers' own circadian rhythms while upending the domestic rhythms of their households. "When my dad was on the graveyard shift we'd have to stay very quiet in the house; if he woke up from his sleep we were in trouble," remembers the daughter of a mucker working rotating shifts in Creighton mine.[5] Walking the picket line was also a chance to blow off steam. With their habitual rough humour, the strikers invented new insults for Inco's managers as they meandered in front of the plant gates or hunkered inside the picket trailers, "Parker is the turd that won't flush," referring to Inco's Canadian vice president, to which another would echo, "I wouldn't give him the steam off my piss."[6] Although the strike was a kind of liberation, it was transitory, for all too soon mouths would need feeding and bills paid.

Some strikers already had part-time jobs that provided some income. For instance, Cameron, a welder in the plate shop at Inco's Frood mine, worked as the public address announcer on Friday nights for the Sudbury Wolves hockey games at the Sudbury Arena.

But with three children, and his wife Olive pregnant with another, the small income from moonlighting could not be stretched to cover the family's costs. Olive began using Multi-Milk, a powdered milk from Standard Dairies around the corner from their West Sudbury home, and stocked up on Puffed Rice in the three-feet tall bags so big in circumference that their eight-year son could wrap his arms around and still not meet his hands. Even the changes to the family's breakfasts and the occasional $25 cheque from Cameron's brother in Ottawa could not meet the family's requirements, and so towards the end of the strike Olive went to work for Revenue Canada, a job she found so satisfying that she remained in the labour market until the mandatory retirement age of sixty-five.[7] Olive was not alone: out of necessity, many women sought paid work during the strike, and in stepping out of the home they also stepped out of the conventional gender roles of the times that dictated men as the breadwinners and women doing the unpaid work at home. Only in the mid-1960s did women join the paid labour force en masse in Canada, and even then, their work was considered as supplementary income.

The newspaper coverage of the first day of the strike featured the exodus of Inco workers seeking work elsewhere and included interviews with Sudbury's business owners proclaiming the anticipated disastrous effect of the strike for the city's economy.[8] While the high rates of unemployment in the 1958 recession dissuaded some from looking for work, others left for nearby Elliot Lake's uranium mines or the pulp and paper mills in Espanola, Sturgeon Falls, and Kapuskasing.[9] Harvey found work 100 km away with his brother and sent money home to support the family of seven. Left without a car, Harvey's wife Freda and seven-year-old daughter Beth walked to the Dominion store for groceries. The groceries included ingredients for "strike food," Freda's version of chili with lots of beans, a smidgen of ground beef, and enormous quantities of pasta, all flavoured by Bravo spaghetti sauce. "We *loved* strike food," Beth exclaimed: "for years after, whenever [my mother] would make that version of the recipe, we reminisced happily."[10] Men like Verne, a labourer in the Copper Cliff smelter, were lucky to get other jobs in the district so they didn't have to leave their families. Verne drove a taxi during the day and worked as a bartender during the evenings at the Laurentian Hotel on Lasalle Blvd across the street from where he lived with his young family.[11] His combined income rivalled his weekly earnings as a labourer at the rate of $1.8975 an hour.[12]

By the time the Inco workers hit the picket line in September 1958, employment rates were slowly rising and markets had begun to rebound after a trough lasting the first eight months of the year.[13] The metal markets in particular made headlines on the financial pages of the newspapers, although prices were still below what were needed to bring the twenty closed mines and milling operations back into production.[14] Despite the upswing in the economy, Inco remained an enthusiastic adherent to the hold-the-line-on-wages policy of the federal government, justifying its position on the basis of its stockpile of nickel.

HELICOPTERS FOR SALARIED STAFF

On the first day of the strike, Inco's non-unionized office staff reported to work at the Copper Cliff headquarters as usual, but this day they carried picket passes and enjoyed a police escort. In anticipation of violent clashes, Inco police formed two lines at the front gates of the main office buildings to shelter the several hundred of Inco's salaried employees from the thick crowd of picketers forming at the front entrance. Felicia, a keypunch operator in Inco's tabulating department in the Copper Cliff offices, had no difficulty crossing the picket line. "There were good relations between the strikers and us office workers and some of her fellow workers even brought coffee to the picketers."[15] The police escorts were soon found to be unnecessary, and the office workers came and went according to their regular eight to five work schedule over the course of the strike. For instance, Kirk, a draftsman, maintained his practice of catching a ride to work with a co-worker. After parking in the large car lot patrolled by Inco police for the duration of the strike, the two men walked together across the railroad tracks, entered the office building, and made their way to the general engineering department where they continued their work on various surveying projects.

Some of the senior salaried employees had already occupied the buildings the night before the start of the strike. In rotation, each of the three groups of these employees would spend one entire week over the course of the strike in their workplace followed by two weeks off. Tucked away for a week at a time, the men slept on rollaway cots and enjoyed free meals provided by local restaurateurs and cooks from Crawley and McCracken, a firm servicing northern lumber camps; they were equipped with laundry facilities, televisions and radios and even films for entertainment, along with a canteen fully stocked with chocolate bars and cigarettes. More than a month before the strike began, Inco had formulated these plans for the three groups of senior employees, setting up supplies such as refrigerators and bedding in their plants. The problem of transport in and out was addressed with a fleet of helicopters contracted to spirit these non-unionized employees across the picket line.[16]

Salaried employees like Bastien, a machine shop foreman who regularly took the streetcar to work, were instructed to walk through the fields and come at night to avoid crossing the picket lines. Other salaried employees such as Glen, maintenance supervisor of Inco's Levack housing who had mine rescue experience, were assigned additional duties as part of emergency strike operations. Bastien, Glen, and other salaried employees working the weekly rotations had to tell their wives and children they wouldn't be at home for a whole week. When Glen's four-year old son heard his father's news, it didn't make sense: "It seemed odd. But then, grown-ups were odd altogether."[17] Bastien's wife, Beatrice, had started working at age sixteen, weighing the four-inch copper billets, twenty to twenty-four at a time on trailers wheeled in and out of the scale house in Inco's copper refinery. Like the few other women employed by Inco during the war, Beatrice lost her job when the enlisted men returned from service.[18] Her time in a workplace overwhelmingly occupied by men had given her skills on how to keep herself safe. Yet during one of her husband's week-long shifts early in the strike, when Beatrice awoke from her sleep at 3 am one morning to an intoxicated stranger knocking on the door, she was afraid. As a young mother without a husband at home, she worried there might be more threatening and even violent encounters if the strike persisted and wondered about being able to protect her eight-year-old son.

Shortly before the strike, landing pads for the helicopters appeared at each of the plants where searchlights were installed for night landings. The small two-seater bubble helicopters made for some bumpy rides, especially when navigating updrafts and downdrafts. On landing, a few white-knuckled senior staff told the pilot, "Don't bother picking us up in seven days. We're going to find our own way out of the property somehow."[19] In future strikes, Inco enlisted larger helicopters for smoother flights.

THE GRIM REALITIES BEGIN TO SINK IN

Just as Inco was proudly announcing to the press that their plans to use helicopters were "unique to Canadian strikes,"[20] the strikers and their families were pitched headlong into the prospect of hardship and sacrifice. The strike had no promise of being settled quickly and though some of the more fortunate families could call upon their monied relations for help, none were exactly wealthy.

Just prior to the strike, Emmet and Eileen had bought a house on McFarlane Lake Road, vowing to change the colour of gaudy red walls in the living room when they moved in. Living from paycheque to paycheque in the years before the strike, like so many others they had no savings. Emmet, a twenty-seven-year-old machinist, found a job at a gas station in Toronto a couple of weeks into the strike, but it didn't pay enough for him to drive to and from Sudbury to visit his family for even the occasional weekend. The strike was financially devastating for the family and it was years before they could afford to buy paint to get rid of the tawdry colour of the walls.[21] Financial implications were not limited to the striking families but rippled outward in the nexus of economic relationships, for instance Dolores remembered her widowed mother casting about for a way to support her and her young brother after losing the income from her regular boarders – strikers who left town to find work elsewhere. Her mother turned to selling makeup "which nobody had money to buy."[22]

The news coverage during the first weekend of the strike brought further attention to the potential economic impact of the strike. Companies supplying Inco with lumber, dynamite, and drilling equipment were destined to "lose their best customer."[23] More local business owners were trumpeting their anticipated fears of economic fallout. Only later did they admit their initial panic was exaggerated.[24] Hardware businesses in particular did quite well during the strike. After working at Inco for seven years as a nipper carrying the materials for the miners at the worksite, Obert took over his father's hardware store in Azilda, the francophone community seven miles west of Sudbury. He recalls that some strikers, especially those confident in an early settlement, took advantage of the time away from work to attend to overdue home renovations, and the store's business actually increased.[25]

For the strikers, the first weekend of the strike was an interruption to their usual Saturday night family ritual of driving to the slag dump for the spectacular display of molten nickel as it was poured onto "slag mountain" – like going to the drive-in movies but with no admission charge. The trains would trundle up the slag hill from underground every hour, each one loaded with twenty or thirty pots of molten nickel to be skillfully poured by the labourers swinging the pots by their heavy, hot handles. Each pot took five minutes to pour and had to be emptied quickly to avoid the hardening of the ore. With each pouring, the slag hill grew higher. The dumping was done around the clock by men working eight-hour shifts, but the spectacle was most dazzling at night, even more dramatic than fireworks, and attracted Sudburians in addition to tourists from across Canada.[26]

Saturday nights in young Jack's family centred on CBC's *Hockey Night in Canada*. Kevin's family moved from Moncton, NB in the mid-1950s for his father Henry to work as a miner in Creighton, one of the world's deepest mines fifteen miles west of Sudbury.[27] Before settling in to watch the Saturday night hockey game on the black and white television in their pocket-sized, Inco-owned house, Kevin remembers, "from the time we were little kids, we would get in our pajamas; even the older ones because if the older ones didn't the younger ones wouldn't want to." Henry would walk downtown to Creighton's Red & White and buy a six-pack of pop. "There was a Coke, a ginger ale, mine was root beer. Four kids and two parents, and we'd each have our favourite and they were all different. That was like heaven!"[28] For a large and growing family on strike, the five cent per bottle cost of the pop was a hardship. Yet for the thirteen weeks of the strike, Kevin's parents made the sacrifice in order to hold fast to the crucial Saturday night ritual.

As the grim realities of what it would take to survive a strike against one of the most powerful North American companies were beginning to sink in, Alexandre Boudreau arrived, unnoticed, in Sudbury. He was a man on a mission to wash the town clean of the communists. Perhaps Boudreau's arrival on the second day of the strike didn't raise any suspicions because Sudburians were quite familiar with clerics coming forward to lead study clubs with miners and smelterman, the majority being Catholic.[29] Only a few years prior, church leaders like Father Con McKee led a study group to apply the Church encyclicals and social teachings to the everyday lives of Sudbury workers.[30] The real purpose of Boudreau's mission in Sudbury would not become apparent until after the strike.

STRIKE COMMITTEES KICK INTO GEAR

The first weekend of the strike brought the union's national and international executive, together with the executive members of the two Inco Locals 598 and 637, to the Regent Street union hall for a strike policy and strategy development meeting. A national strike coordinating committee was formed with equal representation from each of the two locals and the national office: Nels Thibault and Bill Longridge from the national board; Bill Cryderman and Mike Solski from Local 598, and Ronald Methot and Ray Berrick from Local 637.

In those few hours of the meeting, the basic pillars of the strike protocols were established, drawn from the 1941–42 Kirkland Lake strike as well as the 1946 strike wave that included the United Steelworkers' strike in Hamilton and the United Mine Workers' strike in Nova Scotia. Consequently, it was decided that strike benefits in the form of food vouchers would kick in after the first month of the strike, based on need. Every effort would be made to procure produce in bulk from area farms for distribution to members at reasonable prices. Also, there would be extensive recreation, games, and entertainment for strikers and their families to make full use of the union halls. The union's national newspaper, *The Herald*, would be issued twice instead of its usual once a month to provide extensive coverage of the strike. Furthermore, financial appeals would be written on the committee's pending letterhead. In order to conserve funds, the union leaders agreed to cut their own wages in half, a reduction from $90 per week to $45 for the duration of the strike. The local's office staff, union hall janitors, and dance teacher would be asked to accept the same 50 per cent pay reduction.[31]

Two weeks into the strike, the voice of Mike Solski boomed over the airwaves on the semi-weekly television and radio programs. Every Tuesday and Friday morning, he would walk the two blocks north from the union hall to the CKSO studios atop the Regent Street hill (see map in chapter 3) to deliver the fifteen-minute broadcasts known as the "Local 598 Reports." The public broadcasts were also heard in French on CHNO Radio. In addition to the frequent membership meetings at the union halls, these broadcasts, together with the printed excerpts in the *Sudbury Star*, served the dual purpose of keeping the membership and larger community updated on events related to the strike while saving the expense of printing and distributing the union newspaper, *Local 598 News*, to its more than fifteen thousand recipients. To reach the new Canadians within the union's membership, the contents of broadcasts, union bulletins, and press releases were sent for translation to *Ukrainian Life*, *Courier German Weekly*, *Slovak Voice*, *Latvija Amerika*, and thirteen other ethnic newspapers with distributions covering southern Ontario.

The first broadcast of the "Local 598 Report" began with the prescient, rallying assertion by Solski that the strike would "require sacrifice, it will mean a tightening of belts for all of us. But unless we come through this struggle successfully, there are no guarantees of any sort for any one of us."[32] Close on the heels of this prognostication came the reporting of measures taken to ensure the strike's success: "A large body of stewards, picket captains and members of various committees has been assembled to manage the strike."[33]

Working under the Local 598 Strike Coordinating Committee headed by their recording and financial secretaries Stan Racicot and Norm Jaques, the various committees spanned close to four hundred members performing a panoply of vital tasks including picket detail, strike benefits, public relations, insurance plans, and recreation. Perhaps the most important of these announced in the first "Local 598 Report" was to determine the "question of caring for those of our members who may, for good reason, find themselves unable to care for themselves during the strike."[34] The newly formed committees, comprised of men with little strike experience, were soon springing into action.

Issues soon arose that required the attention of the strike committees, for instance to the letters that swamped the Regent Street mailbox; each was reciprocated with a carefully written response with carbon copies filed in the union office for future reference.[35] Some letters came from property owners asking the union to cover their tenants' rent payments.[36] The Strike Coordinating Committee took their cue and began pressing landlords and mortgage holders for leniency in financial dealings with the strikers and advocating for moratoriums on their financial obligations with the business owners.[37] In radio and television broadcasts, the union directly addressed the uncooperative landlords and mortgage holders, asking them to reconsider: "Surely, if your tenants or mortgages were trustworthy enough to do business with during normal times, they justify your trust in them to continue payments just as soon as they are able to do so."[38] In response, many of the property owners deferred their tenants' payments and local merchants further extended credit to their long-standing customers. Perhaps surprisingly, Inco, landlord to a myriad of workers living in company housing in the outlying areas of Creighton, Coniston, Garson, and Levack, also deferred rental payments for the duration of the strike.

Other letters arrived from members concerned about the confusion over the coverage of hospital insurance plans, especially since Inco had let its payments to Imperial Life and Blue Cross lapse in the early weeks of the strike.[39] Over the years of negotiating with Mine Mill, Inco had gradually covered more benefits for its unionized employees, including hospitalization coverage, pension plan, and sick, accident, and life insurance. But contributing to the health and well-being of idle workers was not in the company's repertoire of labour relations. In the void, the union arranged for Imperial Life to accept premiums from members for their medical and surgical coverage during the strike. After a period of confusing communications with Blue Cross, at the end of October the union eventually paid the $60,000 to cover the members' premiums for November, which they repeated for the month of December.

Still other letters landing in the Regent Street hall mailbox were from members who had found employment elsewhere in response to the union's appeal to seek jobs to alleviate the strain on union finances. Men like Kelly Thurlow, Inco employee number 3128, diligently wrote the union to notify of his move to Pointe-au-Baril, seventy-five miles south of Sudbury, where he found work with his father-in-law in exchange for his own and his family's room and board.[40] Because he was not receiving a wage, Kelly Thurlow was exempt from the union's request of a financial contribution from members employed elsewhere in order to support their fellow members walking the line in Sudbury.

One letter in particular would have corralled the executive into a huddle. In his letter, Inco employee number 15076 who identified himself as a long-time "rank and file member of Local 598," complimented the executive on "the ingenuity with which you have been able to secure gains for labour in every contract," and suggested a negotiating strategy that might have avoided the strike had the executive adopted it: "When Inco cut the hours to 32/week in July, that was the time to accept a no-wage increase and a 32-hour week. Once the demand for nickel increased, as it inevitably would, and Inco had to boost production, the overtime rate of time and a half would kick in. But in the meantime, think of the possibilities for public opinion with our weekly wage lower than any other parallel industry."[41] The union's democratic structures and practices encouraged rank-and-file members like this Inco employee to comment freely on the leaders' tactical errors. While the suggested strategy to avoid the strike might have been effective, now that the strike was underway its only use was to remember it for the next time Inco cut the workers' hours. In the meantime, letters such as these reminded the leaders of the diversity within the membership. Along with those who favoured war-like forms as the appropriate expression of virile industrial resistance, there were others who relied on written, reflective modes of expression.

The activities of the Strike Coordinating Committee took a distinctly political turn in the third week of the strike. A six-member delegation drove overnight to Montreal's docks to picket the freighter bound for Wales with "hot nickel."[42] The blockade of the shipments was planned with the help of the Brotherhood of Locomotive Firemen and Enginemen, whose battle for a contract with CNR four months earlier the Inco workers had actively supported. Members of the brotherhood shared their insider knowledge of the scheduling of the transport of nickel to Montreal from the Buffalo, New York storage locations. Unfortunately for the picketers, authorization for members of the International Longshoremen's Association came from the union's New York headquarters too late, and the vessel carrying 1,900 tons of semi-refined nickel and other cargo sailed two days after the picketers arrived in Montreal. News coverage of the picketing on the Montreal docks was closely followed from inside Inco's plants by the salaried employees on their rotations, as their newly assigned responsibilities included tape-recording all news on the strike coming across the freshly installed television and radios.

By the end of October, the Entertainment Committee headed by the union local's recreation director ensured the halls were brimming with social and recreational activities for the striking families. With the local's extensive cultural programming already well established, the committee continued the dance school, family bowling nights, and choir groups, but put performances of high-profile singers on hold to save expenses. In a special effort to include the Levack members and their families who were located in the most remote of Inco's operations, the committee organized a Halloween dance for the members and their wives. Following the dance, arrangements were made for free afternoon and evening screenings of the 1954 movie, *Salt of the Earth* at Levack's Rio Theatre in early November.

The story of the victorious eighteen-month strike by IUMMSW members at the Empire Zinc company in New Mexico was sure to boost spirits.[43] In making a movie about a successful strike of a union embattled by relentless red-baiting, the movie's director and producer, both blacklisted Hollywood Ten members, were directly challenging the prevailing Cold War propaganda. The production and distribution of the movie had encountered numerous delays and obstacles by the anti-communist crusaders in Congress, the Senate, the popular press, and the movie industry including the promoters, studios owners, the Screen Actors Guild, and the projectionists' union.[44] The injunctions, anti-trust suits, and other counter litigation dragged on for years after the final cut, although the filmmakers could never prove the boycott of the film was conspiratorial.[45] Despite the steady political attack during every aspect of its making, the film was successfully completed and enthusiastically applauded by civil libertarians, religious leaders, and minority group representatives. Its Sudbury screening was among the few until the 1960s when the anti-communist fever had begun to dissipate.[46]

The movie, named in deference to the Chicano culture of the southwest, drew attention to the union's history of interethnic organizing and featured many of the Mexican American strikers and their wives in all but the leading roles.[47] Since the war years, IUMMSW was guided by an anti-racist policy in the name of a shared solidarity that crossed ethnic lines. As president John Clark declared in his opening speech to the union's 1955 convention "our goal is complete integration. We look forward to the day when promotion of the Negro, Mexican or other minority person will no longer be news, when equal opportunity for jobs, on-the-job training, upgrading and promotions will be the rule."[48] One of the main union's demands that led to the strike at the Empire Zinc Company was a reduction in the dual-wage system that paid the Mexican American miners less than their Anglo counterparts.

In addition to challenging the established class and racial orders of the 1950s, the strike and its film depiction confronted the gender order of the times. Perhaps more so than the men, the women attending the Sudbury screening would have enjoyed the movie's portrayal of an alternative to the conservative gender roles of the 1950s. Nine months into the strike, the company obtained a court injunction that prevented the men from picketing. In an ingenious move, the strikers' wives took over the picket line for the six months it took to bring the company to the bargaining table in January 1952.[49] The unprecedented reversals of gender roles called for a rethink of the established gender division of labour and household relations. Men were required to take on their wives' domestic responsibilities while the women held the line against violent law enforcement, strikebreakers, and anti-union community members.[50] The movie's theme directly challenged the widely held assumption that women could only be passive supporters in any strike. At the time of *Salt of the Earth*'s screening, the wives of the Sudbury strikers had not yet proved the significant role they would play in the Inco strike.

CHANGING FAMILY ROLES

Family life necessarily continued from day to day as the strike proceeded. Babies were born. Kids learned how to ride bikes. Couples became engaged and were married.[51] In order that three-year-old Maria could attend her uncle's wedding, her mother and Frood miner father scrimped and saved so they could purchase a new dress: "I'll never forget that yellow dress with the pink embroidered flowers! It lasted me for years as my mother cut the skirt towards the bottom and added a piece of fabric between the two original pieces to make it longer so it could still be worn for other special occasions after the strike."[52]

Family roles evolved as wives went out into the paid labour market and husbands freed up from their Inco shifts took up the domestic work. With her teachers' college certification, Faye went back to work as a teacher while her husband Leo set aside his skills as a miner to learn how to look after their four children. As it turned out, Faye relished the revised division of labour within the family, upgraded her academic qualifications over the years to come, and enjoyed a rewarding, long-lasting career as a music consultant in the school system.[53]

Camila found a waitressing job at Local Lines bus terminal on Durham Street, which required her husband Marcel to care for their two pre-school boys. When she set out to look for paid work, she expected it would be easy to find with a resume featuring typing skills and work experience that included switchboard operator, drug store clerk, and hospital dietary supervisor. However, her numerous job applications were rejected once it was revealed that she was a striker's wife. The Local Lines lunch counter job was hers only because her uncle, a bus driver, put in a good word for her and didn't reveal Camila's status to the manager. These were the times when a man's endorsement of a woman's skills was crucial, even for women like Camila with jam-packed resumes; and especially for the wives of Sudbury's strikers. As the only dishwasher and waitress serving store clerks, doctors, and other downtown workers at the thirteen-stool counter and three tables, Camila worked from seven in the morning to six at night. The work was hard, the boss unpleasant, but she "loved being out in the public on a daily basis and Norman fell right into the role very easily and was a much better cook."[54]

When Doris was born several weeks into the strike, her mother took time off work from her job at the Dominion Store meat counter, returning as soon as she could to work, leaving her husband, Konrad, to look after the baby. When the baby was sleeping, Konrad would shovel driveways for a little bit of cash. For Konrad, an end to the strike was going to be a victory, regardless of whether there would be a wage increase, because returning to his job as a mucker machine operator at Creighton mine would be nothing but a relief after these domestic duties. "He wasn't a person to stay at home and take care of a baby, I'll tell you that," his daughter would recall drily years later.[55]

Like most one-resource company towns in North America at the time, Sudbury offered few paid job opportunities to women.[56] Husbands were expected to earn a wage adequate to support a family, while women were to raise the children and keep the home, adjusting the rhythms of the household to accommodate the varying schedules of their husbands who worked afternoon and graveyard shifts. The Inco strike upended these established gender roles, which likely would have given way in some cases to marital conflict and domestic strife that would have been rarely exposed to public scrutiny, least of all the archival documents.

THE LEADERS SPLIT

The union and its presumed communist leadership was a favourite target of the mainstream media's red-baiting. One month into
the strike, they took a new tack to further drive a wedge between the
members. Stepping beyond their usual area of expertise on economic
conditions into commentary on the jurisdictional battles within the
labour movement, the financial columnists characterized the strike
as but one chapter in a long-standing struggle between Mine Mill
and the United Steelworkers of America (USWA). "If MMSW loses
face among its members because of the Inco strike, it will be weakened in its finish-fight with Steelworkers."[57] The media's coverage
fuelled USWA's pitch to recruit MMSW members that had started
immediately after MMSW's certification in 1944 and was punctuated
by anti-communist rhetoric.

The constant din of the Cold War was as pervasive as rain drumming on a tin roof. As described in chapter 2, the reds-under-the-
bed ethos painted communists as ubiquitous, destructive, and
wholly under Soviet direction. The presses of political organizations
joined the uproar of recrimination against communist leadership
during the strike. For instance, the Pan-Canadian Anti-Communist
League's printed material distributed to Sudburians claimed, "Mine
Mill's communist leadership has been itching for years to find a convenient excuse to start a strike in the nickel industry [spurred on
by] their Kremlin masters."[58] The accusation that the strike was a
communist plot was coupled with critics' long-standing allegations
of the union's effort to fuel dissent within the membership. Some of
these critics went so far as to suggest that the union leadership regularly abdicated their responsibility to represent the members' best
interests by negotiating collective agreements whose sole purpose
was to sow dissatisfaction, a tactic they speculated would instigate a
communist revolution on Canadian soil.[59]

By 1958, in the fever-pitched climate of the Cold War, accusations of MMSW's communist leadership were incessant. In reality,
very few held communist beliefs and fewer still were card-carrying
members of the Communist Party. National vice president Harvey
Murphy, who wore his communist beliefs without apology, was an
exception. And contrary to the allegations of the union's critics, a
strike against a stockpile estimated to last nine months was the last
thing the union's national and international leaders wanted! Far

from promoting the strike as an act of willful subversion, they were against it on the basis of the stockpile and the union's finances.[60] Considering their overarching concern for the stability of the membership, any move to oppose the local's negotiating team and executive would have risked a disastrous split in the union. The Inco workers had voted to go on strike, and for the sake of solidarity and cohesion within the union, the job of the national and international leaders must be to support them despite any nagging doubts about the strike's potential for success.

"NOT TO CRACK": SUSTENANCE IN THE STRIKE

The Strike Coordinating Committee was charged with distributing the limited financial resources to the strikers. Since there wasn't enough in the kitty to feed the near fifty thousand mouths of the strikers and their families, how should the limited funds be distributed? To win the strike, the weakest link had to be buttressed. As one leader recounted years later, "No matter if the guy who has been opposed to the union all his life, if he can't survive, he'll be the first one to crack. The important thing in a strike is not to crack."[61] With insufficient funds for everyone to receive support, distribution would be based on need, following the union's past practice in other strikes. Determining who was in greatest need was the complex and sensitive task of the committee, for strikers denied support could become intensely disgruntled and express anger in ways that could seriously undermine the strike.

In the early weeks, the Strike Coordinating Committee established a food voucher system by identifying supportive local businesses. Soon, members could line up at the union halls to register for assistance in the form of food vouchers. As supplementary resources, the committee established relationships with local farmers so large truckloads of potatoes and other produce arrived regularly in front the Regent Street hall for distribution in a food bank set up in the basement of the hall. Additionally, the union's women's auxiliary organized clothing depots in the union halls to distribute coats, boots, and other garments for men, women, and children. Most days of the strike, as many as one thousand people passed through the Regent Street hall alone for food vouchers, clothing, and items from the food bank. In mid-November, as winter encroached in earnest and accelerated the need for fuel to heat homes, the Strike Coordinating

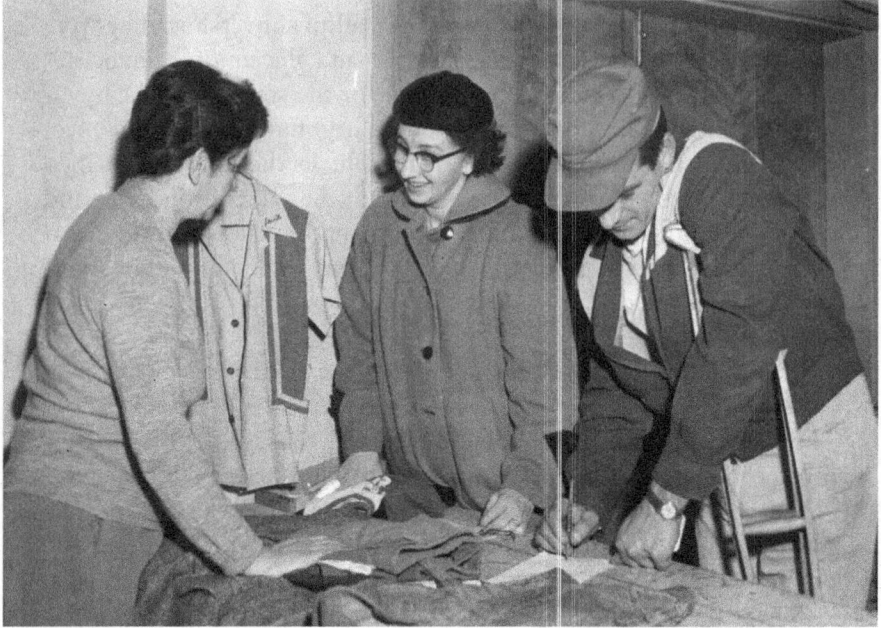

Figure 6.3 | Ladies auxiliary set up a clothing depot in union hall.

Committee urged the Sudbury and District Fuel Dealers' Association to accept vouchers for coal and oil.

Members without another source of income qualified for vouchers even if they weren't active union supporters. The vouchers were non-transferrable with the names of the supportive local merchants and dealers written on them and listed with the union. Eligible members brought the names of their favourite grocers, bakers, and dairy merchants so the vouchers could be customized.[62] The allocations were $8 per week for single men; $10 per week for married men; an additional $2 for each child up to two and $1 for each child thereafter.[63]

Strikers applying for benefits were screened closely in order to conserve the strike treasury. Some members, including loyal union supporters, were outraged when asked to show their bank books as evidence of need.[64] When Sean's father Owen went to the union hall to collect his food vouchers, he was interrogated: "Don't you have a son who is 18? Well, he should be out working." Owen responded, "He's in school, and I've paid my dues since 1944, where has all the money gone?" It seemed inconceivable that a local of so many members had such limited financial reserves after a prolonged strike-free period. But, as the post-strike accounting audit would reveal, the expenditures on property and building costs for the five union halls and summer camp at Richard Lake had reduced the resources considerably and during the strike, all available funds were dispersed to the strikers and their families.[65]

Owen's son Sean did in fact have a part-time job during the strike. Being the first born and only son of a man who loved his job and believed in hard work, Sean was cast to take his place in the paid work world with pride and gratitude. His father had been a potato farmer in PEI before riding the boxcars during the Depression and hopping off in Sudbury like so many others to be hired by Inco in 1933. His first job was among the most dangerous in the smelter. As a puncher, he slaved in front of the flaming two-storey-high furnaces, pounding the vents to allow a continuous flow of oxygen into the furnaces. Over time, he worked his way up to be a skimmer, one of the most skilled jobs in the smelter. During Owen's twenty-seven years at Inco, Sean watched his father keep studious track of the number of tons of ore moved out on each of his shifts along with Inco's overall production, and in the spirit of friendly competition drew comparisons to the production of other shifts. Like so many of the "Depression boys," work was integral to his sense of self-worth and indeed to his very identity.

During his last two years of high school, Sean worked part-time job at the school lunch counter in addition to the paper route he held for several years. Aware of the struggle his parents faced to feed the family of six during the strike, Sean at age eighteen "was old enough to know what their whispers meant." It was the same one faced by almost the entire community of Gatchell, which produced a strong collective sense of "we're all in this together,"[66] as Sean remembers. He voluntarily handed over his paycheque to his parents and brought home any hamburgers, salad, and grilled cheese sandwiches left over from the lunch counter. The family's large backyard garden, overflowing with potatoes and other produce, also helped to sustain the family.

Potatoes were a staple for Homer's family during the strike. The smelterworker took a job at a Blezard Valley spud farm and was paid in a portion of the produce he picked each day. The five-member family ate potatoes for all three meals. Homer's wife, Claire, was an inventive cook and found every possible way to vary the preparation of the potatoes – potato soup, baked potatoes, potato pancakes, boiled potatoes, and more.[67]

Growing gardens came naturally to the myriad of Inco workers from farming backgrounds and canning was a regular fall activity. When Geronimo arrived from Italy in 1952 with his three-months-pregnant wife, Hortensia, to work Inco's copper refinery, they immediately planted an enormous garden.[68] Similarly, Ian, who came from his home on Manitoulin Island to work at Inco two years before the strike, recalled, "We had a big garden, always. Oh, heck yes. When you're from the farm, you know how to grow everything." At the beginning of the strike, Ian made a pact with his drinking buddy: "We just had coffee at each other's place instead of beer. That's how we saved our money. My mom and dad, that generation, they saved their money and taught me to do that. So, actually we were fine, we didn't mind having nothing."[69] In addition to gardens, larders were augmented with regular fishing in the many nearby lakes, and hunting the plentiful deer, moose, and wild fowl in the region.

For Inco, the strike was reduced to a set of numerical calculations. The time needed to empty strikers' stomachs was estimated and compared to the time it would take to deplete the stockpile. The extent of the stockpile, metal market conditions, and the mood of the strikers were frequently evaluated by Inco's corporate leaders. One month into the strike, John Thompson reported to the press, "1959 looks like a good year for the firm. Existing stockpiles will last 7 or 8 months and there is little possibility of the strike going on that long."[70] There would be no need to compromise profits as long as the company resumed negotiations just as the last of the stockpile was being shipped out. In the meantime, Inco continued to extol its virtuous relations with its employees in full-page advertisements in several Ontario papers and attribute its lack of a wage offer to the reduced markets, rising competition, and lower profits.[71] The collusion between the mining companies and mainstream media was nothing new, as the Kirkland Lake strike had taught the union seventeen years prior. It would persist throughout the 1958 strike and into the next few years of the union local's struggle for survival.

For the vast majority of union members, the strike was more than a matter of numerical calculations. To be starved into submission was a real possibility. Using their best judgment, the Strike Coordinating Committee continued to dispense the limited funds to those most in need, which included the most inactive members and even those with suspended memberships.[72] It was an approach that required other members with some money in the bank, oil in their furnaces, or financial help from family members, to waive the relief. In line with the criteria for distribution of support, one striker remembers telling the committee, "Of course, as long as I can hold, I'll hold. If I can't hold no more, then I come and get my money."[73]

But not all members were governed by this altruistic attitude that increasingly ran counter to the growing cultural focus on the values of individualism, the supremacy of the nuclear family, and the emerging consumer culture. Inco families, particular Inco wives, were being advised in popular magazines to build homes that were comfortable, clean, bright, beautiful, healthy, and cheerful. *Chatelaine*, with a readership of over two million, regularly featured articles on home decorating, food preparation, and family money-management alongside suggestions for wardrobe makeovers and new hairstyles.[74] Many Canadian women were indifferent to the marketing efforts, often recovering older furniture to fit into existing décor and continuing to make cautious purchasing choices as they had during the previous decades of depression, war, and the first decade of postwar reconstruction.[75] In the main, however, the striking Inco families, like other Canadians, wanted a share in the country's fabulous wealth being generated from their labour as the nation's overall productivity spiralled upward. The steady improvement in their wages and benefits achieved through the union's negotiation of collective agreements over fourteen years had raised the hopes of Inco families, which the strike was now undermining.

In the months following the strike, the most-needy-first approach that had governed the distribution of strike benefits would prove to be one of the most piercing criticisms of the strike advanced by the union's opponents. While nobody starved, the material sacrifices that were necessary during the strike eroded the confidence the workers had in the union's ability to deliver regular and continued improvements. In the jurisdictional battles between the union and USWA that were to play out shortly after the strike, the hardships of the strike became a crucial argument for replacing Mine Mill with a union that promised a prodigious strike fund.

"Any Goddamn Fool Can Call a Strike; the Secret Is to Get a Settlement"

For Nina, wife of a striking Levack mechanic, one of the most difficult times in her life was the autumn of 1958. Faced with no means of supporting the family, her husband Eric relocated to Elliot Lake for work at the beginning of the strike, leaving Nina in sole charge of the young family. Within days of his departure, she gave birth to their fourth child following a rocky pregnancy. Isolated in the remote community of Levack, post-partum depression was a constant challenge. The paycheques coming from Eric's employment at Dennison Mines in Elliot Lake weren't enough to meet the family's living expenses and Nina noticed her wedding ring loosening on her finger. In the cloudy, gloomy days of late October, with the drizzle and fog anticipating snow that would soon materialize, she wondered how things could be worse. When the children came down with chicken pox, she found out. Exhausted, lonely, and unwell, Nina turned to her neighbour. Together, over afternoon cups of weak tea, they poured out their troubled circumstances as strikers' wives, shared the scrapings of a lipstick left in the tube, and exchanged ideas on how to disguise the same ingredients for their daily soups: beef-bone broth for its nutritional value, vegetables left from last summer's garden, and rice or pasta from the pantry.[1]

Women like Nina had instantly become single mothers with husbands relocating for employment elsewhere during the strike. Like those women whose husbands were stationed overseas during the war years, all at once there was no one to shovel the snow-filled walkways, haggle with the landlord for a reduction in rent, and help dress the children for church on Sunday mornings. Such women were excluded from the many community activities once made possible by leaving the children with their husbands to slip out for the occasional evening meeting or the welcome reprieve that a social occasion could provide. They were alone to deal with the pre-bedtime hubbub of one child loudly sobbing over a favourite teddy gone missing while the other in his pirate pyjamas tore around the living room swiping at the air with a plastic sword. Single-parenting strikers' wives like Nina who could not count on a free evening were also kept from attending the weekend-long Women's Institute (WI) conference held in Sudbury at the beginning of November.

The conference agenda of the charitable organization covered the usual items of concern to rural women, yet it was the dire impact of the strike that monopolized the discussion at the WI conference. As members of a community in which thousands of families were on strike, the women at the WI conference were intimately acquainted with the mounting anxiety it caused. The two hundred representatives from the WI chapters in Algoma and Sudbury districts resolved to take matters into their own hands by contacting labour minister Charles Daley. Urging him to re-open the negotiations, they wrote, "This unnecessary dispute is creating very severe hardships for all the people of Sudbury district, particularly women and children."[2]

The WI delegates were not alone in pressing the labour minister to intervene and kick-start negotiations. A breakthrough settlement for the Algoma Steel workers in nearby Sault Ste Marie prompted MMSW leaders to contact labour minister Daley to ask him to break the deadlock with Inco. With its 27-cent wage and benefits increase, the Algoma settlement marked an important breach in Diefenbaker's hold-the-line policy that corporations had been adhering to for several months. A few days later, the United Steelworkers also torpedoed the policy in settling a twelve-week strike with a 27.8 cent increase to wages and benefits for its eight thousand members at the Steel Company of Canada in Hamilton. These breakthroughs in the Tory government's hold-the-line policy seemed to signal promise of a similar settlement for the Inco workers. But Daley refused to convene talks between the union and Inco, turning a deaf ear to both appeals by ignoring two hundred women as well as a union representing over fourteen thousand workers by refusing to use his power to restart negotiations.

FELLOW MINE MILLERS STEP UP

While the union leaders resolved to continue hammering away on the government to convene negotiations, time was slipping sideways and the union's funds depleting with alarming speed. The November frost had already hardened the ground and the strikers' spirits were flagging while Inco continued to flaunt its stockpile in news statements: "We regret that the strike is continuing. Meanwhile our plants are being maintained in satisfactory condition and customers are being supplied nickel from stocks available in our large accumulated inventories."[3] For years, the miners and smeltermen had resolutely turned their faces to the future, knowing that the past was unalterable. But now, doubt was creeping into the decision to take on the corporate titan, Inco. Where could they go for support?

One group of workers Inco strikers could count on were their fellow Local 598 members who worked at Falconbridge, another mining giant in the Sudbury Basin. The three thousand Falconbridge members organized an array of supportive actions throughout the strike and postponed negotiations with their employer until the Inco strike was over. Umberto, an electrician and union steward, recalls the coordinated collections from his fellow Falconbridge members: "We were the stewards and we had to go around to every man and ask him to donate an amount of dollars per pay, which was every two weeks. I had a receipt book, $10 from you and $20 from you and so on."[4] Umberto also spearheaded the food drives from the Falconbridge members: "We passed out leaflets announcing that there'd be a food drive at the gates the next day. There was a list of food, especially baby needs and stuff. We had a truck, one half-ton truck with a box on it, ready to load the food. Oh my God, we ended up filling, I think, five or six trucks. We couldn't believe how generous the men were. They brought everything; everything imaginable."[5] Having arranged for only one truck to be at the gate, Umberto drastically underestimated the extent to which the Falconbridge wives would scour their cupboards for cans of soup, bags of flour, and bins of rice the night before. In addition to material support, Umberto and his Falconbridge co-workers regularly gave up their Saturdays to shore up the spirits of the strikers by walking side by side with them on the picket line.

As November dawned and the weakening sunshine tumbled temperatures in foreboding of the winter to come, another boost arrived in the form of a telegram from the five thousand MMSW members in Trail and Kimberley BC accompanied by a $10,000 cheque. In an additional show of support, they voted two-to-one to approve a deduction of $5 from each member's monthly pay for the length of the strike. As it turned out, the support from the western locals served more than one purpose.

The situation was that it had been a long-standing practice within the union for the Inco locals in Sudbury and Port Colborne to coordinate their bargaining with the four large locals in BC who negotiated with Consolidated Mining and Smelting Company (CM&S), producer of lead, zinc, and copper. Both the western and eastern blocks would hold back until the other had received proposals from their respective companies. This close coordination reinforced the strength of each local in negotiating collective agreements with two of the largest companies in the base metal industry in the country. However, in the spring of 1958 the historical east-west coordination unraveled. Before the MMSW negotiators in the east received offers from Inco, the western locals settled with CM&S for a five-cent per hour supplement to the defined-benefit pension plan, but no wage increase; wage negotiations were to resume in nine months.[6] As a result of the break in the pattern of east-west coordinated bargaining, there were some fences to be mended within the union. The $10,000 from the MMSW members in Trail that shored up the strike fund also served significantly to repair and re-fortify the fellowship between the east and west branches of the union. Over the course of the strike, numerous contributions came from Mine Mill members from other locals working for the sixty-two companies with which the union held collective agreements.

PETITIONING THE LARGER LABOUR MOVEMENT

In the early morning of 2 November, the temperatures dropped below freezing; winter had slid in overnight. At Regent Street hall, the sharp change in weather was the topic of the small talk that started off the meeting of members of both the international and national executive boards, but over the next few hours it was the strike that commanded their attention, now into the sixth week with no prospect of a settlement. The Local 598's financial secretary, Norman Jaques, reported that the cost of the union's food voucher system was mounting and projections to sustain the fourteen thousand plus strikers and their families were at least $125,000 for each week of the strike.[7] There were more and more letters from disgruntled members who had been refused food vouchers, even reports of fist-fights breaking out between disenchanted strikers and Strike Coordinating Committee members. Jaques concluded by stating what everyone else in the room knew: the financial reserves were nearing depletion.

The leaders bent to the task of raising funds. It was decided that the $900,000 in union properties – the four union halls and Richard Lake camp – would be offered as security against loans granted by other unions. The nearly million-dollar value of these assets must have made all those around the table swallow hard, for they represented years of the local's investment of members' union dues – on the line. If they couldn't win a fair settlement from Inco, all that would be left was their dogged belief in the legitimacy of the fight.

The leaders determined to petition the Canadian Labour Congress[8] for support even though donations from that source were unlikely since the union had been cut adrift from the house of labour a decade prior for its alleged communist domination. Since the end of World War I, communist union organizers had been instrumental in the creation of the electrical, textile, fur and leather workers, and fishermen unions.[9] But during the Cold War, Mine Mill and these other left-led unions became targets of smear campaigns and the contributions of the early communist organizers were conveniently forgotten. The Canadian Congress of Labour's (CCL) opportunity to evict MMSW from the House of Labour came at a labour lobby banquet in 1948 when Harvey Murphy, MMSW leader from Western Canada and chief negotiator for the union's large Local 480, staggered to the mic, thoroughly inebriated, to condemn Aaron Mosher, CCL president, for not defending International president Reid Robinson who was deported from Canada for his alleged communist affiliation. Murphy boomed, "If he [Mosher] is going to kiss the boss's ass, he better be sure to pull his pants down first."[10] The outlandish remark was too lewd and boorish for even the many Murphy supporters within the union who were far from paragons of virtue themselves. More to the point, however, was their annoyance that Murphy gave the CCL the excuse it needed to purge MMSW.[11]

In response to MMSW's request for financial support of the strike, the Congress offered to act as a medium through which affiliated unionists could channel their contributions to aid MMSW's members.

But in later correspondence to Mine Mill president Nels Thibault, the Congress castigated the union as irresponsible for calling a strike at a time when Inco had a massive stockpile and warned that "the Congress was not going to be drawn into having Mine Mill leave its ill-conceived strike on the doorstep of the CLC."[12] Other responses from the official organizations of the House of Labour were similarly disappointing. At its conference in early October, the Ontario Federation of Labour, representing five hundred thousand unionized workers, passed a resolution declaring solidarity with the strikers but without mention of a financial donation.[13] Federations of labour in BC and Manitoba followed suit with similar strident declarations of moral support unaccompanied by desperately needed financial support.

At their 2 November meeting, the leaders resolved to cast wide the net for financial aid: Solski undertook to travel to the US headquarters of the International Brotherhood of Teamsters (the Teamsters), United Mine Workers of America (UMWA), and United Electrical Radio and Machine Workers (UE) unions to solicit aid.[14] Meeting with their leaders in New York, he learned that the Cold War attack on that union was so severe that there was nothing to spare after legal costs. In Washington, Solski met with Jimmy Hoffa of the Teamsters, and John Lewis of UMWA. Much to Solski's delight, Hoffa offered $5,000 and pledged to keep the Teamsters' members from crossing MMSW picket lines – an offer that was exaggerated by the newspapers to discredit the union and the strike.[15] By contrast, Solski's reception by the UMWA was markedly cooler: "It was like entering Fort Knox," he recounted, and he never was able to secure a meeting with Lewis.[16] In the first radio address of "Local 598 Reports" following his return, Solski summarized the results of his week-long trip to the United States: "It would be unwise to build all our hopes on these sources in case they do not materialize. We have got to face this present assault of the company on our own determination and strength if we are to survive."[17] The chill of the Cold War, and its atmosphere of confusion, coercion, and fear, had descended on the labour movement at the worst possible time for Inco strikers.

Despite the anti-communist fearmongering within the labour movement, financial contributions did flow in from unions. Far-flung miners' unions in Australia, France, Scotland, and Wales and unions representing Canadian workers in retail, transportation, manufacturing, and the public sector did their part. Closer to home, the United Fishermen and Allied Workers' Union loaned $5,000 to MMSW and cheques arrived from the district labour councils in the major Canadian cities, including Vancouver, Calgary, Halifax, Winnipeg, Oshawa, and Windsor. Conspicuous by their absence on the MMSW's financial ledger were the Canadian Congress of Labour and the Ontario Federation of Labour.[18]

SURGES OF SUPPORT FROM THE COMMUNITY

By mid-November, the Catholic Charities, an organization specifically created to provide material support to the striking families, was in full swing. With headquarters in a *Sudbury Star* building on MacKenzie Street, the organization distributed food and clothing. The bishop of the Sault Sainte Marie diocese, Alexander Carter, had launched the organization, canvassing the priests in the diocese to collect food and clothing within their parishes. Paradoxically, however, Carter chastised the union for striking at the same time as he solicited help for the strikers. In his letter, read aloud in all the Roman Catholic churches in the diocese, Bishop Carter scolded: "It is inconceivable that the officials of the union could have allowed this strike without carefully considering all its implications."[19] By raising the spectre of financial skulduggery on the part of Mine Mill officials in the early days of the strike, the bishop undermined the confidence of the members in their union's leadership, particularly the large Catholic contingent in the membership. The official voice of the Catholic Church raised an even more dangerous speculation by pronouncing that "the union's persistence in holding out so persistently for their demands [when] we have passed the peak of prosperity which we enjoyed few years ago ... makes the outsider wonder whether some outside influence is not at work." The accusation that the strike was a communist plot fed the rampant Cold War hysteria.[20]

Individuals, local businesses, and community organizations made financial contributions. Notably, Aba Bayefsky, the Canadian war artist stationed at Bergen-Belsen camp upon its liberation, made a donation, as did many others who wished to remain anonymous.

Community organizations ponied up too, among them the Canadian Congress of Women, Canadian Chinese Association, Association of United Ukrainian Canadians, United Jewish People's

Order, and Federation of Yugoslav Canadian, among others. Donations came in from local florists, hotels, men's clothing stores, and large and small grocery stores.

The Red Cross and the Salvation Army made use of their existing channels to support the strikers and their families. R.R. Jessup, board chair of the Red Cross, reported that the biggest increase was in the number of cod liver oil doses the organization distributed. Yet spokespersons for both the Catholics Charities and the Salvation Army described the union's food vouchers as insufficient, and Captain D.E. Hammond of the Salvation Army detailed the extreme circumstances of the strikers, some going without food so they could feed their children. He reported that demands on the army's reserves since the strike started had more than doubled, and warned "I shudder to think what will happen when it turns cold."[21] Several days after Captain Hammond's reports of dire circumstances, his superior, Brigadier Bruce Jennings, contradicted him in the press. "Reports of widespread suffering and hunger among families of striking miners here have been exaggerated."[22] Opposing assessments of the strikers' circumstances continued to appear in the press, some vividly evoking dire conditions while others asserted that "many miners and their families are getting more balanced diets now than they ever did because instead of spending their pay on beer, miners can use the vouchers for nothing but food."[23] And there were individual strikers who denied the reports of hardship outright, offering detailed descriptions of the foods their families continued to enjoy.[24]

The United Church set up a watch-dog committee that was prepared to act if needed, but as of the middle of November, Reverend C.R. Newton of St Paul's United Church reported there had been very little demand. And Dr Lautenslager of St Andrew's United Church avowed, "In my ten years in Sudbury I have never had so few come asking for meals, clothing or shelter as has been since the strike. I'm surprised we're getting along so well."[25] He figured that it helped that the "professional panhandlers" were avoiding Sudbury, imagining that the charities they usually relied on would be directing their resources to the strikers.[26] Indeed, as Dr Lautenslager himself confirmed, the few panhandlers involved wouldn't have accounted for the low number of requests. Yet the inflated reports of deprivation took hold in the press and at the pulpits and began to erode the members' commitment to the strike, for it was impossible in the

midst of it to know exactly how many were suffering from fundamental poverty.

But over the course of the strike, there were instances of poignant
material and moral support from unanticipated quarters. Loretta, the
grade 3 teacher at Copper Cliff Elementary School, regularly distributed sheets of foolscap paper to her students so their parents wouldn't
have to buy scribbler notebooks. A few of Loretta's fellow teachers in
the Catholic schools began their lessons with a prayer for the strikers,
which would have shored up those children in ways that cannot be
measured.[27] And the Copper Cliff Credit Union loans officers were
granting vital emergency loans with easy terms to some strikers.

MUSTERING MEETINGS AND RAMPING
UP THE PRESSURE

Now two months into the strike with winter settling in, the international and national MMSW executive board leaders convened
once again. This time, the board met in Toronto to accommodate
those located at the union's headquarters in Denver. For the assembled unionists with their substantial combined strike experience,
the difficulty in forging a settlement with rapacious employers was
all too familiar. As Canadian MMSW president Thibault said to his
young mentee, Robin (who would become president of Local 598
several years later), "Any goddamn fool can call a strike; the secret
is to get a settlement."[28] Bringing about a settlement with such a
ruthless monopoly as Inco would call on all their collective skill
and ingenuity.

As they had done before, the assembled unionists wiped their
hearts off their sleeves, rolled them up, and went right to work on
the Herculean tasks of bringing an end to the strike and supporting
the fourteen thousand strikers and their families for whatever duration ensued. They agreed to increase their publicity efforts, continue
the financial appeals, enlarge the picket lines, and extend the union's
women's auxiliaries activities to more than fund-raising. When discussion turned to strategies for ramping up the political pressure on
the provincial government, the idea was hatched to organize a cavalcade of strikers and community leaders to present petitions signed by
citizens to the Frost government to call Inco to the bargaining table.

Immediately upon returning to Sudbury from these meetings,
Solski delivered the updates in a series of membership meetings at

the union halls: 2:30 pm and 7:30 pm at the Regent Street hall on Sunday, 23 November; and the next day morning and afternoon meetings at Coniston and Garson halls, followed on Monday by a meeting at Creighton-Lively hall. Then on Tuesday, Solski drove the forty-five kilometers over gravel roads to Levack to meet with those members. At each meeting, the members heard that even greater sacrifice and struggle were going to be needed if there was any hope of reaching a settlement before Christmas. Their president reminded them that Inco had engineered the strike to reduce its nickel stockpiles and was punishing its workers who dared ask for a fair share in the wealth created from their labour. And in case anyone doubted that there was wealth to share, he then read off Inco's annual net profits over the past several years: $86 million in 1957, $96 million the year before, and $91.6 million in 1955. In response, boos echoed throughout the halls like the bellow of elephants. The whopping profits recited to the members revealed that although Inco's nickel deliveries had slumped during the first nine months of 1958, Inco was still the largest producer of copper in the country and copper sold at steadily increasing prices from prior to the strike. Taking a measure of the mood, Solski then urged the audience to collect as many signatures as possible on the circulating petitions in preparation for the cavalcade and ramp up the pressure on the picket lines: "You're being too gentlemanly,"[29] he advised. His warning to the company, "things might not be too quiet from now on" brought further cheers.[30] His prompt to turn up the heat on the lines was a marked change from the early days of the strike when the picketers were instructed to let the contractors and Inco managers pass through when the executive's no-interference directive was devised to avoid legal penalties if violence were to escalate on the picket lines. But now that the strike was stumbling into a third month and the executive had to take that risk entailed by focusing the anger and frustration of its membership.

Back at the Regent Street hall meetings on 23 November, two of the union's most prominent leaders addressed the membership. The first was Canadian president Nels Thibault, a riveting orator tutored by observing his lay-preacher father as well as studying the great speakers of the time. Alive to the mood of the crowd, he walked to the mic as his two daughters joined in the clapping from the adjoining kitchen where they were helping to prepare the post-meeting sandwiches. With many such occasions witnessing their father's

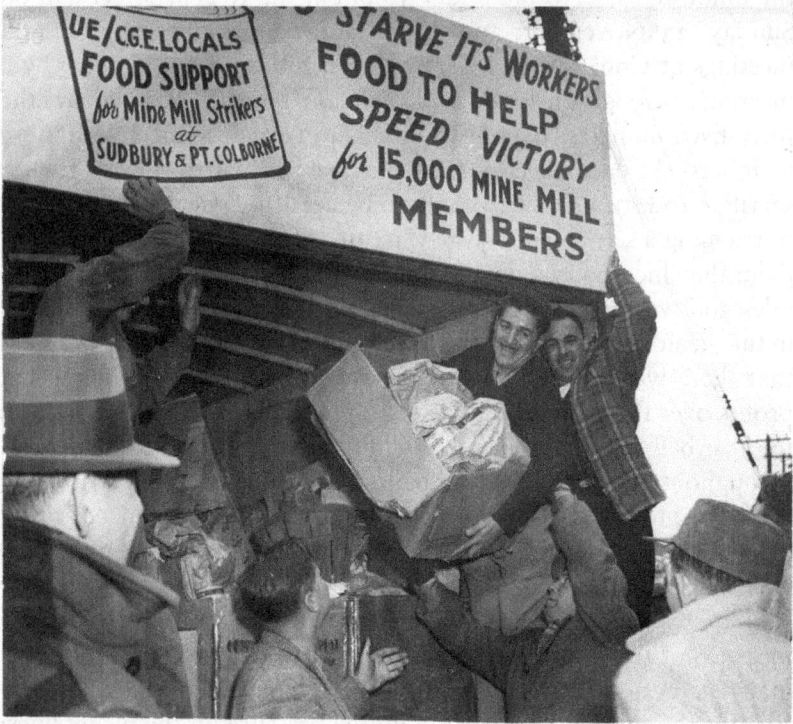

Figure 7.1 | Truckload of non-perishables from United Electrical, Radio and Machine Workers of America (UE).

magnificence behind a mic, they had much to offer years later in explaining his oratorical prowess. Thibault's speech, punctuated with perfectly timed inflection points and his penetrating gaze for emphasis, was crafted to inspire the packed hall at those two late-November meetings to stay focused on the goal of preventing Inco from destroying the union. As though tightly choreographed, his gestures complemented his words in a spell-binding delivery that implored the strikers to stiffen their resolve for a better future. To the crowd, Thibault was one of their own, having been a miner at Inco's Frood mine with first-hand experience of the grinding working conditions and tactics of intimidation. In seeking their own leaders, Inco workers had placed their trust in him and he never failed to inspire them. In exchange, he drew his strength and wisdom from his fellow workers in his crusade for a better life for all. To their euphoric cheers in the Regent Street hall, Thibault brought news of the truck-loads of clothing, food, and other supplies arriving the next day from the locals of United Electrical, Radio and Machine Workers of America (UE) in Peterborough, Hamilton, and Toronto.

International president John Clark followed Thibault on the stage and closed the two Regent Street meetings with promises of the full support of the almost one hundred thousand American MMSW members, resulting in $100,000 from the international office of MMSW. In addition, collections were taken up at the over eighty MMSW locals in California, Alabama, Connecticut, Ohio, Arizona, Illinois, Indiana, Mississippi, and Colorado, including $2,300 from MMSW procreator Local One in Butte, Montana.

With raised spirits, the audience adjourned the Regent Street meeting on 23 November with a march down Elm Street as a prelude to the upcoming cavalcade to the provincial legislature in Toronto. The strikers' radius of action was about to extend well beyond that downtown street of Sudbury.

RAISED HOPES FOR A SETTLEMENT

The Frost government announced it would convene talks between Inco and the union on 26 November. Perhaps Inco decided now was the time to negotiate, but whatever the impetus, hopes ran high for the outcome of the talks, with the cold weather a constant pres-ence pressing in on the strikers and their families. Labour minister Daley was hopeful, too; one less labour dispute on his watch would be a good thing at a time when there were scores of other work-ers heading towards a strike, including twenty thousand construc-tion workers in Toronto, ten thousand employees of the Ontario Hydro-Electric Power Commission, and thirty-two thousand auto workers in Oshawa and Windsor.[31]

Nobody wanted a settlement more than the two men who were to lead the MMSW negotiating team in the talks. But years of expe-rience bargaining with Inco had prepared the local's president and the union's Canadian president to keep their expectations cautious: Although metal markets were beginning to rebound, the stockpile was not yet depleted. Solski and Thibault agreed to start the talks by asking Daley for assurances that Inco was truly prepared to break the ice; and the cavalcade would proceed regardless of the outcome of the talks.

Figure 7.2 | Talks between Inco and MMSW break down, 28 November 1958.

Over the three days of talks under the eyes of the labour minister Daley and chief conciliator Louis Fine in the minister's Toronto offices, Inco made two proposals: to consider a three-year agreement; and to resume the forty-hour week without a commitment on the timing for resumption or the number of workers to be recalled. The reinstatement of a forty-hour week would automatically raise workers' wages by 25 per cent from what they were earning on the thirty-two-hour week, but without knowing how many workers it would affect, the union could not assess the significance of the proposal. The union's negotiating team agreed to the idea of a three-year agreement and developed a series of concessions over the three days based on the revised length of contract. As the hours wound down, it became increasingly clear to the union that Inco had agreed to the talks only to appease the minister and bow to public pressure as well as the threat of the cavalcade. The bargaining finally broke down on Inco's refusal to consider several important planks of the union's demands. The company wouldn't hear of an immediate wage increase; neither was it prepared to guarantee that the post-strike return to work would be based on seniority.[32] Not even the union's demand for Inco to adjust the deduction of union dues from members' paycheques – a demand that would cost the company nothing – was conceded.[33]

Before talks got started on the last day, while the MMSW team was waiting for Daley and Fine, photographer Pete Orfankos of the Sudbury CKST-TV joined the union negotiators in board room number sixty-seven. The friendly joking and repartee with Orfankos while he took a few pictures of the MMSW negotiators was likely the basis of the leak that there was a settlement.[34] It wasn't long before Sudbury's bars and taverns were ablaze with speculations. In the Nickel Range Hotel's Bavarian Room, the Elm Street bar most frequented by MMSW members, the possibility of a settlement combined with the usual salacious discussions that covered the gamut from the identity of communists in the union to friends' marriages that were unravelling. Could Thibault really be Russian, not French, and didn't he come to Sudbury to infiltrate the union, for hadn't the priest said so from the pulpit at last Sunday's service? How soon do you think the strike could be called off? And, what about Mrs X who told her husband that she was pregnant, changed her mind about dates, then after a time announced that all was over – surely she was concealing the ghost of a baby conceived by an Inco supervisor? What are the terms of the settlement likely to be? The media ban about the settlement talks left large gaps to be filled by the active imaginations of the Inco workers and their fellow Sudbury residents.

Membership meetings were held following the collapse of the government-sponsored talks to discuss Inco's closing offer of no wage increase in the first year, 1 per cent in the second year and 1.5 per cent the third year. The membership resoundingly rejected the offer in a series of "No" votes.[35] Planning turned to the cavalcade as the prospect of the strike lasting over Christmas loomed ever larger. Sudbury's shop windows, already aglow with Christmas sale signs and displays of new furnishings, toys, and gadgets, seemed to mock the prospects of the cash-strapped strikers' families for the holiday.

ON TO QUEEN'S PARK: "WE'RE NOT STARVING, WE'RE FED UP WITH INCO STALLING"

The first of December brought snow falling fast and covering roof-tops like vanilla frosting. It was as though the brief respite from the blustery winter had been an illusion. There began several days of high drama and careful stickhandling by Charlie Marcolin, a smelterman at Copper Cliff. With wartime service in the army branch specializing in transport and road convoys, Marcolin went to work to organize a 150-car parade to Toronto. Outfitted with maps and detailed instruc-tions, the cavalcade left Sudbury in brightly decorated cars late on the evening of 2 December. Gasoline and other supplies for the trip were financed by local councilmen, service stations, and small business owners. In order to prevent traffic congestion, some travelled straight down Highway 69 and others took the alternate route through North Bay. The two convoys converged around Barrie and travelled together for the remainder of the trip to Toronto in a single grouping that stretched three miles along the highway. Joining the travelling picket-ers in Toronto the next morning at Queen's Park was the contingent of Local 637 strikers arriving from Port Colborne.

Together, the one thousand strikers, wives, and other supporters marched on Queen's Park, sporting miners' hats and carrying signs that read, "Support the Inco Strikers"; "With You We Can Stop Union Busting"; and "We're Not Starving; We're Fed Up with Inco Stalling." In addition to impelling the government to facilitate talks, the signs aimed to educate the public, for instance those that read "Millions for Wall St – Eleven-week Strike for Us" made explicit reference to the American domination of the Canadian economy. In asserting this position, Mine Mill was spearheading the call for Canadian workers' control over their economic destiny. As MMSW vice president Bill Longridge had proclaimed to a membership meet-ing at the end of November, "It is the responsibility of the government to protect both the natural resources of Canada and its working men against this type of exploitation by a foreign company."[36] Although many of the Inco strikers did not see the strike as reason to nation-alize foreign-owned companies profiting from Canada's metals, minerals, and other natural resources, the concern about American domination of the Canadian economy among Canadian workers generally, including Inco workers, would become widespread in the following decade.

Figures 7.3, 7.4 | Queen's Park cavalcade.

Led by red-bearded Bill Sproule on his guitar and with printed
song sheets, the picketers serenaded the occupants of the sandstone
legislature building in bursts of expansive chants and spirited songs.
The skies were stubbornly cloudy, but the abnormally warm temperatures were in the picketers' favour, as one quipped to a nearby
pressman, "The weatherman has been with us so far. That's one
thing Inco can't control."[37]

Inside the premier's office, the MMSW delegation appealed to the
government for more action. They reminded the premier and invited
guests, including the attorney general, provincial treasurer, several
ministers, and area MPPs, that Inco was alone among the corporate
elites in its stubborn defense of the hold-the-line policy on wages.
Therefore, the delegation argued, it was incumbent on the government to use its offices to secure serious negotiations between the
union and the company, particularly a large American corporation
like Inco only interested in plundering Canada's natural resources. In
the course of the two-hour meeting, the demonstrators outside raised
their voices to several rounds of labour song standards such as "We
Shall Not Be Moved"; "Roll the Cavalcade On"; and "Solidarity
Forever." The picketers also belted out Woody Guthrie's lyrics to
"Union Maid" to pay tribute to the wives, sisters, and mothers who
formed MMSW women's auxiliaries whose provenance was consequential in the early 1940s when the union was gaining a toehold in
mining camps in Northern Ontario.

At the conclusion of the meeting with the premier, Frost signalled
his previous intransigence and unchanged Inco allegiances. In a
press statement, he dismissed the union's appeal that the government take over the operation of Inco. "I at once say the government
has no intention whatever of doing any such thing."[38] Undeterred by
Frost's reaction and the lowering skies, the demonstrators carried on
with their plans. Now joined by Thibault, Solski, and others from
the meeting with politicians, the entire assemblage paraded down
University Avenue, snow falling fast and mounting, as if the brief
respite from the blustery winter had been an illusion. In well-defined
groups of fifty, they headed to Inco's Canadian headquarters on
Yonge Street in the heart of the city's financial district. Toronto's
deputy police chief and a squad of officers were on hand, but there
was no need, for the demonstrators were well-disciplined and tightly
organized. After lunch served by supporters at the Ukrainian Hall
on Bathurst Street, the cavalcade fanned out to the large industrial

plants in the city to distribute handbills and collect donations of money, food, clothing, and children's toys.

Unfortunately for the union, the cavalcade did not produce the immediately desired effect of government intervention to bring Inco to the table and the IUMMSW executive, having been appraised of the cavalcade's results, devised new ways to raise funds from the distribution of "Inco Strike Support" buttons among the union's American members.[39] Rather, the success of the cavalcade lay in the demonstration of a masterfully enacted strategy of resistance that challenged the media's portrayal of the strike as merely a tactic to boost the wages of Inco workers and the government's intention to make Canadian workers pay for the economic recession with a wage restraint policy. The media coverage of the cavalcade drew the public's attention to the American domination of Canada's natural resources, the unequal distribution of wealth among Canadians, and the ill effects of unbridled corporate power.[40] In another few years, these concerns would count as serious political consciousness-raising in the demonstrations for Canadianization of the labour movement across the interlinked movements of anti-war and women's liberation.

WOMEN CAST AS SABOTEURS

At the end of the eleventh week of the strike, the Sudbury local of the women's auxiliary stepped on the accelerator. Having actively raised funds, organized clothing drives, delivered coffee and cheer to the picket lines,[41] and performed life-sustaining emotional and domestic labour from the early days of the strike forward, the auxiliary women were ready to become more political. As one member recounted, "[We supported the strike] because we wanted our men to have decent wages and to have the security you needed and to have the safety. Especially safety, because when you're underground, good God! I don't think men were made to be groundhogs!"[42] Now it was time to do more, so the auxiliary called an open meeting at the Regent Street hall for 10 December.

The crowded hall of nine hundred women cheered when Kay Carlin took to the mic. Kay was a veteran auxiliary member who supported the gold miners in the 1941–42 Kirkland Lake strike in their fight for union recognition and had been involved in organizing the Inco local as described in a previous chapter.[43] In sisterhood with Kay, the women in the Regent Street hall voted in favour of the resolution to support the strikers' fight for a fair settlement. Then they developed an action plan to write letters to Inco president Henry Wingate in New York, and the very next day to march on City Hall to press the mayor to intervene.

The 10 December meeting was chaired by Millie McQuaid, vice president of the MMSW auxiliary's Local 117. The auxiliary, comprised of wives, sisters, and mothers of the MMSW members, had been active in union and community affairs since being officially chartered as Local 117 under the union's constitution in 1943. Like their sister MMSW auxiliaries in Canada and the US, the women of Local 117 created a vibrant social life in Sudbury by organizing movie nights, bazaars, and Christmas parties, while making costumes for the dance school recitals and the local's theatre troupe, the Haywood Players. The auxiliaries undertook ambitious political campaigns for a national health care plan, price controls, childcare, and public housing well before these social and economic reforms became the platform of Tommy Douglas and other high-profile politicians or second-wave feminist groups.[44] Millie joined the women's auxiliary in the late 1940s and was a regular delegate to the national MMSW conventions and Local 598's membership meetings at home.[45] Growing up with a father who worked at Inco's refinery in the 1930s and was fired for his efforts to organize the union, Millie took an active interest in union affairs. During each round of Local 598's bargaining with Inco, she would raise the topics of pensions, health and safety, and sick leave with her husband Tom, a miner at Creighton: "I'd start discussing the next negotiation sessions. And I'd tell him, 'You need something there for security, there's nothing there. I mean it's all very well to get a few more cents an hour but it's not going to do you any good when you get older."[46] Millie was likely an exception among the women gathered in the Regent Street hall. In the late 1950s, a woman's role in the nuclear family limited her involvement in public as well as sometimes private discussions of the terms and conditions of her husband's work. Details discussed at union meetings would be conveyed to the wives who had not attended the meeting, engaged as they were with reading bedtime stories to the children and filling the lunch buckets for the next shift. In many homes, reports of union meetings would have been delivered in tones that made it clear a woman's view was not welcome. In such a milieu, women like Millie were in the vanguard.

Figure 7.5 | Sudbury Arena meeting, 12 December 1958.

The women's auxiliary laid their plans at the 10 December meeting for a march on City Hall where they would confront Sudbury's mayor, Joe Fabbro. To avoid the embarrassment of a contingent of angry women on his doorstep, Fabbro thwarted the women's plans by announcing a meeting with the strikers' wives and the area's elected provincial representatives at Sudbury's civic arena. Although it was dubbed by the press as the "strikers' wives' meeting," men, children, and women with non-striking partners attended the arena meeting. The union leaders suspected that the mayor's true motive in calling the arena meeting was to fuel a fledgling back-to-work movement and urged the auxiliary women not to attend the arena meeting; consequently, very few auxiliary members showed up.

At the arena meeting, the mayor's singular method of conducting the vote on a resolution advocating a back-to-work motion was designed to ensure it would pass. All those NOT in favour were to step forward to the ice surface, an entirely unknown parliamentary procedure. As expected, amid the noise and confusion only a handful of the attendees left their seats to vote against the resolution. The women favouring the back-to-work resolution were given full coverage from the national and local media, instantly prompted as the leaders of an amorphous movement calling for a return to work. Their incendiary quotations such as, "It's been like living in a Communist-occupied country since the strike began" and provocative headlines like "Inco Wives Defy Goons, Yell 'Go Back to Russia'"[47] were fodder for the Cold War warriors keen to dismantle the union.

The fiasco of the arena meeting invigorated a back-to-work movement portrayed as initiated by a group of strikers' wives. The historical record lacks clear indication of the number of individuals identifying with the movement, along with the nature and extent of the support they received from groups such as the Catholic Church. Yet, its extensive media attention produced the impression that it was women – with no distinction made between auxiliary and non-auxiliary women – who sabotaged the strike.

The impression that women were responsible for undermining the strike lingered among Sudburians and tainted relations between the women's auxiliary and the union leaders for decades to come. The leaders blamed the auxiliary women for walking into a trap set by the mayor and thereby contributed indirectly to the creation of a back-to-work movement. During the 1978 strike of Inco workers, the Women Supporting the Strike group of wives began their organizing with a vow to "not repeat the mistakes of the women of '58."[48] More than thirty years after the strike, the auxiliary had to continue to disabuse the notion that it had subverted the strike. In their letter to the president of Local 598 announcing the official cessation of the auxiliary's Sudbury chapter, their trumpeted achievements include "the organizational drive in 1942–43, to the memorable experiences in the 1958 strike and in particular, the help of the sisters in blocking the back-to-work, strike-breaking efforts of local politicians."[49] Furthermore, to the auxiliary women, being directed by the male leaders to stay in their place and not attend the arena meeting undermined their agency to enact their planned strategy of confronting the local politicians, although it was in keeping with the generally held expectations of women's role of the times. The auxiliary women saw themselves as "intelligent women organized to continue improvements not because of charity, but because it is the democratic right of every person to have the essentials and luxuries of this life."⁵⁰ They had good reason to assume that the union's male leaders shared their belief that security, dignity, and health for working people would need to be won at both the bargaining table and the kitchen table. After all, "a union without women is only half-organized" was a long-standing MMSW slogan and women's equality was a foundational pillar of the union constitution. The union leadership had promoted a model of militant masculinity to effectively challenge corporate dominance; however, and at the same time, it promoted the idea of working-class solidarity that encouraged women's participation in union activities, thereby disavowing the established sexual politics within the local and the larger community. To have proceeded under an assumption of equality only to face evidence to the contrary would have been confusing and disappointing for the auxiliary women. And their dedication to supporting the strike, the union, and the labour movement more generally would have inhibited their open discussions of the difficulties they encountered with entrenched male union leadership – a dilemma that must have as vexing to deal with as it was evident.

Like many strikes before and afterwards, the 1958 strike opened the eyes of workers to their place in the economic order and the nature of their relationship with the capitalist class. A parallel awakening to the systemic sexism in trade unions, and the labour movement generally, was incubating during the 1940s and 1950s in the work of auxiliary women. As labour feminists they carried the torch for working-class women's equality in the intervening years between the triumphs of the suffrage movement and the middle-class feminism of the 1960s.⁵¹

INCO TO THE TABLE

Labour minister Daley called a meeting of the union and Inco for 10 am, Tuesday, 16 December. Inco negotiators came to the meeting predisposed to negotiate a contract based on a new confidence in the resurrected nickel markets and their continued expansion into 1959, whereas the union leaders came with full knowledge that if the strike continued much longer it would be the death knell for the union with its nearly exhausted finances and the ever-intensifying red-baiting from the media and the pulpits. But they also carried with them the knowledge fresh from meetings held only days before that the membership had re-affirmed their desire for a decent contract.

In anticipation of the talks failing, the Strike Coordinating Committee made plans to revise the schedule over the Christmas holiday for food voucher issue, clothing depots, and the informal Regent Street food bank. In response to the committee's continued appeals to other unions, word came from Peterborough that members of the UE working at General Electric were organizing Christmas hampers, toys, and clothing to send to Sudbury. But the strikers hadn't felt the dearth of their resources so keenly since the beginning of the strike. The possibility of a bleak Christmas and a miserable New Year was casting a long shadow on their spirits and they wondered how long they could realistically hold out.

The talks that were to span four days in the minister of labour's office began with introductions. Joining the union's negotiating team was Orville Larson, international vice president of MMSW from Denver who brought years of experience negotiating with mining companies in the US along with an imposing physique. Inco's six-member team led by Mockridge, assistant secretary to Inco's Canadian president, remained the same as for the November talks.

Over the first half of the negotiations, proposals toggled back and forth between union and company. Most of the recesses were called by the union side to give the thirteen-member team time to discuss and vote on their responses to Inco's proposals and to develop counter proposals. Sometimes the proposals were issued to either side by labour minister Daley and his deputy, Louis Fine; other times the union and company teams spoke directly to each other under their scrutiny.

The first topic was the return of the forty-hour week and terms of how production would be resumed following a settlement. The union's pressing questions concerned the timing, numbers, and relevant criteria for a return to work. After Inco's spokesperson Mockridge spent time dodging, Daley asked him outright for the assurances the union wanted: "Can we assume, in all good faith, that you will employ as many employees as possible?" to which Mockridge shot back, "We don't like our good faith to be questioned." Realizing that assurances on the numbers of men to be put back on a forty-hour week and other conditions of the start-up of production weren't going to be forthcoming, Solski switched the topic to wages. In response, Mockridge offered $1.33 per hour more than their previous offer made in the end-of-November talks in the same offices. Finally, after nine-and-half months, the negotiations were taking flight. Evidently, this round of bargaining would take a strike to get the wage increase that in previous years could be resolved with the skillful, arduous negotiating on the part of the MMSW team without job action on the part of the workers.

Interspersed with the topic of wages was discussion of terms and conditions of work in the two new departments Inco was soon to establish and the plans for development of a mine in Thompson, Manitoba. The union negotiators wanted assurances that workers transferred to the two new departments – Levack Mill and Exploration Diamond Drilling – would have their seniority and bidding rights protected. Adding a new mine in Thompson at a time when the nickel markets were frail at best seemed an unwise business decision, and the MMSW negotiators were therefore concerned about a curtailment of production resulting in layoffs for Inco workers, among them the most highly skilled exploration miners who must drill downward to create a mine's first shafts, then upward for raises and horizontally for drifts.

To ensure that the return to a forty-hour week in the start-up would be covered in the talks, the union negotiators added to their demands:

a the conclusion of the new collective agreement would be made
   conditional on the completion of satisfactory negotiations of
   the terms applicable to the start-up period. The Union must
   have a clear understanding of any modification of seniority,
   hours of work and overtime and recall rights, and so on during
   the start-up period, and
b a concise statement of the proposed scale of operations under
   which the company will operate.

Fearing the company's retaliation for members' participation in the strike, the union appended a final non-discrimination clause to their demands.[52]

In the exchange that followed, although the Inco team offered verbal reassurance, they refused to give the exact numbers of men who would be taken back to work. A guarantee was given on the non-discrimination for strike participation and a start-up in

January staggered over four weeks with workers recalled on the basis of seniority.

At the start of the third morning of the talks, negotiations were proceeding well. Important topics were being covered. "They've talked sensibly for the first time," Thibault commented, referring to Inco's negotiators. And so it is strictly a matter for speculation as to the reason for the minister's sudden insistence on cutting the talks short. Perhaps Daley was anxious to move on to the other labour disputes that needed his attention, but without any obvious precipitating cause, he suddenly interjected a request to meet individually with the four spokespersons on the MMSW team, Solski, Thibault, Larson, and Murphy. Before agreeing, Solski demanded a recess to consult with the other three members of the team and seek their approval for the minister's unusual request, which would divide the team.

Once in his office, the minister put forward his wage recommendation of 0 per cent, 2 percent, and 2.5 per cent increases respectively over the three-year period under negotiation. With a confident air, he assured the MMSW team that he could convince the company to accept the recommendation. As if that wasn't enough of an abuse of power by a publicly elected official in the role of mediator, he then announced to the MMSW spokespersons that if they didn't accept it, he would go public, thereby breaking the previously established agreement to a media blackout until the talks were over.

When the minister's recommendation was reported to the rest of the MMSW team, they promptly rejected it with certainty that the membership would find it equally unacceptable.[53] With their backs against the wall, the MMSW team insisted on a day-long recess, hoping that would give them enough time to call in their US chips.

Precisely who in Inco's New York headquarters Larson spoke with over the next twenty-four hours is beyond the historical record, but it is known that the conversations were fruitful. At 8 am on 19 December, Larson convened the MMSW team with a proposed "peace formula"[54] crafted during his conversations with the New York office. The formula contained the eventual wage settlement and a strategy of how to circumvent the minister who had significantly deviated from his mediator role and become a vexatious obstacle. Both the proposed settlement and the strategy were voted on by the thirteen-member team and carried unanimously. Any concerns about the formula being devised over the heads of the two government officials Daley and Fine were set aside in light of what the MMSW team had now experienced as a treachery to rival Inco's.

At the start of the day's morning meeting with Daley and Fine, Solski stated that the MMSW team couldn't accept the minister's recommendation but were prepared to make an offer that should be acceptable to the company. Long seconds passed. Daley was so mystified by the union's brazen position that Solski's statement seemed to echo and hang in the air, every word sounding twice. The minister choked with fury, "As we said before, you are not in a bargaining position."[55] He continued to reprimand the MMSW team for rejecting his recommendation until Fine, seated beside Daley and quicker to realize what had been happening over the past day, kicked Daley under the table. From the corner of his eye, Solski caught the action, and as he reminisced years later, in that instant it became clear to both the mediators that they had been snookered, so they beat a hasty retreat to beckon the Inco negotiators back into the meeting. From then on, the pre-scripted exchange of proposal and counterproposal was enacted, and an agreement was reached.

The agreement included the resumption of the forty-hour week with indications that nearly all men would be taken back to work; improved sickness and accident insurance coverage; union security (the deduction from workers' paycheque each month administered by the company would be increased by $1); protections for workers transferred to Inco's new departments of Levack Mill and the Exploration Diamond Drilling; a $25 Christmas bonus; the reclassifications that the union argued for in the opening negotiations in March; protection against retribution for participation in the strike; and wage increases of 1 per cent, 2 per cent, and 3 per cent over the three years of the agreement. The wage offer was a marked drop from the union's original proposal of 10 per cent increase, but higher than industry comparators if restoration of the forty-hour week is taken into consideration.[56]

Later that afternoon, the media cameras descended on the two teams as they shook hands and signed the memorandum of agreement to append a collective agreement once it was ratified by the union members. Back at the hotel, the MMSW team coordinated plans for upcoming meetings to present the terms for their members to accept or reject, presented Orville Larson with a pen and pencil set along with earrings and brooch for his wife in appreciation for his assistance, and packed their bags to catch the 10:30 pm train back to Sudbury.[57]

"IN UNITY THERE IS STRENGTH"

Within minutes of the first news report of the strike agreement, Bell Telephone's Sudbury switchboard was so jammed that appeals were made to subscribers to reduce their calls to allow for emergency messages.[58] The −20° C temperatures, two-foot snow mounds, and vicious, northerly winds couldn't quash the waves of jubilation that swept the district. Young Dolores remembers that she and her brother were home for lunch: "Mom had the radio on to listen to the news when the news came. Mom screamed! The three of us joined hands and danced all around the kitchen!"[59] Store clerks were suddenly busy ringing in Christmas purchases. Mr A.G. Orr, principal of Copper Cliff Elementary School, announced over the PA system that afternoon that the strike was over to the students' loud claps and cheers.[60] MMSW negotiator Albert Routliffe shaved off the beard he had grown into a full Garibaldi from the beginning of the strike as Solski's voice boomed over the last radio broadcast dedicated to the strike: "All of us have learned through our struggles and sacrifices during this trying period that for working people there is only one way to security and that is through unity. We have proved this. A victory was won, not so much in the material gains we made, but rather in the new confidence we have achieved in ourselves, in our union, and in the new knowledge that in unity there is strength."[61]

After being on strike for eighty-nine days, the members ratified the proposed contract in a nine-to-one vote, setting the smelter stacks back to billowing on the second of January 1959.

In the autumn of 1958, thousands of Inco strikers and their families had refused to be intimidated by the egregious actions of one of the largest, wealthiest monopolies in the mining industry, pushing against the government's punishing hold-the-line wages policy. Inco had badly miscalculated the workers' commitment to the righteousness of their struggle for healthy and dignified lives. The union leaders had lived up to their reputation as having "balls of iron," but an even bigger challenge than an eighty-nine-day strike would soon confront these intrepid labour commandos and cause upheaval in the entire community for the next six years.

The "Damn Devil's Brew"

Spirits ran high in Sudbury as the calendar rolled over into the new year of 1959. The shops, beer parlours, street corners, and dinner tables were abuzz with the recall schedule for Inco workers' return to work. By 3 January, as a pristine layer of snow was covering the city and surrounds, seven thousand men were descending into the mines and entering the smelters' gates; the rest of Inco's workforce would soon follow. Four days later, the first pouring of the slag restored the familiar, spectacular glow to the Sudbury sky: "When the smelter furnaces were being restarted and the stacks reheating, acidic particulate was floating everywhere. During the start-up, the acidic particulate floating down was from material stuck on the cold stack walls and sluffing off as it heated up. The wet substances, like tar, burned the paint on people's cars and on metal buildings, fences, and eavestroughs. People didn't care; it was back to work time."[1]

A three-year collective agreement, effective 2 January, was signed between the company and the union, the first agreement of such an extended duration. Inco workers had more protections and job security than ever before. The sickness and accident coverage were increased in both duration and amount, and the full cost of the insurance plans that lapsed during the strike was covered by Inco. Significantly, the restoration of the forty-hour week alone represented an average gain of 44 cents per hour.

But for many Inco workers the outrage that precipitated the strike was further fuelled by what they saw as the paltry settlement of annual wage increases of 1 per cent, 2 per cent, and 3 per cent over the three years.[2] During this time, Inco had refused to dignify its workers with safe working conditions and bestowed reasonable wage packets only when forced. Now the workers saw the miserly wage settlement as punishment for daring to challenge Inco's authority by striking. They said to each other, "We'll bide our time and get those bastards when the time is right," envisioning a time when the union would be back in the Canadian Labour Congress with full support from the country's organized labour movement.[3] Indeed, during the next decade, Inco workers would face down the company several more times in a series of militant strikes. In the meantime, Inco could bask in the immediate afterglow of the strike.

IMMEDIATE CONSEQUENCES OF A FIRST-TIME SHUT DOWN

In more than one regard, Inco was well served by the strike. First, of course, was the reduction in its stockpile of nickel. Then there was the dramatic cut in labour costs over the thirteen-week strike that enhanced the financial reports to stockholders and enriched the capital reserves required for the planned expansion into Thompson, Manitoba the following year. As the first shutdown in Inco's long history, the strike also illuminated the advantages of a planned shutdown to the company directors.[4] Equipment had never before been serviced according to a schedule but rather when it broke down, which was often at the most inopportune time. Over the course of the strike, contractors and salaried staff rebuilt the fire bricks of the nickel reverberatory furnaces, cleaned many sections of flue pipes, and had opened up the hoppers under the one-and-a-half-mile-long network of ductwork that ran throughout the smelter. To everyone's surprise, the hoppers were found to contain many tons of copper-nickel dust that had accumulated over the years. The dust was placed back into the production circuit following the strike, prodigiously boosting the profit margins.[5]

However, not all unexpected findings were as beneficial, particularly not for the Inco workers. During the strike, the salaried staff had kept the smelter furnaces going so they wouldn't freeze but the temperature was not kept high enough to prevent crusts from forming inside the cauldrons. During one of their first shifts back at work, the smelter workers took the brunt of Inco's lack of experience with shutdowns when Owen, one of the skimmers at the Copper Cliff smelter, came face to face with the problem in the very instant of the pouring process.

As a skimmer, Owen's job was to stand, hour by hour, on a platform at the edge of one of the several twelve-metre-diameter cauldrons of boiling molten metal that were suspended by immense
chains and controlled by a crane operator. With the ladle-like industrial skimming tool, he would skillfully determine the exact moment
when the copper was sufficiently separated from the nickel in the
cauldron and ready to be poured off. At that instant, he would signal
to the crane operator to position, then tilt the cauldron over the train
car on the track twenty feet below so the liquid copper could spew
into the train car for transport a mile and a half away to the refinery.
During the pouring, the skimmer closely monitored the process so he
could signal to the crane operator when to return the cauldron to its
upright position. Only their precision timing maintained the process
within the very narrow margin of error and maximized the amount
and purity of the poured copper. The minute-by-minute synchroni-
zation of the actions of skimmer and crane operator was managed
solely by hand signals at far-off distances and over the deafening
roar of the smelter, an exacting coordination that produced deep
friendships and brooked ethnic and language divisions, fostering a
team ethic. Each Christmas, Owen and his son, Sean, made their
annual drive to Sudbury's Italian enclave to deliver season's greet-
ings and the usual bottle to a workmate. "Our lives, and the lives of
the entire crew, hang in the balance all the time and this guy is the
crane operator of crane operators" was Owen's answer when Sean
asked his father why this particular workmate warranted a bottle
every Christmas.

As Owen stood on the platform during the first post-strike shift,
he spied a large crust formed because the maintenance of the furnace temperature was not kept hot enough during the strike. There
was no time to stop the pouring process; within a split second,
it was about to fall and splash the scorching molten metal far
and wide. The safety of the crew was Owen's first thought: while
the scalding metal hurled down, his imploring screams had them
running for cover, peeling off the outer layers of their clothes as
they fled. In the scramble to safety, Owen was unable to avoid the
metal splashing inside his boot, and the 1,400°C glowing alloy
delivered an excruciating burn to his foot. While his workmates
escaped unharmed, the accident landed Owen in the hospital for
a full two months recovering from the injury, the only break in
his twenty-seven years of faithful attendance in the Inco smelter

and his meticulous record-keeping of his crew's output, for daily, weekly, and monthly comparisons proudly shared with crewmates, family, and friends.[6]

"WHERE DID THE MONEY GO?"

In the weeks and months following the strike, Inco workers hotly debated its causes and consequences. Each had his own version of events, depending on political views, religious beliefs, perceptions of the union leadership, and the extent of union involvement. As one said sixty years later, "Yes, we survived. I can't say it shouldn't have been called. It was one of these things that you're damned if you do, damned if you don't."[7] Opinions differed on various points, but the months of 1958 lost to sacrifice were not readily forgotten. Many of the strikers found it inconceivable that a union of thousands of members, each paying monthly dues, had accumulated such small financial reserves after a prolonged strike-free period.

Defeatism and disunity had been seeded in the early days of the strike when questions about the union's lack of funds were first raised by Bishop Carter[8] and media editorials such as, "Where Did the Money Go?"[9] Shortly after the strike, rumours began to circulate that the shortage of financial support during the strike was because money from the union's treasury had been stolen. Other accusations, boosted by the Cold War fever, attributed the limited funds to the union's subsidization of political causes elsewhere. Also, the distribution of funds and food vouchers on the basis of need during the strike had required members to reveal their financial status, a contentious invasion of privacy for many. "It was the biggest mistake that the union made by asking the members for the bank books to prove that they had little or no money and needed support. Most members involved never forgave MM [Mine Mill] for the slight."[10] The election of the local's executive that followed three months after the strike gave the members an opportunity to express their displeasure. And so it was that these issues predominated evaluation of the local's executive by the members in the election of March 1959.

The election toppled the local's president, Mike Solski and all but three of the executive members who had overseen the strike. The national and local media were quick to feed the Cold War mania in reporting the election results: "No longer will stacks of the *Canadian Tribune*, a communist publication, be found in the boardroom of the Mine Mill headquarters when the newly elected group takes over."[11] The new executive initiated an audit of the local's finances in the hopes it would reveal the strike executive's malfeasance. In fact, the audit did the opposite by exonerating the strike's executive and reporting that the various expenditures over the previous several years had been spent strictly for the benefits of the members.[12]

PRONOUNCEMENTS FROM THE PULPITS
AND THE LEADERSHIP COURSES

The official voice of the Catholic Church, the *Catholic Register,* regularly commented on the major developments of Mine Mill as part of its relentless war against communists. Within the first month of the 1958 strike, the *Register* asserted the outlandish claim that the strike was a plot orchestrated by communist agents to induce economic chaos as a precursor to overthrowing "all our democratic institutions so that North America will fall like an over-ripe plum" directly into the lap of Moscow's despots.[13]

From their pulpits, local Catholic priests regularly called out Mine Mill leaders as Stalin's messengers.[14] Mine Mill's concerted efforts to reach into the communal life of its membership with the extensive social programs constituted a challenge to the Church's promotion of traditional values, especially those associated with the patriarchal family structure,[15] and threatened its ability to retain its large following in the region's population. Even though the Church appealed to some of the same values of support thy neighbour, honour hard work, and sacrifice one's own needs for the sake of collective well-being, its anti-communist focus during the Cold War became myopic, leaving many working-class Catholics confused and alone to cope with the problems that confronted them in their workplaces.[16] During the fractious election for the local's executive of MMSW following the 1958 strike, Catholic Church spokesmen characterized the vote as "a choice between Christ and Stalin" and urged the Catholic union members to "vote against the Communist conspiracy."[17] Although the full extent of measures taken by the Catholic Church to dismantle Mine Mill is a matter of the historical record that has yet to be fully revealed, the installation of Alexandre Boudreau in Sudbury at the start of the strike is a measure that bears scrutiny and is plainly evidenced by his own account.

ALEXANDRE BOUDREAU

Ostensibly, Boudreau was recruited by Dean Ferland to teach in the Extension Division of the University of Sudbury, the newly formed Catholic university and outgrowth of Sacred Heart College established by the Jesuits in Sudbury in 1913.[18] Given the coincidental timing of Boudreau's arrival, however, we might surmise that other Catholic Church notables were involved in his Sudbury assignment. On just the second day of the strike, Boudreau arrived in Sudbury by train from his hometown of Cheticamp, Cape Breton, with his wife and seven-year-old son, and an impressive set of credentials: a graduate degree in public administration from Harvard and a ten-year stint as chief commissioner of the federal civil service.

Boudreau's anti-communism, which began during his studies at Harvard, had recommended him for his position as chief commissioner. In this capacity, he would have fulfilled the Cold War mandate of identifying suspected communists within the public service workforce and been granted access to the RCMP files on the eight hundred thousand Canadians under surveillance, including Harvey Murphy and other Mine Mill leaders.[19] Boudreau made several international missions to Pakistan and Southeast Asia in his decade-long career as chief commissioner that were part diplomatic and part intelligence-gathering for Canada's Cold War foreign policy. The year before the strike, Boudreau was stationed in Boston as consul general representing Canada in the New England states with intelligence duties, reporting to the Canadian ambassador in Washington and Canada's Department of External Affairs. There, he enjoyed frequent and lengthy meetings with then-senator J.F. Kennedy, during which they discussed strategies to stem the surging tide of communism both were convinced was wrongly redefining the world's political map.

When Boudreau arrived in Sudbury at the beginning of the strike, he went straight to work to recruit students for his leadership training courses to start within ten days of his arrival. He focused on MMSW members, many of whom had limited formal education and were hungry for any form of enrichment. Boudreau travelled to North Bay to meet with Bishop Carter, bishop of the diocese, to solicit his help in recruiting members of the union.[20] Bishop Carter was eager to oblige and contacted the parish priests within the diocese for names of potential recruits from their congregations. Boudreau's Acadian background was guaranteed to endear him to the large contingent of francophone MMSW members. His January training session registered over 140 Mine Mill members, recruited with the help of James Kidd, a hired organizer for United Steelworkers.[21]

On paper, the curricula of the leadership courses included economic history, trade unions, and world problems delivered by Boudreau with his commanding presence and skillful use of the chalkboard; however, the courses were thinly veiled anti-communist polemics. Ever the diplomat, he never raised his voice and his piercing eyes were the only signal of his anger, ignited when he spoke about the dangers of communism and "Sudbury's reputation of being known throughout the world as a centre of communist activities in Canada."[22] The courses ran under the banner of the Extension Division of the University of Sudbury and shared similar aims with other Catholic labour schools in Ontario such as the Pius XI Labour School in Windsor and the Toronto Catholic Labour School, whose purpose was to influence the affairs of the local labour unions and in particular to rid the leadership of anyone suspected of being sympathetic to communist ideas – which included those who were critical of Canada's foreign policy.

At one of Boudreau's first leadership classes, a tall, blond, young man, sitting in the front row and attentive to every detail of the lecture, presented himself to Boudreau at the end of the evening and offered his help.[23] From that moment on, Raymond Poirier, a Levack miner, became Boudreau's "right hand man in the struggle against the communist stronghold in Sudbury."[24] The post-strike elections for the Local 598 Executive in March 1959 delivered Raymond Poirier as financial secretary along with other Boudreau students elected to executive positions such as Don Gillis as president and Don McNabb as recording secretary. Bishop Carter, who was away in Rome at the time of the post-strike election, sent a congratulatory telegram to Boudreau. Boudreau left Sudbury in late 1959, as he wrote, "without worry. The Mine Mill union had just been kicked out of Sudbury, to be replaced by the Steelworkers of America, and calm has returned."[25] Boudreau's leadership courses were of great service to the steelworkers' union. However, his confidence was misplaced. The inherent militancy of Inco workers would ensure the promised calm was unattainable in 1959 and would remain so.

STEELWORKERS' RECURRENT RAIDS: "DOING THE BOSSES' WORK"

The attempts by the USWA to obtain bargaining rights for the Inco workers had started almost immediately after MMSW was certified and negotiated its first contract in 1944.[26] USWA had built up its membership in war industries and subsequently lost thousands of members in the immediate postwar years.[27] As a consequence, it was intent on usurping the large memberships and the bounty of their union dues from MMSW's locals like Sudbury and Trail, BC.[28] The ensuing turf wars between Mine Mill and USWA distracted the workers from the bosses who were the main source of their hardships. Setting the USWA raids within a historical frame, one old-timer mused, "Looking back to the 1930s, there was only one enemy and that was the boss. The challenge was to organize and get enough support from your fellow workers to take them on. We did that and succeeded, but then afterwards comes in all these raiders doing the bosses' work for them."[29] Buttressed by the prevailing Cold War climate, USWA's practice of raiding MMSW locals became respectable, and even patriotic. Unable to attack MMSW's record of representing its members, USWA resorted to anti-communist rhetoric and thinly veiled suggestions that MMSW was disloyal to Canada.[30] From the first of the jurisdictional battles between Mine Mill and USWA, the *Catholic Register,* declared its allegiance to USWA and urged "patriots and Christians to stand up and be counted" in the fight against communism.[31]

Notably, the USWA's interest in recruiting more members into its ranks had coalesced with the Cold War campaign of the House of Labour leaders to stamp out communists within the labour movement. Immediately after Mine Mill was expelled from the Canadian Congress of Labour (CCL) in 1949, fights broke out over MMSW's jurisdiction.[32] Even as the United Mine Workers argued to be the obvious inheritor,[33] USWA's counter claim was accepted along with a $50,000 cheque to the CCL; and shortly thereafter, the executive council of the CCL granted jurisdiction in the mining and smelting industries to the USWA.[34]

Having secured the jurisdiction from the CCL in 1950, USWA quickly set up temporary offices in the Coulson Hotel in downtown Sudbury, from where it mounted a recruitment drive to capture the signatures of Inco members to apply for the bargaining rights of the local's fourteen thousand plus members given that they were in a legal position to displace MMSW within the last sixty days of the collective agreement. All that was needed were the signed USWA membership cards for a total of 45 per cent of Inco workers to be presented in an application for certification to the Ontario Labour Relations Board.

With a nearby office in place, USWA recruiters invited Inco workers to a meeting in the Coulson Hotel's beverage room. Amid the fast-flowing pints of beers covered on USWA's tab in the smoke-filled bar, the Inco workers were told they should trade their Mine Mill card for a USWA membership because the USWA was not a communist union. After a few minutes, Nels Thibault, then-president of Local 598, stood up, ablaze with fury directed at the USWA recruiter, to say: "The Sudbury miners are not interested in your red-baiting nonsense, and since a CPR passenger train is leaving for Toronto in a few hours, you should be on board. A ticket will be provided for you free of charge and we will accompany you to the train to make sure you don't miss it."[35] Although this episode summarily aborted USWA's bid for supremacy of the union local in 1950, several other raids followed on the Sudbury and other MMSW locals in the subsequent years. MMSW withstood the many USWA attacks, indeed even gained strength because of them in some workplaces.

Notwithstanding its vigorous and widespread promotion, USWA's anti-communist propaganda failed to persuade many MMSW members. As Mike Farrell remembers from his time as a young miner, "We really didn't know too much about the Mine Mill union, but we knew that the boss hated the union. And, since the boss hated the union, the union had to be a damn good thing for us workers."[36] Under the union's constitution, leaders had the freedom to join political parties of their choosing and were protected from discrimination on the basis of their political activities with the consequence that contenders for elected union offices were appraised strictly on the basis of how they would advance workers' rights. To the majority of Inco workers, allegations of communist infiltration in the union were eclipsed by the union's record of tangible advances made in their lives. In ridding itself of MMSW, the CCL neither destroyed MMSW nor strengthened itself[37] for outside the Congress umbrella, MMSW continued to evolve into one of the most powerful centres of workers' strength in the heart of the Canadian mining industry. It was the Inco strike of 1958 that sounded the death knell for Mine Mill's representation of Inco's miners and smeltermen.

"HOW DOES THE LITTLE GUY MAKE UP HIS MIND?"

For the six years following the strike, war was waged between USWA and MMSW for the representation of the Inco workers. The battle for the bargaining rights of the largest local in Canada spilled over into the courts, as it did into every corner of Sudbury. Fists would fly. Men would run at each other with broken beer bottles. In the schoolyards, insults of "commie" were hurled at children of Mine Mill stalwarts. The pubs and bars were awash with threats and shouting matches. Smashed windows, fire hoses, and illegal brass knuckles featured in several large-scale riots while police stood by with arms folded. Ties between family members would remain broken for years to come.

The war of the lunch-bucket stickers was one of the tamer manifestations of the struggle between MMSW and USWA. The "Steel, Go Home" stickers, applied to the lunch buckets of USWA supporters when left unattended for a split second, were vigorously peeled off and replaced with "Inco loves Mine Mill, But workers like Steel," only to be covered over again by Mine Mill loyalists at the first opportune moment.[38] Many of the Inco workers were aware there were larger forces at play during the three successive votes in which they had to decide which of the two unions would represent them. "The propaganda, CIA [Central Intelligence Agency], the church, everybody had a finger in the pie. Then, the dumb little guy like me, he had to make up his mind."[39]

In its vigorous campaign for the bargaining rights of the Inco workers in the aftermath of the 1958 strike, USWA invoked anti-communist rhetoric and promised to bring Inco workers back into the Canadian Congress of Labour so workers could count on their support in the eventuality of a strike. In addition, the USWA made higher wages a recruitment staple, building strategically on workers' growing concern about their economic security. The deprivations of decades of war and economic depression were still dominant in the minds of Inco's miners and smeltermen. A tremendous appetite among Inco workers, as Canadian workers generally, had been unleashed at the end of the war to purchase what had been denied for so long. The rapidly expanding array of consumer goods and services in the postwar economy was appealing on several counts: novelty, time and labour savings, and the allure of possessing what only the moneyed class had previously enjoyed. As they assumed the increasing burden of monthly payments on furniture, houses, and cars, Inco workers would often come to work when sick because even with their relatively good wages a day's absence would be a blow to the family's perilously balanced finances.[40] It was not, therefore, surprising that economic gains were a paramount emphasis in the battle between MMSW and USWA following the strike.

In the first of three representation votes by Inco workers in 1962, the USWA's victory carried by only fifteen votes, or 0.1 per cent of the membership. The vote established Inco's miners and smeltermen as Local 6500 of the USWA, one of 507 USWA locals spanning the country, and increased the count of USWA members in Canada to one hundred thousand.[41] The *Catholic Register* applauded the vote, as did the national and local media.[42] Two more representation votes followed. Both returned USWA as the winner. The battle for the bargaining rights of the Inco workers ended with the third vote in 1965.

ENTER USWA: LESS MILITANT UNION, SAME MILITANT RANK-AND-FILE MEMBERS

USWA ultimately secured the bargaining rights at Inco but paid dearly for the achievement. The more senior MMSW members were especially difficult to sway because their loyalty to Mine Mill stemmed from firsthand experience of working conditions prior to the establishment of MMSW and the substantial improvements made by that union to their lives. At a monetary level, there was the significant cost of estimated millions from the USWA coffers for advertising on prime-time television, and the winter jackets, chicken dinners, and other expensive promotional give-aways they offered to entice loyalties.[43] Since it seems unlikely that the USWA's rank-and-file members in the US would have endorsed such a large outlay to woo workers away from a legitimate union in a remote part of northern Canada, a more probable scenario for the extravagant spending is that it was authorized by the top USWA officers in the union's American offices, activated by the colluding interests of the power elite as discussed, rather than the members. Regardless of the source, USWA's exorbitant recruitment expenditures far surpassed any MMSW spending on counter initiatives during the raids. The MMSW leaflets for distribution at the plant gates were printed on the office mimeograph machine and the morning radio program was no cost. An artist was paid $10 for each cartoon appearing in the leaflets. And registered letters to each member's household outlining the procedure to disavow their signature on the cards authorizing the certification votes if falsified on their behalf cost just ten cents apiece.[44]

In addition to the heavy recruitment costs to secure the bargaining rights, the strikes at Inco over the next decades were expensive for USWA. By the 1960s, the expectations of workers were shifting and unions were assumed to provide regularized financial support for all strikers regardless of their level of need. According to one estimate, for instance, the financial support for Inco members during the 1978–79 strike cost USWA more than the total expenditures over the sixteen years it took them to win the right to represent the Inco workers.[45] The spending on Inco workers coupled with USWA outlay for another large, militant local at Hamilton's Stelco plant added up to a heavy subsidy by the international USWA for the Canadian section of the union.[46]

Additionally, Local 6500 members and its elected leaders required extensive disciplining by the international USWA, having inherited a militant rank and file.[47] In the mid-1960s when USWA negotiations with Inco had stalled, the rank and file were ready to take on the company in retribution for "the shit-kicking Inco gave the workers during the 1958 strike."[48] A wildcat strike was sparked by the otherwise common occurrence of a shift boss misusing his power. When a Levack miner was fired for taking an extended coffee break, word spread instantly throughout the plants, and illegal pickets shot up at the gates of Inco's operations. For the next twenty-four days, rank-and-file members bust loose. Cars were set on fire, Inco's telephone lines were cut, bulldozers poached from the Copper Cliff smelter blocked the highway to Inco's offices, and pot shots were fired at helicopters from the open fields around Inco's landing strip. The USWA leadership vowed never to let the rank and file assert such control that could result in violence again. The union leaders learned, "we had to be leaders and direct any strikes, and that the strikes would be run properly with discipline," the precise lesson that the corporate architects of postwar industrial legalism wanted unions to learn. By the next strike in 1969, the local's executive had instituted measures to ensure greater discipline in the event of a strike.

The combative spirit of the Inco workers continued into the 1970s. Twenty years later almost to the day of the 1958 strike, the Inco members organized as USWA Local 6500 struck against a stockpile again. Their pugnacity took them out and kept them out on the picket line in Inco's longest strike up until then. The conditions were very similar to those leading up to the strike of 1958: layoffs prior to negotiations, an escalating cost of living that was undercutting workers' real wages, and a stockpile of nickel.[49] The members were enraged about the rollbacks to gains previously negotiated by the union, rollbacks that included a weakened grievance procedure put forward by the company in the protracted bargaining. Charging Inco as a "corporate welfare bum" in the popular press, the strikers were able to garner strong community support.[50]

Eight months into the 1978 strike, the impulse to challenge the company's dominance still burned in the bellies of the members. The nickel markets had turned around, stockpiles were reduced, and the shift bosses were calling the workers to report back to work. Sam, an Inco tradesman, responded to the voice over the phone: "I don't have to do shit. I'm busy putting a roof on my garage. You didn't mind keeping me out of work for close to a year, now you can kiss my ass if you think I'm going to jump back to work right away."[51] At the time of the strike, the USWA local was a thorn in Inco's side. It also spelled trouble for the conservative USWA's international officers, particularly with the outspoken "long-haired radical" president the members had elected on a platform of greater independence for the local from the dictates of the international office.[52]

In the years following the 1958 strike, Inco workers thwarted the company's plan to orchestrate a graduated transition from MMSW to USWA to a compliant staff association.[53] They had no desire to trade USWA for a company-led association. In the main, they elected USWA executives who represented their needs and aspirations at the bargaining table, many of whom were former MMSW stewards, committee members, and trustees. The few former MMSW stewards who had thrown their badges down the mine shafts in early protest of the transition to USWA were urged by other Mine Mill stalwarts not to abandon their steward duties: "We were elected by the membership and we'll represent the membership no matter what executive is in place."[54] In its militancy, Local 6500 remained an exception in a union dominated by staff representatives appointed by a top-heavy international office with the expectation of support for their compromising positions on job cuts, affirmative action, and other politically sensitive topics.[55]

Despite their expressed militancy, once Inco workers were organized as a USWA local, they became part of the large bureaucratic and hierarchical structure of an international union. USWA's convention voting procedures favoured large locals through its fixed membership-delegate ratio.[56] Member dues were funnelled first to the national and international offices, then doled out to the locals. The union's press remained under the tight control of incumbent union administrations to exclude vigorous controversy or opposition to prevailing administrative policies. And significantly, collective agreements, strike votes, and other important decisions affecting the locals' members required national and international authorization.

Thus, in the transition from MMSW to USWA, Inco workers sacrificed the decidedly democratic structure and procedures of a rank-and-file union. MMSW had retained its horizontal structure from its origins as the Western Federation of Miners (WFM), born in the late 1800s in remote mining camps as a federation of locals.[57] Because communication between the locals and their international headquarters was extremely limited by virtue of geography and technology, the WFM locals had a great deal of autonomy to make decisions independently.[58] In contrast to USWA, voting at MMSW's conventions ensured that small locals were adequately represented in decisions on important matters of union policy by allotting a number of votes for each delegate on the basis of the number of members in the delegate's local. Furthermore, MMSW's constitution ensured the pages of the union's journal were "open to all officers and members of the organization for the discussion of social affairs, industrial, economic and political questions, or any other questions pertaining to the interest of the working class." An additional manifestation of MMSW's rank-and-file unionism was the limit on salaried officers who were paid no more than the highest paid worker in the union.[59] And perhaps of most significance was the provision that MMSW locals' executives were free to sign the collective agreements and call for strike votes without the approval of the union's national or international officers, a provision that rested on the assumption that workers in each local know their own circumstances best and consequently should be authors of their own destiny.

A further sacrifice in the transition from MMSW to USWA's bread-and-butter unionism was the women's auxiliaries. The wives of the miners and smeltermen, organized formally into auxiliaries with their own charters, conferences, and social and political agendas, had been instrumental in MMSW's activities from the war years of the Kirkland Lake strike and organizing of the Inco local through to the rich social programming in the 1950s,[60] to say nothing of their efforts (sabotaged and otherwise) during the 1958 strike. Under the newly installed USWA leadership, stricter guidelines and more limited roles for emerging auxiliaries were introduced.[61] It would be a full twenty years later, and another strike, before a fledgling wives' organization, emboldened by the second wave of feminism, challenged the USWA local's leadership for a recognized role in formulating strategy during a strike.[62]

Finally, in the transition of union representation, Inco workers lost the social, recreational, and cultural programming so vital to communal well-being. By the end of the 1960s, the theatre troupe, dance school, and concerts were a thing of the past, and the summer camp had been greatly diminished. Social cohesion had been considerably shored up by bringing families together in such inclusive spaces as the badminton club, Saturday morning movie screenings, and dance school recitals, to name a few. As opportunities for members and their families to come together and share their lives, these programs fostered relationships, bridged ethnic divisions, and redistributed social power. The cultural programs sustained by MMSW were also an alternative to the high art found in museums, galleries, and concert halls of the elite, providing cultural forums to express the truth of working peoples' lives and fuel their desire for equality, freedom – and importantly, beauty. The subversive potential of such expressive fare lay in the reclamation of the means of cultural production through amusement, satire, and vision, and brought balance to lives regularly consumed by the mind-blunting work of the union members and the unpaid labour of women who supported it.

"WHEN YOU PUT THIS ALL TOGETHER ... THE WRONG PEOPLE WERE ON TRIAL"

The 1958 strike showed the world's mining giant that its workers could bring production to a standstill for a full thirteen weeks. To safeguard its monopoly in the nickel market, it was necessary for the company to have complete control of its supply of the metal. Despite the fact that Inco had encouraged the strike, the question became how the company could ensure that the workers wouldn't halt production in a time without a stockpile.

The ideological war being waged against left-led unions during the Cold War was as convenient for Inco as it was for others in the business elite intent on rolling back the gains made by workers and their unions during the war and heading off further advances. Certainly, the corporate class would have accurately perceived the threat behind an emergent, vibrant union movement, emboldened as it was by the postwar industrial legalism that guaranteed workers' rights to collective bargaining.[63] Many capitalists held the view that the balance of power must be restored in their favour, although there were diverse opinions on which levers of the postwar political economy should be used to achieve that goal. One such lever was the business lobby's pressure on the Canadian government to introduce legislation mirroring the American Taft-Hartley legislation that was demonstrating its effectiveness in hobbling the advances of workers in the US by attacking their unions.[64]

The anti-communist fervour whipped up enough panic to override the American public's concern about the erosion of personal liberties from the Taft-Hartley bill, the *Smith Act*, the *McCarran Act* that launched the creation of concentration camps to detain designated subversives,[65] and other repressive legislation introduced by Republican senator Joe McCarthy, Barry Goldwater, and other red-baiters.[66] By the early 1950s, the Cold War machinery was bombarding the left-led unions with grand jury sessions, denial of security clearances, and subpoenas by the House Committee on Un-American Activities hearings.[67] Under the *Taft-Hartley Act*, the unions were required to submit affidavits attesting to non-communist affiliations. Even when affidavits were filed, union officials were often charged with conspiracy to defraud the government on the premise that the affidavits were false. As the American MMSW president remembers, "Well, when you go back and put this all together, you can't help but come to the conclusion that if there was a conspiracy, the wrong people were on trial. The conspiracy was against MMSW because it was militant, it was outspoken and it was ready, willing, and able to take on the mining industry at the table."[68] It was not until November 1965 that the tide began to turn when the Supreme Court unanimously reversed previous convictions. Although all who had been charged were exonerated by mid-1966, the union in the US was severely weakened by the decade-long struggle that made it difficult to provide adequate financial support to the Sudbury members during the 1958 strike.[69]

In Canada, a similar fear of communist subversion triggered a wave of political repression. Canada had neither the Taft-Hartley legislation, the House on Un-American Activities Committee, nor the spectacle of the Hollywood Ten. But this country had its own Cold War and many of its victims were in the labour movement.[70] It was enough that a handful of MMSW's leaders held communist sympathies, some of them Communist Party members, for the union to be swept up in the frenzy. The purges took place at all levels within the labour movement, from the international congresses down to the local union halls, despite the fact that the total membership of communist-led unions in the late 1940s was at most between 10 and 20 per cent of all unionized workers.[71] The ideological war depleted the labour movement of its militancy and in doing so, its ability to effect the proper balance in industrial relations.

The Cold War rhetoric served the array of power brokers who were threatened by a highly decentralized, democratic union such as MMSW in a position to interrupt the all-important flow of nickel from Inco's mines and smelters. The Dulles brothers stand out as exemplary Cold War warriors with a direct connection to Inco. Both Dulles brothers were partners in Sullivan and Cromwell, the large corporate Wall Street law firm that served as Inco's legal counsel. These two Cold War warriors were central figures in the power elite on Wall Street, in the CIA and the State Department, all of which had very clear and vested interests in Inco, its monopoly in the nickel market, and the consequent assurance of a steady supply of nickel for the production of armaments during the most frigid years of the Cold War. John Foster Dulles, the secretary of state at the time, was a former top-level Inco executive secretary on the company's board of directors and executive council. His younger brother, Allen, director of the CIA from 1953 to 1961, was responsible for establishing worldwide surveillance networks to monitor and disrupt international communist movements as a crucial component of the Eisenhower administration's Cold War national security policy.

While it is true that debates about political interference in MMSW's Sudbury local will continue into the long after-light of history, the more connections are made that generate new questions, the more clearly a picture begins to emerge that high levels of church, state, and business had a hand in dismantling MMSW and thereby delivering Inco workers to the far less militant USWA.

The unholy trinity of political, economic, and social forces within various institutions and organizations – what one old-timer called "the damned devil's brew"[72] – would likely have been successful in dismantling the union even if there hadn't been a strike in 1958. As discussed, a key element was the USWA, ever keen to usurp the dues of one of the largest union locals in Canada. But also, the CLC was intent on cleaning the House of Labour of reds. And further to these factors, MMSW's social unionism was a secularizing force that threatened the Church's ability to attract large segments of the area's population. Add to this the US State Department's intention to wrestle from left-leaning leadership the representation of a workforce delivering a nickel supply critical to production of armaments. Finally, there was the company itself, for if Inco's aim in fomenting the 1958 strike was to dismantle the Mine Mill union, this eagerness was only increased after a strike that clearly revealed Inco's vulnerability to labour disruptions.

9

The Significance of the Inco Strike

Measured in terms of both magnitude and duration, the MMSW strike against Inco was one of Canada's greatest strikes in the early postwar period. The strike and the subsequent conquest by USWA in 1962 mark an important inflection point in the history of Canada's labour movement. The events described in this book contain elements of both the shop floor militancy of the war years and the subdued union leaderships of the neoliberal era in the decades that followed, positioning the strike between these two epochs.

One decade prior to the strike the federal legislation governing labour relations was introduced. The *Industrial Relations and Disputes Investigation Act* (IRDIA) of 1948 grew out of the wartime legislation designed to provide a legal framework to regulate unionization and collective bargaining. Together with the provincial labour legislation that followed, the IRDIA formalized the postwar settlement between capital and labour. On the other side of time, the strike came a little more than a decade before the postwar settlement buckled under the weight of the economic stagnation of the 1970s, closing the door on workers' increased share of the country's wealth and opening the door to business unionism.

The postwar accord ensnared unions in a complex net of expensive and time-consuming legal procedures that undercut their role of fostering shop-floor militancy. The actions of workers have since been constrained by the contractual arrangements between unions, the state, and private corporations. Although this legalism gave workers and their unions much-needed recognition, it robbed them of the spontaneous job actions that can express resentments and justifiable demands directly. Under the new industrial legality after

World War II, unions and their leaders were subject to fines in the event of violations of the law. The legal edifice shifted the role of union leaders away from response to their members' needs and aspirations toward the posture of disciplining the members and channeling workers' grievances into bureaucratized procedures with the result that spontaneous direct actions by the rank and file were effectively thwarted. Most unions fell in line; and many of their leaders adopted conservative recommendations to their members, and in so doing betrayed the working-class interests of the memberships in their fight for dignified, healthy lives.

During the 1958 strike, the MMSW leaders straddled the line between conforming to the new requirements of postwar industrial legality while striving to stay true to their historical commitment to working class struggle. They supported the Inco workers' urge to challenge the all-powerful mining giant in striking against a stockpile. Despite their reservations about the possibility of a successful outcome, the leaders stood behind their members. At the same time, they stayed on the right side of the law in censuring the eruption of wildcatting in the few days prior to the start of the strike.

We have yet to see in all dimensions the actors behind the scenes during the 1958 strike and secession four years later of the Inco workers to USWA. What emerges from the existing record, however, is the rare blend of courage, creativity, and commitment on the part of the MMSW leaders, including those who argued against the strike. They came up through the ranks, elected first as stewards, then members of their plant's grievance committees, chief plant grievance officers and on to the negotiating team and the Local's executive. Some had been bonus miners with large paycheques for the ore they pulled out but were prepared to put down their drills and give up their bonuses in solidarity with their fellow workers' grievances. In leading the strike, these men were responding to the militant impulse of the members who were "fed up and determined to fight for what they thought was just and right."[1]

Before and during the strike, the leaders were required to constantly assess the volatile balance of forces at play, and evaluate the likely outcome of different responses. In order to come to terms with the significance of the strike, however, we must move beyond uncritical applause for the union leaders. Perhaps under the pressures of shepherding a union under attack, a siege mentality sometimes gripped them that impaired decision-making. Perhaps in the fog of battle, they didn't try hard enough to persuade the members to wait for the stockpile to diminish before striking. Explaining the reasons to avoid the strike to the members would have required an honest assessment of the bargaining weakness of the union, which the members were not anxious to hear. And as elected representatives, the leaders knew that any terms of settlement that fell short of their membership's justifiable demands would be unpopular enough to trigger defeat in the next election.

Whatever their deficiencies, the strike leaders were certainly not the communist agitators imported from Russia that they were painted to be. For one thing, while the union gave workers some say on their working lives, the leaders did not advocate for companies to put them on the board of directors as a truly communist agenda would suggest. They spoke a principled truth to power, sturdy in their conviction that they were acting on behalf of their fellow workers toiling under Inco's domination and gruelling conditions of work. Over its hundred-year history, MMSW stood for rank-and-file unionism; as such, it is noteworthy that Mine Mill was one of the few unions to boast a record without evidence of fraud, gangsterism, or dictatorial control among the leadership.

THE TREND OF BUSINESS UNIONISM: "I SWALLOWED MY PRIDE AND VOTED FOR THE GODDAMNED THING"

The 1958 strike facilitated the successful raid on the Sudbury local and the eventual annexation of all but one MMSW local by the USWA. The conquest is emblematic of the sweeping trend in Canada's labour movement towards bureaucratic business unionism that continues to the present day.

The Inco strike sounded the death knell for Mine Mill's representation of Inco's miners and smeltermen, and the eventual loss of that large Sudbury local severely weakened the union as a whole. MMSW's coffers were depleted, and the membership severely undercut. With the representation of the fourteen thousand Inco workers lost to the USWA, Local 598 had shrunk to the three thousand members who worked for Inco's competitor, Falconbridge. The Trail and Kimberly, BC locals consisted of approximately seven thousand members, bringing the total Canadian membership to approximately ten thousand.

MMSW and USWA finally merged in both the US and in Canada in 1967 following year-long negotiations between national and international leaders. Similar mergers between other unions throughout North America would be seen in the 1980s and 1990s as an organizational adaptation to declining memberships, persistently high levels of unemployment, and the changing nature of work.[2]

As a result of the merger with USWA, the MMSW leaders were absorbed into their structure and scattered across Canada, necessarily undermining connections with their members. Even the self-declared communist, Harvey Murphy, was acceptable to the USWA apparatus as part of the merger agreement.[3] As one MMSW member reflected on the hypocrisy, "It's very funny that all those fellas, the so-called communists, all of a sudden became angels and they were all given good staff jobs within the Steelworkers union."[4] The assimilation of the former MMSW leaders revealed the spuriousness of USWA's accusations of MMSW's communist domination during the raids. Although the MMSW leaders were formally accepted into USWA after the merger, the USWA's bureaucratic culture was a difficult adjustment for most. "Sitting in a corner and told not to do anything very much" and "having to consult with the secretary before taking a shit"[5] were untenable and they soon found the exit door.

At MMSW's Canadian convention in 1967, there were many impassioned speeches about the pro and cons of merging with a union that had been warring for their turf for close to two decades. Arguments in favour included the need for strong links between the unions in the face of the metal industry's increasingly globalized corporate networks and the consequent growth of their influence on governments, legislatures, and the courts.[6] Surely a merger with USWA was the most palatable alternative to MMSW's slow decline. Even the most committed Mine Millers were among the two-thirds of the Canadian members who voted for the merger with USWA. "I swallowed my pride and voted for the goddamned thing, because in my mind, there was no alternative."[7] Members voting for the merger were swayed by the argument that greater strength for MMSW members would be achieved through unity with USWA, uniting approximately 90 per cent of workers in the non-ferrous metals industry in the US and Canada. In protracted debate at the convention, the Falconbridge workers, still organized as MMSW Local 598, vociferously protested. Addressing his fellow delegates, one member argued, "All the reasons that have existed for the past 15 or 20 years for not joining Steel exist today, and I just can't see myself altering my course 180 degrees so fast that I meet myself coming back."[8]

BUCKING THE TREND:
"SAYS JOE, 'BUT I AIN'T DEAD'"

In comparison with Inco, Falconbridge was a smaller operation with a closely knit group of workers who called each other by nicknames. They were fiercely loyal to MMSW and had provided significant support to their fellow Local 598 members during the 1958 Inco strike, as described in chapter 4. During the early 1960s as Inco workers seceded to USWA, the Falconbridge members resisted no less than three recruitment drives in which USWA failed to obtain the 45 per cent of signed member cards required for a formal certification vote to be called and supervised by the Ontario Labour Relations Board. Moreover, the number of signed cards by members wishing to join the USWA declined in each successive drive. Having mounted an effective defensive against USWA's incursions, the Falconbridge workers were not going to capitulate now. To these MMSW loyalists, joining USWA would only further support the Cold War policies that had corrupted the labour movement, paper over the human fallout from the booms and busts of the mining industry, and protect the expanding profit margins for shareholders. Accordingly, the merger was viewed as surrender by the three thousand Falconbridge members who chose instead to continue as an independent union maintaining democratic procedures and unabashedly militant politics.

With the Falconbridge workers no longer overshadowed by the size and dazzle of the local's contingent of Inco workers, a new chapter in their history opened up. In the midst of a rapidly bureaucratizing union movement following the merger with USWA, the Falconbridge workers survived to become the remaining solo MMSW local until 1993, when the local merged with the Canadian Auto Workers.

Significantly, following the merger the surviving MMSW Local 598, consisting of the Falconbridge workers, won the legal right to retain the assets of the Regent Street and Richard Lake properties purchased in the late 1940s and early 1950s. These holdings, considerable by any standards but particularly if owned by a union, would have been coveted by USWA. The fact that USWA did not inherit the assets is "one of labour history's greatest ironies."[9] One Falconbridge old-timer recounted the twist of events: in the early 1960s, when Inco workers were seceding to USWA, the Falconbridge members tried to establish their own MMSW local. They applied to the Ontario Labour Relations Board for certification as a separate MMSW local.[10] Persuaded by USWA's arguments, the board denied the application: "In compelling us to continue to belong to Local 598, eventually when the merger took place, Local 598, then consisting of Falconbridge workers only, had all of the MMSW properties. If we'd have had a separate local, we would have lost all of that, but as it was, we have only the steelworkers to thank for having defeated us in setting up a separate local, and then later installing us with all of the wealth of Local 598."[11] In any final tally of USWA financial accounting of the hefty costs of acquiring the bargaining rights of the Inco workers, the loss of MMSW Local 598's properties must be added to the ledger. That the loss was a result, at least in part, of USWA's own doing would have made the sting worse.

As the vestige of MMSW Local 598, the Falconbridge workers continued the union's tradition of pugnacity in holding back the power brokers seeking to eliminate a robust centre of workers' strength in the heart of the Canadian mining industry. Following the loss of their fellow MMSW members to USWA, they contributed to the wave of spirited resistance among Canadian workers that blossomed in the 1970s. Through the local's alliances with the New Left, anti-colonial struggles, and the women's and anti-war movements, the Falconbridge workers extended MMSW's arc of bestowal to the labour movement by continuing to bolster picket line militancy and fighting back against incursions on organizing Canadian workers. As the sole descendants of a union that understood the basic aspirations of hard-rock miners with a militant history, this small group of Sudbury workers stood as a bulwark against the trend towards corporate-like unionism.

> I dreamed I saw Joe Hill last night,
> Alive as you or me
> Says I, 'But Joe, you're ten years dead,'
> 'I never died,' says he.
> 'I never died,' says he.
> 'In Salt Lake, Joe,' says I to him,

Him standing by my bed,
'They framed you on a murder charge,'
Says Joe, 'But I ain't dead,'
Says Joe, 'But I ain't dead.'

'The copper bosses killed you, Joe,
They shot you, Joe,' says I.
'Takes more than guns to kill a man,'
Says Joe, 'I didn't die,'
Says Joe, 'I didn't die.'

———

History is in the story of the 1958 strikers, as they are in history. Once that history has been fully comprehended, we can more easily broach the formidable challenges we face as workers. When the future asks, what new actions and forms of organizing will workers need to defend themselves, how will we respond? How can we use our collective ingenuity and strength to respond to the manifestation of ever more formidable issues ahead? A full accounting of our past – the achievements, along with the mistakes and shortcomings – will lift us up to our full height and grant us confidence to create more dignified forms of work, an equitable distribution of the world's resources, and mechanisms that foster human connection, shared purpose, and a sense of belonging.

In the decades since the 1958 strike against Inco there has been a steep downward cycle of decreasing union membership that correlates with a reduction in the power of organized labour. Unions have struggled to retain influence under the impact of labour-saving automation, restructured workplaces, new patterns of consumerism, and the decline of identities tied to social class. While the strike can be understood as the death knell of one of Canada's most militant, democratic unions, it must be seen as part of the general ascendency of globalized networked capitalism that has tilted the frontier of control further towards employers and weakened labour unions leaving few avenues of recourse for workers to defend themselves against indignities and injustices.

The postwar accord between capital and labour brought a vital recognition to unions and enhanced the capacity to negotiate higher wages for their members. Yet, as the recent decades have revealed, the chronic features of capitalism of inflation and unemployment cannot be resolved at the bargaining table, and the policy levers used to address each seem only to make the other one worse. As long as prices continue to rise, workers are no further ahead, and increasingly collective agreements have taken on the appearance of walking up the down escalator. Further, significant number of workers continue to find themselves in precarious employment and outside labour unions: women, ethnic and racial minorities, the differently abled, and those in the low-skilled occupations in particular.

Implicit in the postwar accord was the nuclear family model with the male as the only full-time worker, the head of a dependent household kept afloat by women's unpaid labour – a model that deviated from the reality for many workers then, as it does now. Inequities by sex and race within the Canadian working class has steadily increased in the past decades. Another threat to the well-being, and indeed the very existence, of workers that has come to light since the 1958 strike is the environmental degradation resulting from the unrestrained power of resource extraction corporations such as Inco. For all these reasons, the struggle for workers' rights and dignity is as necessary in this day and age as it was when Mine Mill members struck against Inco.

Notes

PREFACE

1 Privy Council, *Royal Commission Appointed under Order.*
2 Collins, "Learning from the Outsider Within," 514–32. Patricia Collins coined the term outsider-within.
3 Solski interview by Jim Tester, 15 May 1981, page 19, Laurentian University Archives, P019, series I, sub-series B, file 1.

CHAPTER ONE

1 Angus, *Cobalt,* 12–13.
2 Saarinen, *From Meteorite Impact to Constellation.*
3 MacDowell, *Remember Kirkland Lake,* 40.
4 Angus, *Cobalt,* 12.
5 Clement, *Hardrock Mining,* 142–44.
6 Ibid.
7 Research participant AC34.
8 Saarinen, *From Meteorite Impact to Constellation,* 62–96.
9 Mercier, *Anaconda,* 21–30.
10 Ibid. In Laurie Mercier's comprehensive description of a smelting town in Montana comparable to Sudbury's Copper Cliff, she demonstrates that while masculinity and the frontier trope has long predominated our understanding of the development of one-resource towns, in fact women were a significant force for civic improvement and key contributors to the town's development.
11 Research participant AC38.
12 *The Hole Story,* directed by Richard Desjardins and Robert Monderie.

13 Ontario Department of Mines, *Annual Report Mines Inspection Branch 1940–1960*, bulletin nos 131–60 (Toronto: Printer to the Queen's Most Excellent Majesty, 1940–1960).

14 Seguin. *Fighting for Justice and Dignity*, 18.

15 Ibid.

16 Swift, *The Big Nickel*, 17–21.

17 Ibid.

18 Saarinen, *From Meteorite Impact to Constellation*, 62–96.

19 Solski interview by Jim Tester, 15 May 1981, page 3, Laurentian University Archives, P019 Solski fonds, series I, sub-series B, file 1.

20 *The Hole Story.*

21 Pederson, *International Directory of Company Histories,* 196.

22 Non-ferrous metals are those that do not contain iron. The category includes both base metals (i.e., nickel, copper, lead, zinc, aluminum, tin) and the precious metals (i.e., gold, silver, platinum, rhodium, palladium).

23 "Inco Smelter Reports," 1958, author's own archive.

24 Radio and television broadcast, 25 November 1958, Archives Ontario, F1280, series 2, box 7, file 9.

25 Inco annual reports cited in Black, "An Analysis of Inco."

26 The point here is profits rose faster than wage increases.

27 The unions railed against the war industry, pointing to the war expenditures as a net subtraction from the nation's output available for civilian purposes and thus at the expense of living standards. The expenditures redistributed income in favour of the wealthy, increasing the profits particularly of the largest corporations, most of which were and still are US-owned or US-controlled (p. 46 of MMSW's 1956 submission) and widened the gap between growing productive capacity and workers' limited purchasing power (p. 45 of submission). The position was a contradictory one for a union that represented workers in the industry. The union addressed its own contradictory position by advocating for further development of markets for nickel for civilian purposes such as public works projects and manufacturing goods within domestic industries that had been deprived of nickel due to military priorities.

28 Inco president's address to shareholders, Archives Ontario, F1271, series G-II, box MU6691.

29 Lingenfelter, *The Hardrock Miners,* 3–106. The unionization and industrialization and of the western mines were intertwined. The increasing development of lower-grade, base-metal deposits led to more capitalization and larger operations with greater mechanization in which the miner was converted from an individual into a cog in a corporate machine cutting,

drilling, and timbering ever-deeper passageways and operating steam-powered equipment for the hoisting, pumping – all tasks that required high-level skills. The $3.50/day was a symbol of miners' struggle for a wage commensurate with the required skill and dangers of their work.

30 Ibid. Lingenfelter's (1981) analysis of the three decades leading up to formation of the WFM shows that rather than weakening union organization, the fluidity of the mining frontier had the opposite effect. As the miners from the Comstock unions moved into the Montana silver camps to form the Butte Miners' Union, they adopted the constitution and bylaws of the Comstock unions and nearly all the new unions followed the Comstock unions in establishing a minimum wage as their main demand. These early miners' unions set the pattern for union organizing.

31 Mouat, *Roaring Days*, 67–87. Mouat describes the mine owners' inflammatory rhetoric characterizing the union as unruly hooligans under the influence of agitators from south of the border, to discredit the WFM. The owners pointed to the uprising in Coeur d'Alene, Idaho in 1899 as the lawlessness that was being imported into BC. Such hyperbole stood in stark contrast to the calm, non-violent approach of the strikers in the Slocan silver mines the same year. Although WFM's history of brawls, dynamiting, and martial interventions is widely assumed, in his *The Hardrock Miners*, Lingenfelter's analysis of the WFM-formative miners' unions demonstrates that these early organizations of miners often showed restraint in the face of mine owner offensives, rapid industrialization, and the large infusion of outside capital.

32 Mouat, *Roaring Days*. During the 1899 strike in the Slocan silver mines, the WFM leaders appealed to PM Laurier to enforce the federal *Alien Labour Act*, a law that prevented the owners from importing strikebreakers from the US.

33 Dubofsky, "The Origins of Western," 131–54. Dubofsky's (1966) explanation for the violent conflict on the mining frontier goes beyond the general characteristics of the quick-on-the-trigger hyper-masculinity of miners or the greed and short-sighted self-interest of the mine owners. His Marxist analysis, instead, explains the miners' radicalism as a direct and natural outcome of the social and economic forces shaping the early industrialism in the metals-mining industry. Nowhere else in the country were the social and economic arrangements changing so rapidly and drastically. Mining camps like the Colorado gold camp of Cripple Creek and the silver rush boom town of Butte, Montana were changed almost overnight into industrial fortresses as domestic and foreign capital rushed to exploit the assumed bonanza ore bodies. Cleavages in the pre-existing

dense social networks advanced too quickly for smooth adjustment. Mine owners, previously onsite and hardly distinguishable from miners, were now managing remotely and turning to state and federal authorities to control their workers. The close relations between miners and local merchants who had been dependent on the patronage of miners were severed. The consequences of the rapid industrialization and the alliance between corporate capitalism and government, which polarized the social order, convinced the miners of the need for a radical restructuring of the social and economic structure.

34 WFM was a highly democratic organization devoted to the idea of unity of all workers with universal membership card transfer and opposed an apprentice system, arguing it was a method of bondage that reinforced divisions between workers. Turning away from its radical inheritance in 1896, the WFM affiliated with the American Federation of Labor, the conservative craft-based labour organization. However, as Jensen (1968) writes, "the marriage was not a good one and the honeymoon, if there was one, was short" (Jensen, *Heritage of Conflict*, 59). The WFM was critical of the AFL's lack of support for the Leadville miners' 1886–87 strike and the ideological differences between the two organizations manifested in WFM's objection to the AFL's centralization of control and absence of rank-and-file influence. The incompatibility led to the WFM's withdrawal from the AFL a year after it first affiliated. Then, again in 1911, although "strenuously opposed in some quarters of the WFM", the union reaffiliated with the AFL in the hopes that the agenda of industrial unionism could be more easily achieved from within rather than outside the AFL (ibid., 244).

35 The WFM was a major force in establishing the IWW in 1905. The IWW sought working class solidarity that transcended divisions by sex, age, ethnicity, race, and skill level, recruiting workers from far-flung mining camps in the west to the textile mills in the east. During its most active years, the IWW fought bitter strikes with intransigent employers and ultimately suffered defeat in the early 1920s. Within a year of the founding of the IWW in 1905 and the affiliation of the WFM as its mining department, factional feuding took hold within each and between the organizations. With no obvious ways of effecting reconciliation on key questions over the revolution or pure-and-simple industrial unionism, the national leaderships of the WFM and IWW soon drew apart and the WFM severed its IWW affiliation. Caught between the two stools of revolution or reform, the IWW learned too late that the two are not mutually exclusive. As Dubofsky (1988) writes: "At any given historical moment, tangible

reforms may vitiate the spirit of revolution among masses of workers."
(Dubofsky, *We Shall Be All*, vii.)

36 Solski and Smaller, *The History of the International*, 61.

CHAPTER TWO

1 Waiser, *All Hell Can't Stop Us*, 41–55.

2 Stevenson interview, by Rick Stow, 11–12 June 1988, Library and
Archives Canada, Rick Stow fonds, ISN no. 151470.

3 Bill Wright, one of the major owners of the Wright-Hargreaves gold
mine in Kirkland Lake, used the profits from the mine to buy the two
newspapers, *Mail and Empire* and *The Globe*, and amalgamated them
into the *Globe and Mail*, establishing his broker, George McCullagh, as
the publisher.

4 MacDowell, *Remember Kirkland Lake*, 209.

5 The wartime administration of Mackenzie King issued Order-in-Council
PC 1003 in February 1944, which granted the right to Canadian workers
to select a union of their choice to represent them in bargaining with their
employers. In 1948, the *Industrial Relations and Disputes Investigation
Act*, a successor to PC1003, was passed, and in 1967 renamed the
Canadian Labour Code.

6 MacDowell, *Remember Kirkland Lake*, 207–12. By the end of February,
approximately five hundred strikers were back working in the mines,
1,800 remained in town, unemployed, and seven hundred had left town
to seek work elsewhere. The union's wire to the prime minister on
5 February that had conceded defeat announced that the miners would
return to work if the workers were rehired on the basis of seniority and
the government would promise protection against company reprisals. But
the government held firm to its non-interference policy. In the intervening
weeks while production resumed, labour minister Humphrey Mitchell
refused to intervene to prevent the punitive re-hiring policies and the
blacklisting of the strike leaders.

7 Ibid.

8 Stevenson, "Globalization and Armageddon," 274.

9 Stevenson interview by Rick Stow, 11–12 June 1988, Library and Archives
Canada, Rick Stow fonds, ISN no. 151470.

10 Kay Carlin interview by Barbara Dumphrey, 1982, Laurentian University
Archives, Barbara Dumphrey fonds P047, tape no. 4.

11 The names of the attackers on the leaflet included "Stinky Stelmack," the
leaflet authors only knowing Stelmack's surname filled in the first name.

(Stevenson interview, 11–12 June 1988, Library and Archives Canada, Rick Stow fonds, ISN no. 151470.)

12   Solski interview by Jim Tester, 15 May 1981, page 11, Laurentian University Archives, PO19 Solski fonds, series I, sub-series B, file 1.

13   Swift, *The Big Nickel*, 37–9.

14   As other research has confirmed, Inco's hiring strategy during the early postwar years targeted Nazi-sympathizers in order to curtail the strength of the union. See e.g., Terry Pender, "Special Report: Mine Mill and the Mounties," *Sudbury Star*, 11 November 1993, City of Greater Sudbury Library Public Archive.

15   Abella, "International Union, 1936–48," 86–110.

16   Tom McGuire's speech, 26 May 1973, MMSW conference audio recording, Library and Archives Canada, ISN no. 334936.

17   The Coniston smelter was owned by Mond Nickel until 1929 when Inco bought it.

18   Solski interview by Jim Tester, 15 May 1981, page 3, Laurentian University Archives, PO19 Solski fonds, series I, sub-series B, file 1.

19   Ibid.

20   Solski interview by Jim Tester, 15 May 1981, page 9, Laurentian University Archives, PO19 Solski fonds, series I, sub-series B, file 1.

21   Ibid.

22   There were over 1,800 accidents on average each year in the mining industry in Ontario in the early 1940s. At Inco alone, there were forty-two accidents that resulted in fatalities in the first half of the decade. *Source:* Ontario Department of Mines. *Annual Report Mines Inspection Branch 1940, 1941, 1942, 1943, 1944,* bulletin nos 131–5.

23   Research participant AC45.

24   Mercier, "A Union without Women," 315–40.

25   Ibid.

26   Cobble, *The Other Women's Movement*, 23–5. Auxiliaries were not uncommon in unions, particularly left-led unions. Other unions with women's auxiliaries were the United Auto Workers, Teamsters, United Electrical, Radio & Machine Workers, and United Fisherman & Allied Workers Union. During the peak of auxiliaries in the 1940s and 1950s, their membership in numbers almost equalled their membership in unions as paid workers, as Cobble (2004) demonstrates in her US study. Although corresponding Canada data does not exist, it is probable that the same can be said about Canadian women. On the history of the Sudbury's MMSW Auxiliary Mine-Mill, see Mercedes Steedman, "The Red

Petticoat Brigade," 55–71. And, for the auxiliary women's involvement in the radical group of women consumers, Housewives Consumer Association, see Julie Guard, *Radical Housewives*.

27 Nels Thibault interview by Mike Solski 25 May 1981, Part 1 and 2, Laurentian University Archives, P019, Solski fonds, series I, sub-series B, boxes F47, 3.1, and 3.2, file 50.2.

28 International Nickel Company, *Annual Address*, Archives Ontario, series G-II, 1958 Annual Report, box MU6691.

29 Collective agreement, 10 March 1944, page 2, UBC IUMMSW (Canada) fonds, box 145.

30 Local 598's first collective agreement with Inco in 1944 stipulated that monthly union dues would be collected from the volunteering worker. In the third agreement, effective 1 June 1946, Inco became a "closed shop," which means every worker pays monthly union dues as a condition of their employment. In closed shops, the dues are typically deducted from workers' pay-cheques by the employer and remitted to the union, which gives the union security knowing it has the financial means to carry out its programs. Union security was one of the common demands of unions during the strike wave immediately following World War II. The most famous of these strikes was mounted by the United Auto Workers at the Windsor Ford plant, which resulted in the Rand formula, proposed by Supreme Court justice Ivan Rand. The Rand formula, also known as automatic check-off, produced the first closed shops. Justice Rand justified the deduction of dues from non-union members on the basis that these workers benefit from the union representation in the form of higher wages, better benefits, and improved working conditions. As McInnis *Harnessing Labour Confrontation* persuasively argues, the Rand formula provided trade unions with the necessary financial security, but it did so in such a way that relegated organized labour to a secondary role relative to capital's part in the postwar economic reconstruction.

31 Jack Rauhala interview by Marlene Gibson, 1981, Laurentian University Archives, P009 NOLIA fonds, tape no. 92.

32 Nels Thibault interview by Mike Solski, 25 May 1981, Laurentian University Archives, P019 Solski fonds, file 51, tape no. 42.

33 Ibid.

34 Ibid.

35 Ibid.

36 Palmer, *Working Class Experience*, 236–8.

37 Solski interview by Jim Tester, 15 May 1981, page 18, Laurentian University Archives, P019 Solski fonds, series I, sub-series B, file 1.

CHAPTER THREE

1 Research participants E2.

2 *Mine Mill News*, 17 March 1952, cited in John Lang, "A Lion in a Den," 170.

3 McInnis, *Harnessing Labour Confrontation*, 19–45.

4 Buse, "Weir Reid and Mine Mill," 269–86.

5 Stevenson, "We're Still Here," 189–90.

6 Letter to Betty Meakes from Nancy Lima Dent, 8 May 1956, page 2, Dance Collection Danse Archive, Nancy Lima Dent fonds, box 1, folder 11.

7 Duthie, "'What's That Tutti-Frutti Stuff," 43.

8 Crouse School of Dancing and Shirley Simard School, which taught mostly acrobatics.

9 Newspaper article, 20 August 1951, "Union Camp Busy Spot," *Sudbury Star*, City of Greater Sudbury Public Library Archive.

10 Research participant AC46.

11 Local 598 paid $10,000 to cover the camp costs for the summer of 1958 so the fees could remain the same as the previous year. (1 December *Canadian Tribune* article, "Miners Fight for Union, Answer Press Slanders," Library and Archives Canada, RG-146-3 (CSIS) public access files, vol. 19.)

12 *Local 598*, 1959, film, 19:48 minutes, Library and Archives Canada, Meridian Films Ltd fonds, accession number 1990-0369, item no. ISN 166812.

13 Buse, "Weir Reid and Mine Mill," 269–86.

14 Ibid., 269–86.

15 Stevenson, "Ballet Ruse," 87.

16 Lang, "Review of Mick Lowe's The Raids," 271–3; Lang, "A Lion in a Den," 170.

17 Nels Thibault interview by Mike Solski, 25 May 1981, Laurentian University Archives, P019 Solski fonds, file 51, tape no. 42.

18 Canadian Constitution of the International Union of Mine, Mill and Smelter Workers, July 1955, page 23, UBC IUMMSW (Canada) fonds, box 6, file 7. The preamble to the Canadian constitution of MMSW, adopted in 1955, explicitly recognizes that the Canadian membership "has distinct and separate national aspirations and is concerned with distinct and separate national problems ... [and] the International Executive Board and the President shall take no action inconsistent with the Canadian constitution."

19 The history of American domination of Canadian unions that stretches back to the 1920s as documented in Lipton, *The Trade Union Movement*.

20 King and Braid, *Red Bait*, 49.

21 Trade tariffs and quotas were a thorny issue for the union because the American leadership, beholden to the American membership, were inclined to support the lead and zinc quotas proposed by the US Congress since they would ensure that benefits from any economic recovery in the metals market would go first to the American workers, at the expense of the Canadian members. To support both the American and Canadian members, the Canadian and International Boards of the union took the joint position of opposing any barriers against the free flow of base metals between Canada and the US. The autonomy of the Canadian arm of IUMMSW allowed it to press the federal government for a national policy to develop the metals industry under Canadian leadership and control while working out a unified position with its US counterpart. Together the two executive boards recommended sliding-scale quotas on goods being imported by the US that would give preference to those companies in countries with high wage standards, thereby encouraging industries wishing to export to the US to increase wages of their workers, while at the same time offering some job protection to the US workers.
Source: Mine Mill research report, October 1958, "Upturn in Non-Ferrous Prices," volume II no. 1, Research Department of IUMMSW, Denver: IUMMSW, UBC IUMMSW (Canada) fonds, box 58, file 58-10.

22 WFM/IUMMSW collection, University of Colorado Archives, box 274, folder 23. Canadian members continued to have representation on the union's international executive board through the district structure with Albert C. Skinner as the District 2 representative. At the time of the 1958 strike, the other international board members were John Clark, president; Asbury Howard, vice president; Orville Larson, vice president; Albert Pezzati, secretary-treasurer; Ernest Salvas, District 1; Raymond Dennis, District 3; Alton Lawrence, District 5; Irving Dichter, District 6; C.J. Powers, District 7.

23 John Clark speech for March 1955 convention, Spokane WA, University of Colorado Boulder Libraries – Archives, Special Collections, Government Information, & Map Library, WFM-IUMMSW collection, box 8, file 10. The red scare affected Canadian locals in their relationship to the international board, despite the fact that Canada did not pass the same degree of repressive legislation as was enacted in the US. Under the *Tart-Hartley Act,* Canadians elected to the union's international office had to qualify under US law and compelled to sign US government affidavits and show compliance to a foreign government, a state of affairs president John Clark characterized as "colonialism" in a speech to convention delegates.

24 Verzuh, *Smelter Wars,* 232.

25 Canadian Constitution of the International Union of Mine, Mill and Smelter Workers, July 1955, page 23, UBC IUMMSW (Canada) fonds, box 6, file 7.

26 Research participant S16. USWA was actively collecting signature to apply for the OLRB-supervised vote when the young man was approached; USWA was unable to collect signatures from the required 45 per cent of the membership in this raid. Note: In late March 1956, the labour legislation was amended to allow for transfer of jurisdiction. The decision by the OLRB to accept the Canadian MMSW as a legitimate entity, and therefore eligible to hold bargaining rights for groups of workers, came only five days before the legislation was passed 31 March 1956. MMSW had to re-apply to the OLRB for bargaining rights at Inco in 1956 under the changed legislation. *Sources*: newspaper article, 31 March 1956, "Amendment to *Labour Relations Act* May Help Settle Status of Mine Mill," *Sudbury Star*, City of Greater Sudbury Public Library Archive; newspaper article, 21 April 1958, "Union File to Keep Bargaining Rights," *Sudbury Star*, City of Greater Sudbury Public Library Archive.

27 Solski interview by Rick Stow, 29 September 1994 and 24 June 1988, Library and Archives Canada, Rick Stow fonds, ISN no. 566061 and 138003.

CHAPTER FOUR

1 Research participant E12.

2 Research participant S12.

3 Research participant AC35.

4 Newspaper article, 18 February 1958, "Mine Mill Play Draws Full Houses for Two Nights," *Sudbury Star*, Laurentian University Archives, P072, Inco fonds, box 1.

5 Minutes of 15 April negotiations, page 2, Archives Ontario, F1280, box MU 7727, file: "Joint Negotiating Committee, 598/637, Minutes, 1958." In addition to Mike Solski, Norman Jaques, Jack Quenneville, and William Cryderman, previously mentioned in the text, the eighteen-member committee included Lynn MacLean, Stan Racicot, Rene Fortin, Leo Legault, Norm Dupuis, Albert Routliffe, J. McWilliam, H. Leblanc, F. Meilleur, and C. Patterson of Local 598 and Roland Methot, Yves Lemay, Louis Brema, and Mickey Pine of Local 637.

6 Canadian Constitution of the International Union of Mine, Mill and Smelter Workers, July 1955, page 23, UBC IUMMSW (Canada) fonds, box 6, file 7.

7   Delamere is the man in pin-striped suit facing away from the camera: http://www.sudbury.library.on.ca/heritage/imgref.asp?img=main/acc1000 to1499/images/MK1493L.jpg.

8   Inco layoff schedule, 14 March 1958, UBC IUMMSW(Canada), box 38, file 32-2.

9   Telegram to John Diefenbaker, Parliament Buildings, Ottawa from Michael Solski, president MMSW, Local 598, 17 March 1958, Archives Ontario, F1271, series A-I, box 86, file: "Telegrams Outgoing, 1958."

10 Research participants WE8.

11 The proposal for a one-year timeframe for collective agreements ran counter to the trend in the industry towards longer contracts. Longer contracts protected unions' certification since they could only be raided by other unions when the collective agreements were about to expire. Longer contracts also guaranteed the check-off dues for a longer time. But unions like MMSW with their democratic structure and close connection with members were more inclined to shorter term contracts as a means of keeping the membership more closely connected to the leadership.

12 Proceedings of the 10th Annual Canadian Convention of the International Union of the Mine, Mill and Smelter Workers, Winnipeg, 24–28 February 1958, UBC IUMMSW (Canada) fonds, box 3.

13 The 1957–58 recession, which began in the second quarter of 1957, was even more severe than the previous slump in 1954 at the end of the Korean War.

14 Report on development in the metal mining industry, 25 June 1958, UBC IUMMSW (Canada) fonds, box 8, file 8-1.

15 Proceedings of the 10th Annual Canadian Convention of the International Union of the Mine, Mill and Smelter Workers, Winnipeg, 24–28 February 1958, UBC IUMMSW (Canada) fonds, box 3.

16 Minutes of 15 April negotiations, page 2, Archives Ontario, F1280, box MU 7727, file: "Joint Negotiating Committee, 598/637, Minutes, 1958."

17 Diefenbaker's other measures of increased old-age security and unemployment benefits were helpful to workers and more than the wage restraint policy, contributed to the economic recovery that came in later months of the 1958.

18 Newspaper article, 11 January 1958, "'Hold-the-Line' v. Demands for Wage Increases Will be the Opposing Themes During 1958," *Globe and Mail*, York University Archives, Ray Stevenson fonds, box 1998-032:005, file 24.

19 Clement, *Hardrock Mining*, 41.

20 The name of the bureau changed to Statistics Canada in 1971.

21 Letter from H.L. Robinson to Mike Solski, 14 January 1958, Archives Ontario, F1271, series A-I, box MU 6650.

22 Minutes of 6 May negotiations, page 1, Archives Ontario, F1280, box MU 7727, file: "Joint Negotiating Committee, 598/637, Minutes, 1958."

23 Minutes of 6 May negotiations, page 6, Archives Ontario, F1280, box MU 7727, file: "Joint Negotiating Committee, 598/637, Minutes, 1958."

24 Local 598's first collective agreement with Inco in 1944 stipulated that monthly union dues would be collected from the volunteering worker. In the intervening years, through collective bargaining, every worker paid monthly union dues as a condition of their employment, which gave the union a security knowing it had the financial means to carry out its programs. Union security was one of the common demands of unions during the strike wave immediately following World War II. The most famous of these strikes was mounted by the Windsor United Auto Workers at the Ford plant, which resulted in the Rand formula, proposed by Supreme Court justice Ivan Rand and founded on the recognition of unequal power between workers and employers. The Rand formula, also known as compulsory check-off, provides for union security whereby an employer deducts a portion of the salaries of all employees within the workplace to go to the union as union dues ("checkoff"), whether the employee is a union member or not. Rand argued that deducting dues from non-union members was justified because these workers benefit from the union representation in the form of higher wages, better benefits, and improved working conditions.

25 IUMMSW financial statement, 5 June 1958, Archives Ontario, F1271, series A-I, box MU 6650.

26 For 14,337 strikers, which included Local 637 and Local 598 members, the fund would amount to $2.82 of strike support for each striker.

27 Minutes of 7 May negotiations, page 5, Archives Ontario, F1280, box MU 7727, file: "Joint Negotiating Committee, 598/637, Minutes, 1958."

28 Ontario Department of Mines, *Annual Report Mines Inspection Branch,* bulletin nos 143–54.

29 Collective bargaining agreement between the International Nickel Company of Canada Ltd and Sudbury Mine, Mill and Smelter Workers' Union, Local 598, 1 June 1956, page 54, Archives Ontario, F1271, series G-III, box MU 6694.

30 Collective bargaining agreement between the Consolidated Mining and Smelting Company of Canada Ltd and International Union of Mine, Mill

and Smelter Workers' Union, Local 480, 1 June 1956, page 6, UBC IUMMSW (Canada), box 18, file 18-12.

31 Minutes of 7 May negotiations, page 13, Archives Ontario, F1280, box MU 7727, file "Joint Negotiating Committee, 598/637, Minutes, 1958."

32 Zembrzycki, "The Sinter Plant Boys," 257–78. In the early 1960s, the sintering plant was replaced by a nickel refinery, but not before many workers died of early deaths of various forms of cancer.

33 Research participant E8.

34 Research participant S16.

35 Ibid.

36 Zembrzycki, "The Sinter Plant Boys," 257–78.

37 Research participant E17.

38 Research participant E1.

39 Seguin, *Fighting for Justice and Dignity*, 15–17.

40 Minutes of 7 May negotiations, page 10, Archives Ontario, F1280, box MU 7727, file "Joint Negotiating Committee, 598/637, Minutes, 1958."

41 Minutes of 23 May negotiations, page 4, Archives Ontario, F1280, box MU 7727, file "Joint Negotiating Committee, 598/637, Minutes, 1958."

42 Majority report of conciliation board, Inco – L598-637, cited in *MMSW News*, vol. 11, no. 9, September 1958, page 2, Laurentian University Archives, P019, series I, sub-series B, file 37. Protracted negotiations were a significant expense for the union; for instance the agreement in effect previous to the strike cost the union $10,000.

43 Research participant AC30.

44 Minutes of 19 June negotiations, page 1, Archives Ontario, F1280, box MU 7727, file "Joint Negotiating Committee, 598/637, Minutes, 1958."

45 Ibid., 3–4.

46 Ibid., 5.

47 Ibid., 7.

CHAPTER FIVE

1 Report to the membership, 7 July 1958, page 8, Archives Ontario, F1280, series 2, box 7, file 9.

2 Press release, 7 July 1958, page 1, Archives Ontario, F1280, series 2, box 7, file 9.

3 Report to members. 13–14 July 1958, page 4, Archives Ontario, F1280, series 2, box 7, file 9.

4 Ibid., 3.

5 E. Charland and J. Packota were not Local 598 executive members, nor
   were they delegates to the previous MMSW conference, nor were they on
   the Strike Coordinating Committee. However, they might have been
   stewards.

6 Research participant ACI5.

7 Minutes of 11 August 1958 conciliation hearings, pages 4–5, Archives
   Ontario, F1280, box MU 7727, file "Joint Negotiating Committee,
   598/637, Minutes, 1958."

8 *Canadian Business*, January 1958, cited in a union submission to the
   Conciliation Board by Locals 598 and L637 International Union of Mine,
   Mill and Smelter Workers and International Nickel Company of Canada,
   page 21, Archives Ontario, F1271, Series G-I, Box 2 (MU6692).

9 Union submission to the Conciliation Board, submitted by Local 598 and
   Local 637 International Union of Mine, Mill and Smelter Workers and
   International Nickel Company of Canada, page 35, Archives Ontario,
   F1271, series G-I, box 2 (MU6692).

10 Minutes of 13 August 1958 conciliation hearings, page 2, Archives
   Ontario, F1280, box MU 7727, file: "Joint Negotiating Committee,
   598/637, Minutes, 1958."

11 Union submission to the Conciliation Board, submitted by L598 and L637
   International Union of Mine, Mill and Smelter Workers and International
   Nickel Company of Canada, page 36, Archives Ontario, F1271, series
   G-I, box 2 (MU6692).

12 Brief submitted to the Royal Commission on Canada's Economic
   Prospects by Local 802, International Union of Mine Mill and Smelter
   Workers, 23 January 1956, page 24, Library and Archives Canada,
   RG-146-3 (CSIS) public access files ATIP request 1025-9-91039, vol. 4
   "The IUMMSW – Women's Auxiliary, BC, 1932–1966." The beneficial
   effect of consumer spending during recessions was proposed by other
   business luminaries, such as the president of the Bank of Nova Scotia:
   "in general, high and rising wages are a good thing, and it must be
   admitted that the momentum of rising wages and salaries has helped to
   sustain buying power during the present year."

13 Minutes of 14 August 1958 negotiations, page 2, Archives Ontario, F1280,
   box MU 7727, file: "Joint Negotiating Committee, 598/637, Minutes, 1958."

14 Ibid., 4.

15 Minutes of Local 598 executive board meeting, 2 March 1958, Laurentian
   University Archives, P048, N37: 3, box 1.

16 Minutes of joint meeting of Local 598 executive board and plant
   executive, Laurentian University Archives, P048, N37: 3, box 1.

17 Report to members on conciliation hearings, n.d., page 11, Archives Ontario, F1280, series 2, box 7, file 2.

18 Research participant AC30.

19 Research participant E1.

20 Parr, *Domestic Goods*, 64–118. As Joy Parr demonstrates the architects of Canada's postwar reconstruction focused on stimulating the capital-goods sector and export capacity. To these postwar planners, only a slow lifting of prohibition on imports of many consumer durables, and a corresponding cautious increase in demand for consumer goods, would avoid an inflationary boom that could abort the planned reconstruction. They only needed to look south of the border for a counterexample where inflation was rising at an alarming rate. Despite the policy interventions by Canada's postwar planners, inflation continued in the late 1940s in Canada, and while it was less dramatic than in the US, an economic downturn followed in 1953–54. The 1957–58 recession, which began in the second quarter of 1957, was even more severe.

21 Ibid. Parr points to the distinctiveness of the Canadian experience in her analysis of Canadian women's continued use of the more arduous wringer washer over the modern automatic washers well into the 1960s. Her analysis highlights Canadians' more pragmatic, conservative approach to domestic consumption in comparison to the American sconsumer trends.

22 Liverant, *Buying Happiness*, 14–43; 157–83.

23 Report to members on conciliation hearings, n.d., page 11, Archives Ontario, F1280, series 2, box 7, file 2.

24 The prior year, Joseph Scioli was subpoenaed by the House Committee on Un-American Activities regarding the alleged communist activities in the Buffalo area. Like so many others called before the committee, when he was on the stand, Joseph refused to answer the questions, pleading the Fifth Amendment that affords citizens the right to not provide testimony that could incriminate them.

25 Quenneville interview by Jim Tester, 17 November 1978, Archives Ontario, C97, Jim Tester fonds, reel no. 57.

26 Letters to Inco employees from R.H. Waddington, assistant vice president and general manager, Ontario division, 25 August 1958, UBC IUMMSW (Canada), box 41, file 41-10.

27 Inco's nickel deliveries dropped by 41 per cent in 1958 compared to the previous year. Inco annual report, 2 March 1958, Laurentian University Archives, Regional Collection HD N52, 1532.

28 Lang, "A Lion in a Den," 210. The US government stopped stockpiling nickel at the beginning of 1957. Falconbridge, Inco's main competitor also located in Sudbury, had a proportionately larger share of the European market with its refinery in Norway and its US contracts didn't expire for another two years. So, the company was in a much better economic position than Inco.

29 One month into the strike, Inco lost production of approx. 15,542,460 pounds of nickel. *Source:* "Inco Smelter Reports," 1958, D-1, author's own archive.

30 Report to membership on Inco conciliation, 10 September 1958, page 1, Archives Ontario, F1280, series 2, box 7.

31 Strike vote twelve and thirteen, September 1958, Archives Ontario, F1280, series 2, box 7.

32 Ibid. Inco's miners voted 88 per cent in favour of striking, versus 77.6 per cent of the surface workers.

33 Research participant AC36.

34 Research participant E21.

35 Research participant WE7.

36 Minutes of 16 September 1958 negotiations, page 1, Archives Ontario, F1280, box MU 7727, file: "Joint Negotiating Committee, 598/637, Minutes, 1958." The province's labour legislation did not specify a time frame for notifying the company of an imminent strike, so it was left up to the union.

37 Ibid., 2.

38 Mike Farrell interview by Rick Stow, 15 September 1988, author's archive.

39 Strike vote bulletin, 15 September 1958, UBC IUMMSW (Canada), box 2, file 2-1.

40 "Inco Smelter Reports," February 1958, pages 48–9, author's own archive.

41 "Inco Smelter Reports," March 1958, page 59, author's own archive.

42 "Inco Smelter Reports," May 1958, page 80, author's own archive.

43 Research participant E16.

44 "Inco Smelter Reports," September 1958, page 118, author's own archive.

45 Solski and Smaller, *The History of the International*, 133–4.

46 Newspaper article, 11 June 1956, "Wildcat Strike at Smelter," *Sudbury Star*; newspaper article, 20 June 1952, "Miners at Levack Stage Walk-Out," *Sudbury Star*; newspaper article, 4 June 1954, "Work Stoppage at Murray Mine," *Sudbury Star*; newspaper article, 18 June 1956, "Rumors

to Contrary, No Weekend Walkouts," *Sudbury Star*, City of Greater Sudbury Public Library Archive.

47 Report to membership on Inco conciliation, 10 September 1958, page 4, Archives Ontario, F1280, series 2, box 7.

48 Research participant S25.

49 "Inco Smelter Reports," 1958, author's own archive.

50 Report to membership on Inco conciliation, 10 September 1958, page 4, Archives Ontario, F1280, series 2, box 7.

51 Research participant E15.

52 Minutes of 17 September 1958 negotiations, page 1, Archives Ontario, F1280, box MU 7727, File "Joint Negotiating Committee, 598/637, minutes, 1958."

53 Research participant AC4.

54 CBC Radio program, *Raid or Liberation,* aired 10 January 1962, production credit: writer, Wilfred List, Library and Archives Canada, Dave Lehto fonds, accession number: 1983-0350, https://www.bac-lac.gc.ca/eng/CollectionSearch/Pages/record.aspx?app=filvidandsou&IdNumber=14713.

55 Canadian Constitution of the International Union of Mine, Mill and Smelter Workers, July 1955, page 23, UBC IUMMSW (Canada), box 6, file 6-7.

56 Rosswurm, "An Overview and Preliminary Assessment," 1–18; Whitaker and Marcuse, *Cold War Canada,* 310–41.

57 Schrecker, "McCarthyism and the Labour Movement," 139–57.

58 Skinner interview by Alice Hoffman and Greg Giebel, part 2, 19 June 1973, pages 16–17, 30–8, Laurentian University Archives, P019, series I, sub-series B, file 48; Kinoy, *Rights on Trial,* 63. Under the US *Taft-Hartley Act* union leaders were required to file affidavits asserting their non-communist affiliations. Unions that did not comply with the Taft-Hartley regulations were denied access to the National Labour Relations Board for rulings on complaints of unfair labour practices put forward by the unions on behalf of their members. In union certification votes, supervised by the board, the non-compliant unions were prevented from appearing on the ballot and thus put in the awkward position of having to advise their members to vote "no union." So, to not file affidavits severely crippled the unions' ability to properly serve their members, even when affidavits were filed, union officials were often charged on conspiracy to defraud the government, allegedly because they had signed false affidavits. By the mid-1950s, most of the top leaders of the communist-alleged

unions in the US were "involved almost full time in staying out of prison," including sixteen MMSW officials.

59 Ibid. The $500,000 was raised over a period of ten years. "Not a dime came from the dues money of the union."

60 Letter to Mr Solski from "An Outraged Inco Wife," 11 September 1958, Archives Ontario, F1280, series 2, box 7.

61 Telegram to Mike Solski from Peter Zahavith, 21 September 1958, Archives Ontario, F1280, series 2, box 7.

62 Solski, "Struggles in Sudbury," 175–7.

63 Solski interview by Jim Tester, 15 May 1981, page 23, Laurentian University Archives, P019 Solski fonds, series I, sub-series B, file 1.

64 Ibid., 23.

65 Jack Quenneville interview by Jim Tester, 17 November 1978, Laurentian University Archives, P009 NOLIA fonds, taped interview no. 4.

CHAPTER SIX

1 Dominion Bureau of Statistics, *Census of Canada 1956,* https:// publications.gc.ca/collections/collection_2017/statcan/CS92-504-1956. pdf. The population of Sudbury alone was 46,482. In the larger Sudbury region, the population was 141,975 in 1956.

2 Minutes of meeting of picket captains and stewards Local 598 executive board meeting, 21 September 1958, Laurentian University Archives, P048, N37: 3, box 1.

3 Inco strike footage, September to October 1958, Library and Archives Canada, Inco fonds, ISN no. 99434; Solski interview by Jim Tester, 15 May 1981, Laurentian University Archives, P019 Solski fonds, series III, sub-series I, file 1.

4 Report to members, second week of strike, page 4, Archives Ontario, F1280, series 2, box 7, file 9.

5 Research participant AC47.

6 Research participant E2.

7 Research participant AC1.

8 Newspaper article, 24 September 1958, page 1, "14,000 Inco Workers Strike Today," *Globe and Mail,* ProQuest Historical Newspapers, https:// www.proquest.com/historical-newspapers/14-000-inco-workers-strike-to-day/docview/1323481323/se-2.

9 Newspaper article, 24 September 1958, page 3, "Taxi Business Booms Carry Miners Away," *Toronto Daily Star [1900-1971],* ProQuest Historical Newspapers, https://www.proquest.com/newspapers/page-3/

docview/1434655543/se-2. At the end of the strike, in a letter to Mr Crossgrove, of Inco's personnel department, Solski listed the 630 members who had left Sudbury over the thirteen weeks. Some moved to Toronto and elsewhere for work, others returned to their family farms in Saskatchewan, and still others rejoined relatives in Italy and Spain. Only Inco's personnel files can reveal how many returned to Sudbury at the end of the strike.

10 Research participant AC39.

11 Research participant AC38.

12 $1.8975/hour in 1958 would be $17.94/hour in 2021. "Inflation Calculator," *Bank of Canada*, 27 September 2021, https://www.bank ofcanada.ca/rates/related/inflation-calculator/.

13 Mine Mill research review, October 1960, *Another Big International Deficit,* vol. 1 issue 1, Research Department of IUMMSW, Toronto: IUMMSW (Canada), Laurentian University Archives, P019, series I, sub-series A, file 7.

14 Mine Mill research report, October 1958, *Upturn in Non-Ferrous Prices,* volume II no. 1, Research Department of IUMMSW, Denver: IUMMSW, UBC IUMMSW (Canada), box 58, file 58-10, Laurentian University Archives, P019, series I, sub-series A, file 7.

15 Research participant E6.

16 Newspaper article, 25 September 1958, page 2, "Use Six Helicopters as Shuttle Service for 2,500 at Inco," *Toronto Daily Star [1900-1971],* ProQuest Historical Newspapers, https://www.proquest.com/newspapers/page-2/docview/2202184715/se-2; chronological record of company meetings in regard to the 1958 strike, L.R. Wilson Archive, Port Colborne Historical Museum, 992.16, uncatalogued binder.

17 Research participant AC5.

18 During the war, Inco hired women, but only in the smelter not for jobs underground. Returning soldiers were granted their jobs and seniority equivalent to their time in the military.

19 Research participant S12.

20 Newspaper article, 24 September 1958, "Use Six Helicopters as Shuttle Service for 2,500 at Inco," *Toronto Daily Star [1900-1971],* ProQuest Historical Newspapers, https://www.proquest.com/newspapers/page-2/docview/2202184715/se-2.

21 Research participant AC40.

22 Research participant AC41.

23 Newspaper article, 27 September 1958, page 2, "Sudbury Strike Hits Several Communities," *Globe and Mail,* ProQuest Historical Newspapers,

https://www.proquest.com/historical-newspapers/widening-effects-noted/
docview/1288806350/se-2.

24 Newspaper article, 11 October 1958, "Business Not as Bad as Some
Anticipated," *Sudbury Star*, City of Greater Sudbury Public Library.

25 Research participant S19.

26 The first step in the smelting process was roasting to drive off the sulphur,
accomplished in multi-hearth roasters in the late 1950s. The product of
the roasting was then sent to the reverb furnaces where high temperatures
created a molten mixture, with the heavier matte settling at the bottom.
The lighter slag was skimmed off and went to the slag dump. After a
hundred years of dumping, the slag mountain was very large with mineral
content quite high from the original days of under-developed separation
and smelting processes.

27 The Creighton mine is now the world's largest neutrino research lab 2 km
underground. The "SNOLAB" is a five thousand square metres underground scientific research lab staffed by more than one hundred researchers
and other personnel conducting various astrophysics experiments. See
https://www.snolab.ca.

28 Research participant AC12.

29 Saarinen, *From Meteorite Impact to Constellation*, 2013. In the decade of
the 1950s, 60 per cent of the population of Sudbury were Roman
Catholic.

30 Hogan, "Hard Rock and Hard Decisions," 13.

31 Official report on financial contributions to 1958 strike, n.d., Laurentian
University Archives, P059, series: "Strike," box 9. Barbara Cook, the
dance teacher had just signed a year contract for $75/week. The MMSW
constitution specified that the officials would never earn more than the top
earning union member. The staff and officers' pay reduction to half their
regular wage amounted to $12,277 over the course of the strike.

32 Radio & television broadcast, 7 October 1958, Archives Ontario, F1280,
series 2, box 7, file 9.

33 Ibid.

34 Newspaper article, 7 October 1958, "First Statement on Policy,"
Sudbury Star, Laurentian University Archives, P072, Inco fonds, box 6,
F32:2.

35 Except those that came from unknown sources, e.g., the words "We Want
to Go Back Work" on a piece of lined paper with no date, no name, no
return address.

36 Letter from Anna Lovsin to Mike Solski, 24 October 1958, Archives
Ontario, F1271, series A-I, box 85, file: "Strike Inquiries."; letter from

Mike Solski to Anna Lovsin, 27 October 1958, Archives Ontario, F1271, series A-I, box 85, file: "Strike Inquiries."

37 The postwar period saw tens of thousands of Canadians purchasing household durables of furniture and appliances on credit. By 1956, the average Canadian family owed over 12 per cent of its total income and the average per capita installment debt had increased threefold since 1942 (Liverant, *Buying Happiness*, 171). Borrowing for household durables was on the increase while credit for fuel, food, and other immediate consumables was waning except in close-knit mining communities like Sudbury where the new patterns of consumer credit were taking hold alongside the long-standing tradition of local merchants extending credit to customers for food, fuel, and other immediately consumable goods.

38 Newspaper article, 17 October 1958, "Medical Plans, Mortgages," *Sudbury Star*, Laurentian University Archives, P072, Inco fonds, box 6, F32:2.

39 Radio & television broadcast, 31 October 1958, Archives Ontario, F1280, series 2, box 7, file 9. Imperial Life, carrier of hospital insurance for the two thousand Inco employees, was accepting communication from members and continued their coverage, but negotiations with Blue Cross remained strained and uncertain until the end of October.

40 Letter from Kelly Thurlow to Mike Solski, 15 October 1958, Archives Ontario, F1271, series A-I, box 85, file: "Strike Inquiries."

41 Letter from Inco employee no.15076 to fellow union members, "Brothers," n.d., Archives Ontario, F1280, series 2, box 7, file: "Letters."

42 Newspaper article, 14 October 1958, page 20, "U.S. Won't Stockpile Nickel Third Year," *Toronto Daily Star [1900-1971]*, ProQuest Historical Newspapers, https://www.proquest.com/newspapers/page-20/docview/1425708279/se-2.

43 Lorence, *The Suppression of Salt*, 47–64, 113–48. Clinton Jencks, the strike's lead organizer and IUMMSW representative, first alerted the director to the strike as a potential film subject and starred in the movie. Although both Jencks and the union had been under scrutiny by government anti-communist watchdogs for at least a full year before *The Suppression of Salt*, Jencks's high profile in the origins and production of the movie marked him as a logical target for escalated harassment. In 1954, at the height of the organized boycott of *The Suppression of Salt*, the militant unionist was convicted of perjury in signing the Taft-Hartley noncommunist affidavit and sentenced to five years and a $20K penalty. Jencks's protracted legal battles, spanning almost eight years, began to wane in 1957 when the Supreme Court reversed the verdict, largely

because the government's star witness, Harvey Matusow recanted his testimony against Jencks and by that time, the Court was beginning to abandon the anti-communist crusade.

44 Ibid.

45 Ibid.

46 Verzuh, "Remembering Salt," 165–98. In 1954 MMSW Local 480 in Trail, BC screened the film to nine hundred residents of the Trail area. The four thousand MMSW members were also treated to an address by the movie's female star, Anita Torres, who spoke forcefully on the battle of both the strike and the making of the movie.

47 Baker, *On Strike and On Film*, 45–118.

48 John Clark speech for March 1955 convention, Spokane WA, University of Colorado Boulder Libraries – Archives, Special Collections, Government Information, & Map Library, WFM-IUMMSW collection, box 8, file 10.

49 Baker, *On Strike and On Film*, 119–76.

50 Ibid., 173. As Baker shows, in some cases, a husband's latent home-making skills were a pleasant surprise to both husband and wife. In others, the men resisted their newly assigned duties in the households, feeling their masculinity threatened, and even the most committed of union leaders admitted to his fellow unionists, he stopped short of changing diapers.

51 Newspaper article, 8 January 1959, "Record Year for Births as 4,744 Born in Area; August Bride's Month," *Sudbury Star*, City of Greater Sudbury Public Library. Births were a record number in 1958, for the third straight year. The number of marriage licenses issued in 1958 exceeded those issued the year before. Death rates were on the decline in 1958, dropped to 534 from 590 the previous year.

52 Research participant AC42.

53 Research participant AC43.

54 Research participant WE2.

55 Research participant AC47.

56 Mercier, *Anaconda*, 30–42.

57 *Financial Post*, 25 October 1958, "Here's What Inco Strike Really Means," Laurentian University Archives, P072, Inco fonds, box 6, F32:2.

58 Press release, 29 September 1958, Archives Ontario, F1280, series 2, box 7, file 9.

59 Gilbert Godin, "The Autobiography of a Labourer," 50. Godin became president of Northern Workers Adult Education Association, the legacy of Boudreau's leadership courses. In his book, Frank Southern promotes the

notion that the communist leadership of the union pushed for the strike in an impossible economic climate in order to foster class cleavage: Southern, *The Sudbury Incident.*

60 Harvey Murphy articulated the national leaders' position in the *Raid or Liberation.* CBC Radio program, *Raid or Liberation,* aired 10 January 1962, production credit: writer, Wilfred List, Library and Archives Canada, Dave Lehto fonds, accession number: 1983-0350.

61 Joe Astgen interview by Gaston Belanger, 1981, Laurentian University Archives, P009, NOLIA fonds, taped interview no. 107.

62 Newspaper article, 21 October 1958, "Strike Voucher Procedure," *Sudbury Star,* Laurentian University Archives, P072, Inco fonds, box 6, F32:2.

63 Newspaper article, 20 October 1958, "Asks Frost, Daley for New Inco Peace Effort," *Port Colborne Tribune,* Laurentian University Archives, P072. Inco fonds, box 6, F32:2; Brasch, *A Miner's Chronicle,* 48. Note: these amounts contradict Hans Brasch (1997), who writes that he was a married man with no children and received $8/week for food vouchers.

64 Brasch, *A Miner's Chronicle,* 43–56.

65 Seguin, *Fighting for Justice and Dignity.*

66 Research participant AC32.

67 Seguin, *Fighting for Justice and Dignity,* 27.

68 Research participant WE5.

69 Research participant E11.

70 Newspaper article, 23 October 1958, "Nickel Sales Picking Up," *Sudbury Star,* Laurentian University Archives, P072, Inco fonds, box 6, F32:2.

71 Newspaper article, 13 November 1958, "Good Relations Have Been a Tradition at Inco," *Globe and Mail,* Laurentian University Archives, P072, Inco fonds, box 6, F32:2.

72 Minutes of Local 598 executive board meeting, 19 October 1958, Laurentian University Archives, P048, N37:3, box 1.

73 Joe Astgen interview by Gaston Belanger, 1981, Laurentian University Archives, P009, NOLIA fonds, taped interview no. 107.

74 Liverant, *Buying Happiness,* 157–83.

75 Ibid.

CHAPTER SEVEN

1 Research participant AC44.

2 Newspaper article, 1 November 1958, "WI Group Asks Intervention in Inco Strike," *Sudbury Star,* Laurentian University Archives, P072, Inco fonds, box 6, F32:2.

3 Newspaper article, 6 November 1958, "Inco Earnings Less Than Half of Last Year's," *Sudbury Star*, Laurentian University Archives, P072, Inco fonds, box 6, F32:2.

4 Research participant S25.

5 Ibid.

6 MMSW *Herald*, May 1958, "Referendum on Pension Proposal by CM&S Membership," vol. 3, no. 29, page 7, Laurentian University, Regional Collection HD 6528 M6 M55 1958. Up until the 6 and 7 May negotiations with Inco, only reclassifications were discussed; no wage offer had been presented to the union. The settlement with Consolidated Mining and Smelting (CM&S), which was arrived at on 19 June with bargaining on wages to commence nine months later in January 1959, turned out to be advantageous for the CM&S members since by then the metals markets had improved and MMSW achieved a twenty-nine cent/hour increase over three years. This was considerably higher than the final settlement with Inco after the strike, which amounted to a sixteen-cent/hour increase in wages and benefits.

7 Letter to John Lewis, president of United Mine Workers of America from Mike Solski, 24 November 1958, Archives Ontario, F1280, series 2, box 7. By the end of November, the union was spending $125,000/week to maintain the strike. The executive members estimated, correctly, that the strike would last another four to five weeks before Inco would be willing to bargain.

8 The congress changed its name from the Canadian Congress of Labour to the Canadian Labour Congress in 1956.

9 Whitaker and Marcuse, *Cold War Canada*, 311.

10 R. Veruh, "The Reddest Rose: Trade Unionist Harvey Murphy," *The British Columbia Review*, last modified 2018, https://thebcreview.ca/2018/09/12/19-trade-unionist-harvey-murphy/.

11 Research participant E16. This incident triggered MMSW's temporary suspension from the congress. A year later, at the October 1949 CCL convention, MMSW was expelled with no debate and little vocal support from the delegates since other left-led unions had already been expelled and therefore were barred from attending the convention. *Source*: Abella, "International Union, 1936–48," 86–110. The Congress engaged in further strategies to undermine MMSW as part of its agenda to cleanse the labour movement of communist-stamped unions. Shortly after the expulsion, the congress chartered their own local in Sudbury, Local 101, to woo the approximately two thousand members of the Mine Mill General Workers Local 902, which represented the workers at Loblaws,

Dominion, several of Sudbury's department stores, and Garson's civic workers and hotel bartenders.

12 CKSO news report, 11 December 1958, Laurentian University Archives, P0102, box 120:1.

13 Newspaper article, 9 October 1958, "OFL Backs Mine Mill, Asks It to Get Back In," *Sudbury Star*, Laurentian University Archives, P072, Inco fonds, box 6, F32:2.

14 University of Colorado Boulder Libraries – Archives, Special Collections, Government Information, & Map Library, WFM-IUMMSW collection, box 032, file 16: "Strike Poll – 5 November 1958." When the two members from the international executive attending the 2 November meeting returned to their American base, they polled the other international executive with a motion to contribute an additional $25,000 from the IUMMSW strike fund to the Inco strike. The motion passed unanimously.

15 The press inflated both the amount the Teamsters donated, reported as $500,000, and the conditions of the support, suggesting that the financial assistance was dependent on MMSW merging with the Teamsters.

16 Mike Solski, "Review and Critique of Red Bait," 11.

17 Radio & television broadcast, 23 November 1958, Archives Ontario, F1280, series 2, box 7, file 9.

18 Over the course of the strike, the local received over $266,305.83 in financial donations. *Source:* official report on financial contributions to 1958 strike, n.d., Laurentian University Archives, P059, series: "Strike," box 9.

19 Newspaper article, 1 November 1958, "Bishop Carter's Letter to the Clergy," *Globe and Mail*, Laurentian University Archives, P072, Inco fonds, box 6, F32:2.

20 Newspaper article, 11 October 1958, "Editorial: A Sinister Coincidence," *Catholic Register*, 17th year, no. 33, https://www.catholicregister.org/archive.

21 Newspaper article, 17 November 1958, "Sudbury Strikers Go Hungry So Their Children Can Eat," *Globe and Mail*, Laurentian University Archives, P072, Inco fonds, box 6, F32:2.

22 Newspaper article, 19 November 1958, page 1, "Inco Strikers' Situation Said 'Not Desperate,'" *Toronto Daily Star [1900-1971]*, ProQuest Historical Newspapers, https://www.proquest.com/newspapers/page-1/docview/1434656339/se-2.

23 Newspaper article, 21 November 1958, "Union Vouchers Cut Some Sudbury Miners Said 'In Real Need,'" *Toronto Daily Star [1900-1971]*, Laurentian University Archives, P072, Inco fonds, box 6, F32:2.

24 Newspaper article, 19 November 1958, page 4, "Mill Strikers Deny Hardship," *Globe and Mail,* ProQuest Historical Newspapers, https://www.proquest.com/historical-newspapers/mill-strikers-deny-hardship/docview/1288609049/se-2.

25 Newspaper article, 15 November 1958, "Strike Increases Fuel, Clothing, Demands on Welfare Groups," *Sudbury Star,* Laurentian University Archives, P072, Inco fonds, box 6, F32:2.

26 Ibid.

27 Research participant AC15.

28 Research participant E16.

29 Newspaper article, 24 November 1958, page 29, "Talk with Lewis, Hoffa, Sudbury Strikers May Join Teamsters, Get Funds," *Toronto Daily Star [1900-1971],* ProQuest Historical Newspapers, www.proquest.com/newspapers/page-29/docview/1434656112/se-2.

30 Newspaper article, 24 November 1958, "Hoffa Offers Support As Daley Attempts Inco Settlement," *Toronto Daily Star [1900-1971],* Laurentian University Archives, P072, Inco fonds, box 6, F32:2.

31 Newspaper article, 26 November 1958, page 6, "The Vicious Circle," *Globe and Mail,* ProQuest Historical Newspapers, https://www.proquest.com/historical-newspapers/vicious-circle/docview/1288595879/se-2.

32 CKSO news reports, Laurentian University Archives, P019, box 30.

33 Radio & television broadcast, 2 December 1958, Archives Ontario, F1280, series 2, box 7, file 9. Inco's offer included 1 per cent in the second year, and 1.5 per cent in the third year. Over the three days of talks, the union dropped its demands in a series of successive proposals from its starting position of 8 per cent wage increase, equivalent to seventeen cents an hour in a one-year agreement to 3 per cent in the first year, 3.5 per cent in both the second and third year.

34 Minutes of 16 December negotiations, page 2, Archives Ontario, F1280, box MU 7727, file: "Joint Negotiating Committee, 598/637, Minutes, 1958." In a subsequent meeting in the labour minister offices on 16 December, both the minister and the union refer to previous pre-emptive press releases as harmful to the process of negotiations. In the middle of their discussion about the press, Thibault remarked "we found out who the guy was that followed us around last time."

35 The results of the Local 637 membership meeting in Port Colborne were similar.

36 Newspaper article, 1 December 1958, "Members Unanimously Reject Inco Proposal," *Port Colborne Tribune,* Laurentian University Archives, P072, Inco fonds, box 6, F32:2.

37 Newspaper article, 4 December 1958, "Strikers Head Home with Food, Clothing," *Sudbury Star*, Laurentian University Archives, P072, Inco fonds, box 6, F32:2.

38 Newspaper article, 4 December 1958, "Resume Talks, Premier Tells Inco Delegates," *Sudbury Star*, Laurentian University Archives, P072, Inco fonds, box 6, F32:2.

39 International executive board minutes, 2–6 and 8–10 December 1958, University of Colorado Boulder Libraries – Archives, Special Collections, Government Information, & Map Library, WFM-IUMMSW collection, box 032, file 16.

40 Newspaper article, 3 December 1958, "Sudbury Strikers Sing on Queen's Park Invasion," *Sudbury Star*, Laurentian University Archives, P072, Inco fonds, box 6, F32:2; newspaper article, 3 December 1958, page 1, "Won't Take Over Inco Frost Tells Cavalcade," *Toronto Daily Star [1900-1971]*, ProQuest Historical Newspapers, https://www.proquest.com/newspapers/page-1/docview/1425698303/se-2; newspaper article, 3 December 1958, "Women to Join Strikers," *Toronto Telegram*, Laurentian University Archives, P072, Inco fonds, box 6, F32:2; newspaper article, 4 December 1958, page 5, "Delegation of Miners," *Globe and Mail*, ProQuest Historical Newspapers, https://www.proquest.com/historical-newspapers/delegations-miners/docview/1288813923/se-2.

41 National ladies auxiliary newsletter, 1958, no. 256, UBC IUMMSW (Canada), box 56, file 6.

42 Millie McQuaid interview by Mercedes Steeman, 1993, Laurentian University Archives, Mercedes Steedman fonds.

43 The play, "*With Glowing Hearts: How Women Worked Together to Change the World, And Did,*" by Jennifer Wynne Webber, is based on the supposition, grounded in historical research, that the seeds of the women's auxiliary were planted during the Kirkland Lake strike when Kay met Dorothy MacDonald, who later became the national coordinator of the MMSW women's auxiliaries.

44 *The Program for the Coming Year*, n.d., Archives Ontario, F1280 fonds, Mine Mill and Smelter Workers (Local 598), series 18, box 72, file no. 5.

45 The union's Canadian constitution outlines the duties of the officers of the union and chartering branches of local unions to assist the women's auxiliaries however possible. As well, it was the right of the auxiliaries to send their elected delegates to all conventions and to attend all local union meetings and freely express their opinions.

46 Millie McQuaid interview by Mercedes Steedman, 1993, Laurentian University Archives, Mercedes Steedman collection.

47 Newspaper article, 14 December 1958, "Inco Wives Defy Goons, Yell 'Go Back to Russia,'" *Toronto Telegram*, Laurentian University Archives, P072, Inco fonds, box 6, F32:2. For the Catholic Women's League involvement in the strike see Steedman, "Godless Communists and Faithful Wives," 233–53.

48 *A Wives' Tale* directed by Sophie Bissonnette, Martin Duckworth, and Joyce Rock.

49 Letter to Brother Briggs, president L598, 6 June 1990, reprinted in *100th Anniversary. The Western Federation of Miners and Canadian Union of Mine, Mill and Smelter Workers*, page 53, author's archive.

50 Basic fact of interest to prospective members of the Ladies' Auxiliaries of the International Union of Mine, Mill and Smelter Workers, pamphlet prepared by auxiliary vice president, Kay Carlin, UBC IUMMSW (Canada), box 17, file 6.

51 Cobble, *The Other Women's Movement*, 69–93, 145–79. The "Labour feminists" viewed the labour movement as the primary means through which the lives of working-class women could be improved. Unions offered an avenue for women's influence as auxiliary women and as trade union members themselves. They advocated for economic and social rights to cushion the individual against the vagaries of the market through social security. In doing so, these women had a pivotal role in shaping the emerging welfare state. See Cobble's (2004) challenge to the supposed interlude between the first and second waves of feminism, a period when working-class women who used both collective bargaining and legislation in their campaign for "full industrial citizenship." In an era when the labour movement still promoted the idea of a family wage to enable the wives of working men to be stay-at-home mothers, labour feminists insisted that all women should have the right to adequately paid wage work. Eventually eclipsed by the "equal rights" feminism of the 1960s, labour feminists of this era grappled with the tensions between the goals and strategies of equality and difference. For them, it was not a matter of fighting for either rights or benefits, but both. Full economic citizenship required "special" accommodation for women's maternal responsibilities.

52 Minutes of 16 December negotiations, page 3, Archives Ontario, F1280, box MU 7727, file: "Joint Negotiating Committee, 598/637, Minutes, 1958."

53 Minutes of 18 December negotiations, page 3, Archives Ontario, F1280, box MU 7727, file: "Joint Negotiating Committee, 598/637, Minutes, 1958."

54 Ibid., 2.

55 Minutes of 19 December negotiations, page 1, Archives Ontario, F1280, box MU 7727, file: "Joint Negotiating Committee, 598/637, Minutes, 1958."

56 Research associates' report, 14 January 1958, "Data on Wage Rates," prepared for Local 598 IUMMSW, Montreal PQ. The report reviews wage rates from over one hundred collective agreements in the industries employing others in the same occupations as Inco's workforce.

57 Orville Larson second interview by Alice Hoffman, 5 March 1975, page 38, University Penn State, United Steelworkers of America collection, series 9, box 24, folder 10, transcript no. 63471. Shortly after playing such a pivotal role in settling the strike on behalf of the MMSW's Sudbury members, Orville Larson went on to have a distinguished career with the United Steelworkers of America as the non-ferrous mining coordinator. The archival records reveal Larson resigned from IUMMSW on 1 January 1960 because of the difference of opinion with other members of the international executive board concerning the potential of a merger with USWA. Larson believed merging with USWA was the best course of action for IUMMSW because the mine owners would benefit the most from the rivalry between the two unions. In preparation for his departure from IUMMSW, he had made arrangements to work for the Benjamin Franklin Insurance Company in Arizona. When word spread of his imminent departure, several unions approached him with offers, including USWA. As he said in a retrospective interview, "It was a hard decision. On the one hand, I was fed up; I was disgusted. I never wanted to hear of the labour movement again. On the other hand, I'd spent a lifetime in the labour movement." It was Larson wife's blunt remarks that clinched his decision: "Who are you kidding? You're not going to be happy as an insurance agent." Recognizing the folly of such a radical change for a man who had been part of the labour movement for so long, Larson joined the USWA. His exodus from IUMMSW was cast as a breach of loyalty, yet just five or six years later, the IUMMSW executive voted for the merger with the USWA.

58 Newspaper article, 20 December 1958, page 1, "Agreement Brings Joy to Sudbury," *Globe and Mail*, ProQuest Historical Newspapers, https://www.proquest.com/historical-newspapers/agreement-brings-joy-sudbury/docview/1288603099/se-2.

59 Research participant AC41.

60 Research participant AC15.

61 Radio and television broadcast, 23 December 1958, Archives Ontario, P1280, box 7, file 9.

CHAPTER EIGHT

1 Research participant E21. Inco introduced a formal program in late 1960s to reimburse citizens for the sulphur damage to cars, fences, and other metal surfaces that the downdrafts of sulphur destroyed. One car was re-painted four times.
2 Over the three years, the wage increases lifted the labourer rate from $1.8967/hour to $2.0125/hour.
3 Seguin, *Fighting for Justice and Dignity*, 30.
4 The strike introduced the idea of shutdown maintenance. Regular shutdowns and maintenance schedules only became part of Inco's planned activities in the decade following the strike.
5 Research participant E21.
6 Ontario Department of Mines, *Annual Report Mines Inspection Branch 1959*, bulletin no. 159, 62. Within a week of the skimming accident, a process labourer, thirty-one-year-old Christo Barbounis was killed when the bricks of one of the smelter's seven furnaces gave way spewing twenty-five tons of burning metal into the smelter. With his back turned to the furnace at the time, Barbounis heard the rumbling noise of the flowing matte and immediately ran in the opposite direction. Because he stumbled for an instant too long in his rush, he was quickly overtaken and submerged in the scorching matte.
7 Research participant E12.
8 Newspaper article, 1 November 1958, "Bishop Carter's Letter to the Clergy," *Globe and Mail,* Laurentian University Archives, P072, Inco fonds, box 6, F32:2.
9 Newspaper article, 20 November 1958, "Where Did the Money Go?" *Globe and Mail*, Laurentian University Archives, P072, Inco fonds, box 6, F32:2.
10 Brasch, *A Miner's Chronicle*, 48.
11 CKSO News, audio broadcast, 10 March 1959, Library and Archives Canada, Dave Lehto fonds, ISN no. 14167.
12 "Stewart Audit Report," UBC, IUMMSW (Canada), box 11, folder 1. The audit showed the local's finances had been handled responsibly over the years. The union had paid off the debt incurred to purchase the property for the first hall on Regent Street within two years of purchase. And other major expenses of property and building costs for the halls, the camp, entertainers and so on were paid promptly from the available revenues in the form of membership dues.

13 Newspaper article, 11 October 1958, "Editorial: A Sinister Coincidence," *Catholic Register* 17th year, no. 33, https://www.catholicregister.org/archive.

14 Research participant E16.

15 Rosswurm, "The Catholic Church," 119–38.

16 Ibid.

17 Speech by Catholic priest, 1958, Laurentian University Archives, P019, Solski fonds, series I, sub-series B, file 51, tape 50.

18 Bouvier, "Les sciences sociales au Québec," 131–46. http://classiques.uqac.ca/contemporains/bouvier_emile/transformations_sc_soc_UdeM/transformations_sc_soc_UdeM_texte.html. Emil Bouvier was the first president of the University of Sudbury. Prior to coming to Sudbury, he was the director of the Department of Political Economy at Georgetown University, where he had studied under the anti-communist apostle, Father Edmund Walsh (Peake and Horne, *The Religious Tradition in Sudbury*). The Jesuit Scared Heart College opened in 1913. It was a classical college like those in PQ and degrees were granted by l'Université Laval. In 1953 the transformation of the college into a degree-granting institution was initiated and in 1957, the *University of Sudbury Act* was passed in the Ontario legislature. In 1958, a board of regents was appointed, including R.D. Parker, vice president of Inco.

19 *McDonald Commission of Inquiry concerning Certain Activities of the* RCMP *McDonald Commission, Second Report, Volume I, Freedom and Security of the Law* (Ottawa: Minister of Supply and Services 1981). https://publications.gc.ca/site/eng/471402/publication.html.

20 Boudreau, *A l'assaut des défis*, 62.

21 Letter from James Kidd to Alexandre Boudreau regarding list of names recommended for participants in extension course, 6 January 1959, Laurentian University Archives, P1280, series 17, box 71; letter from James Kidd to Alexandre Boudreau assuring him the cost of the requested USWA educational materials would be paid from the general budget of the USWA, 4 March 1959, Laurentian University Archives, P1280, series 17, box 71.

22 Newspaper article, 21 September 1959, "Sudbury Known Throughout World as Centre of Communist Activities," *Sudbury Star*, Laurentian University Archives, P059, box 2, file 11.

23 Boudreau, *A l'assaut des défis*, 63.

24 Ibid.

25 Ibid., 67.

26 Solski interview by Jim Tester, 15 May 1981, page 23, Laurentian University Archives, P019, Solski fonds, series I, sub-series B, file 1.

27 McInnis, *Harnessing Labour Confrontation*, 43–4.

28 Verzuh, "The Raiding of L480," 81–117.

29 Al King interview by Jim Tester, 3 September 1977, page 4, Archives Ontario, Jim Tester fonds, C97, reel no. 26.

30 Stanton, *My Past is Now*, 106.

31 Newspaper report, 1 April 1950, "Freeing Labor Unions from Communist Control," *Catholic Register*, 9th year, no. 5, https://www.catholicregister. org/archive.

32 Jensen, *Heritage of Conflict*, 240. The practice of assigning union jurisdictions by federations of labour was an outgrowth of unionization in mass production and often caused significant tensions between and within unions. For instance, in 1911, WFM's application for AFL affiliation was strenuously opposed by the International Association of Machinists because the latter union's claim to jurisdiction of the engineers in and around mines. In other instances, amicable relations were established early and continued over the decades. For example, the historic agreement between IUMMSW and United Mine Workers, which designated coal mining as the jurisdiction of the latter and hard rock mining was left to the Western Federation of Miners, was formally expressed in the IUMMSW constitution and endured for decades. The practice of labour federations assigning jurisdiction had ceased for all intents and purposes by the early 1970's. The only place where it continues after a fashion is in the building trades and that function is performed by the building trades unions themselves usually through their provincial councils.

33 Abella, "International Union, 1936–48," 86–110.

34 CCL convention proceedings, 1950, cited in Lang, "A Lion in a Den," 118–22; Skinner interview by Alice Hoffman and Greg Giebel, part 2, 19 June 1973, page 13, Laurentian University Archives, P019 Solski fonds, series I, sub-series B, file 48. Similar collusion took place between USWA and the American house of labour in the US. Almost immediately after MMSW was expelled, USWA was given jurisdiction over the non-ferrous metal industry. Phil Murray, the first president of USWA, orchestrated CIO's assignment of the jurisdiction of the nonferrous metal industry to his union, using the Cold War politics as the pretense.

35 Stevenson, "Globalization and Armageddon," 292.

36 Mike Farrell interview by Rick Stow, 15 September 1988, author's archive.

37 Abella, "International Union, 1936–48," 86–110.

38 Don McNabb interview by Francine Charland and Janet Giroux combined videos of various dates, Library and Archives Canada, Ron Mann fonds, ISN no. 3311532.

39 Joe Astgen interview by Gaston Belanger, Laurentian University Archives, P009, NOLIA fonds, taped interview no. 107.

40 Seguin, *Fighting for Justice and Dignity*, 20.

41 Radio and television broadcast by United Steelworkers of America, 1965, Library and Archives Canada, Dave Lehto fonds, ISN no. 14956.

42 Newspaper report, 27 October 1962, "Victory Came After Three Tries by Anti-Red Miners," *Catholic Register*, 20th year, no. 35, https://www.catholicregister.org/archive.

43 Jack Rauhala interview by Marlene Gibson 1981, Laurentian University Archives, P009, NOLIA fonds, taped interview no. 92; Joe Astgen interview by Gaston Belanger, 1981, Laurentian University Archives, P009, NOLIA fonds, taped interview no. 107; research participant E16.

44 Tester interview by Rick Stow, 21 January 1989, 15 September 1988, and 25 August 1989, Library and Archives Canada, Rick Stow fonds. ISN nos 138004, 138006, and 151491.

45 Research participant S18.

46 Mike Farrell interview by Rick Stow, 15 September 1988, author's archive.

47 McKeigan, "The Rise and Decline," 252–4. The rank and file remained militant at least until the early 1980s when apathy among the membership began to set in, with many members convinced that the local's executive elections were not honest.

48 Seguin, *Fighting for Justice and Dignity*, 45.

49 Clement, *Hardrock Mining*, 322–31.

50 Research participant USW2.

51 Research participant E16.

52 McKeigan, "The Rise and Decline," 242, 248–9.

53 Thibault interview by Mike Solski, part 1 and 2, 25 May 1981, Laurentian University Archives, P019, Solski fonds, series I, sub-series B, file 50.2, boxes F47, 3.1, and 3.2.

54 Tester interview by Rick Stow, 21 January 1989, 15 September 1988, and 25 August 1989, Library and Archives Canada, Rick Stow fonds, ISN nos 138004, 138006, and 151491.

55 McKeigan, "The Rise and Decline," 256–9.

56 Bromwich, *Union Constitutions*, 11.

57 In the face of declining membership, the WFM tried to lay to rest its militant past at its 1916 convention and renamed itself the International

Union of Mine, Mill and Smelter Workers (IUMMSW). The chosen new name was to reflect its industrial jurisdiction, international affiliates, and a widened regional focus; and the constitution's preamble was adjusted to reflect the union's move away from radicalism. For example, precepts such as "the working class and it alone, must achieve its own emancipation" were replaced with less revolutionary tenets such as "the occupation of the men employed in the metal mines, mills and smelters is both hazardous and unhealthy, and believing that through organization conditions of employment can be improved and more adequate compensation obtained, we have formed the International Union of Mine, Mill & Smelter Workers." *Sources:* Constitution and bylaws of the Western Federation of Miners, adopted at Butte City, Montana, 19 May 1983, University of Colorado Boulder Libraries – Archives, Special Collections, Government Information, & Map Library, WFM-IUMMSW collection box 2, file 1; constitution of the International Union of Mine, Mill and Smelter Workers, as adopted by referendum 1 November 1918, University of Colorado Boulder Libraries – Archives, Special Collections, Government Information, & Map Library, WFM-IUMMSW collection box 2, file 3. Note: Searches in the University of Colorado and Cornell University archives reveal the first English IUMMSW constitution was 1918. Yet, there is a 1916 constitution in Spanish in the WFM-IUMMSW and Jencks collections. There was no convention held in 1917 for ratification, possibly due to the war.

58 WFM had developed a horizontal structure, unlike most international unions. Inheriting the structure, Mine Mill locals had the power to make their own decisions, which the national and international bodies could not override unless by membership votes. Locals signed collective agreements and held the purse strings. Membership dues were held by the locals; they doled out funds to the national and international offices, not the reverse as is the case with most unions. *Source:* Smith, *The Unfinished Journey*, 515.

59 Bromwich, *Union Constitutions*, 37.

60 Quinlan, "Forward," 27–31; Saarinen, *From Meteorite Impact to Constellation.*

61 Mercier, "A Union without Women," 315–40.

62 The Wives Supporting the Strike Committee was comprised of over two hundred women, including the seven-women steering committee. *Source: A Wives Tale*, https://www.imdb.com/title/tt0137249/.; McKeigan, "The Rise and Decline," 246–7.

63 McInnis, *Harnessing Labour Confrontation*, 53–60.

64 Whitaker and Marcuse, *Cold War Canada*, 193.

65 Izumi, "Prohibiting 'American Concentration Camps,'" 165–94.

66 Kinoy, *Rights on Trial*, 61–96.

67 Schrecker, "McCarthyism and the Labour Movement," 139–57.

68 Skinner interview, by Alice Hoffman and Greg Giebel, part 2, 19 June 1973, page 16–17, 30–8, Laurentian University Archives, P019, series I, sub-series B, file 48.

69 The *Smith Act* was another legislative pillar of the anti-communist crusade. The main targets were high-ranking Communist Party members. More than 140 people were charged and tried, resulting in a range of outcomes from dismissal to conviction with incarceration. In doing so, it contributed to a climate of fear that curtailed the ability of left-led unions to effectively serve their members, However, the *Smith Act* posed fewer concrete obstacles to the union in comparison to the *Taft-Hartley Act*.

70 Eiden, *Labor and the Class Idea*, 191–213.

71 Whitaker and Marcuse, *Cold War Canada*, 315. This figure of 10–20 per cent refers to the proportion of all the unionized workers in Canada who were members of Communist-led unions (i.e., those unions that were expelled from the House of Labour on allegations of being Communist-led). Since there were roughly five to ten thousand Canadians who identified as being communist, the 10–20 per cent is somewhat misleading. For instance, the members of MMSW members would have been included in the 10–20 per cent, but very few of those members would consider themselves communists.

72 King and Braid, *Red Bait*, 70.

CHAPTER NINE

1 Solski interview by Jim Tester, 15 May 1981, page 23, Laurentian University Archives, P019, series I, sub-series B, file 1.

2 Chaison, "Union Mergers," 97–115.

3 Verzuh, *Smelter Wars*, 233. Murphy was a prominent member of the Communist Party of Canada, often declaring himself as the "reddest rose in the garden" until 1957 when he resigned to stem the red-baiting attacks on the union. Both Murphy's resignation and appeal – "Let a man's political views be that of his own and not be dictated to by anyone out of fear or favour. I think they are just like religious views. They belong to the man himself. Our union is absolutely free of any domination of any outside organization" did little to stop the accusations that the union was communist dominated. *Source:* debate between Larry Sefton and Harvey Murphy, 1961/1963, Laurentian University Archives, P009, NOLIA fonds.

Note: there is some confusion over the date of the debate, labelled in the archive as 1963. The debate was held on Port Colborne to address the Mine Mill members of Local 637, yet other sources indicate the debate led to the local voting for USWA representation in 1961.

4   William Lockman interview by Gaston Belanger and Marlene Gibson, 1981, Laurentian University Archives, P009, tape no. 80-81.
5   Research participant E16.
6   Official proceedings, 10th Special Merger Convention, 23–24 June 1967, page 19, IUMMSW, Winnipeg, Manitoba, UBC IUMMSW collection, box 3.
7   King and Braid, *Red Bait*, 151.
8   Official proceedings, 10th Special Merger Convention, 23–24 June 1967, page 75, IUMMSW, Winnipeg, Manitoba, UBC IUMMSW collection, box 3.
9   Jim Tester interview by Rick Stow, 21 January 1989, 15 September 1988, and 25 August 1989, Library and Archives Canada, Rick Stow fonds, ISN nos 138004, 138006, and 151491.
10 Sudbury Star, "Sudbury in the 1960s," *Sudbury Star,* 15 October 2011, https://republicofmining.com/2011/10/15/sudbury-in-the-1960s-by-sudbury-star-unknown-date/.
11 Jim Tester interview by Rick Stow, 21 January 1989, Library and Archives Canada, Rick Stow fonds, ISN no. 138004.

Select Bibliography

PUBLISHED BOOKS, BOOK CHAPTERS,
AND JOURNAL ARTICLES

Abella, Irving. "The International Union of Mine Mill and Smelter Workers, 1936–48." In *Nationalism, Communism, and Canadian Labour,* edited by Irving Abella. Toronto: University of Toronto Press, 1973.

Angus, Charlie. *Cobalt: Cradle of the Demon Metals.* Toronto: Anansi House Press, 2022.

Baker, Ellen. *On Strike and On Film: Mexican American Families and Blacklisted Filmmakers in Cold War America.* Chapel Hill: The University of North Carolina Press, 2007.

Boudreau, Alexandre. *A l'assaut des défis.* Moncton: Editions d'Acadie, 1994.

Bouvier, Emil. "Les transformations des sciences sociales à l'Université de Montréal." In *Les sciences sociales au Québec, continuité ou rupture,* Tome premier. Chapter VIII. pp. 131–46. Montréal: Presses de l'Université de Montréal, 1984.

Brasch, Hans. *A Miner's Chronicle: Inco Ltd. and the Unions, 1944– 1997.* Sudbury: United Steelworkers of America, Local 6500, 1997.

Bromwich, Leo. *Union Constitutions: A Report to the Fund for the Republic.* New York: The Fund for the Republic, 1959.

Buse, Dieter. "Weir Reid and Mine Mill: An Alternative Union's Cultural Endeavours." In *Hard Lessons: The Mine Mill Union in the Canadian Labour Movement,* edited by Dieter K. Buse, Peter Suschnigg, and Mercedes Steedman. Toronto: Dundurn Press, 1995.

Canada. Privy Council. *Royal Commission Appointed under Order of* PC
    411 to Investigate the Facts Relating to and the Circumstances
    Surrounding the Communication, by Public Officials and Other Persons
    in Positions of Trust of Secret and Confidential Information to Agents
    of a Foreign Power. Last modified 2013. https://publications.gc.ca/site/
    eng/472640/publication.html.
Chaison, Gary. "Union Mergers in the US and Abroad." *Journal of*
    Labour Research 25, no. 1 (2004): 97–115.
Clement, Wallace. *Hardrock Mining: Industrial Relations and*
    Technological Changes at Inco. Toronto: McClelland & Stewart Ltd,
    1981.
Cobble, Dorothy Sue. *The Other Women's Movement: Workplace Justice*
    and Social Rights in Modern America. New Jersey: Princeton University
    Press, 2004.
Collins, Patricia. "Learning from the Outsider within: The Sociological
    Significance of Black Feminist Thought." *Social Problems* 33, no. 6
    (1986): 514–32.
Dominion Bureau of Statistics. *Census of Canada 1956 Population.*
    Bulletin 1–4. Ottawa: Queen's Printer and Controller of Stationary,
    1957.
Dubofsky, Melvyn. "The Origins of Western Working-Class Radicalism,
    1890–1905." *Labor History* 7, no. 2 (1966): 131–54.
– *We Shall Be All: A History of the Industrial Workers of the World.*
    Second Edition. Chicago: University of Illinois Press, 1988.
Eiden, Barry. *Labor and the Class Idea in the US and Canada.* Cambridge:
    Cambridge University Press, 2018.
Guard, Julie. *Radical Housewives: Price Wars and Food Politics in Mid-*
    Twentieth-Century Canada. Toronto: University of Toronto Press,
    2019.
Izumi, Masumi. "Prohibiting 'American Concentration Camps': Repeal of
    the *Emergency Detention Act* and the Public Historical Memory of the
    Japanese American Internment." *Pacific Historical Review* 74, no. 2
    (2005): 165–94.
Jensen, Vernon. *Heritage of Conflict: Labor Relations in the Nonferrous*
    Metals Industry up to 1930. Ithaca: Cornell University Press, 1950.
King, Al and Kate Braid. *Red Bait: The Struggles of a Mine Mill Local.*
    Vancouver: Kingbird Publishing, 1998.
Kinoy, Arthur. *Rights on Trial: The Odyssey of a People's Lawyer.*
    Cambridge: Harvard University Press, 1983.

Lang, John B. "Review of Mick Lowe's The Raids: The Nickel Range
Trilogy." *Labour / Le Travail* 77, no. 1 (2014): 271–3.

Lingenfelter, Richard. *The Hardrock Miners: A History of the Mining
Labor Movement*. Berkeley: University of California, 1981.

Lipton, Charles. *The Trade Union Movement of Canada, 1927–1959*.
Toronto: NC Press, 1967.

Liverant, Bettina. *Buying Happiness: The Emergence of Consumer
Consciousness in English Canada*. Vancouver: UBC Press, 2018.

Lorence, James. *The Suppression of Salt of the Earth: How Hollywood,
Big Labor, and Politicians Blacklisted a Movie in Cold War America*.
Albuquerque: The University of New Mexico Press, 1999.

MacDowell, Laurel Sefton. *Remember Kirkland Lake: The Gold Miners'
Strike of 1941–42*. Toronto: University of Toronto Press, 1983.

McKeigan, Bruce. "The Rise and Decline of L6500 USWA." In *Mining
Town Crisis: Globalization, Labour and Resistance in Sudbury,* edited
by David Leadbeater. Halifax: Fernwood, 2008.

McInnis, Peter. *Harnessing Labour Confrontation: Shaping the Postwar
Settlement in Canada, 1943–1950*. Toronto: University of Toronto
Press, 2002.

Mercier, Laurie. *Anaconda: Labor, Community and Culture in Montana's
Smelter City*. Chicago: University of Illinois Press, 2001.

– "A Union without Women is Only Half Organized: Mine Mill,
Auxiliaries, and Cold War Politics in the North American Wests."
In *One Step over the Line toward a History of Women in the North
American Wests,* edited by Elizabeth Jameson and Sheila McManus.
Edmonton: University of Alberta Press/AU Press, 2008.

Mouat, Jeremy. *Roaring Days: Rossland's Mines and the History of
British Columbia*. Victoria: University of British Columbia, 1995.

Palmer, Bryan D. *Working Class Experience: The Rise and Reconstitution
of Canadian Labour, 1800–1980*. Toronto: Butterworth & Co, 1983.

Parr, Joy. *Domestic Goods: The Material, the Moral and the Economic in
the Postwar Years*. Toronto: University of Toronto Press, 1999.

Peake, Frank and Ronald Horne. *The Religious Tradition in Sudbury
from 1883–1983*. Sudbury: Journal Printing, 1982.

Pederson, Jay. *International Directory of Company Histories, Vol. 45*.
Detroit: St James Press, 2002.

Quinlan, Elizabeth. "Forward." In *With Glowing Hearts – How Ordinary
Women Worked Together to Change the World (And Did),* by Jennifer
Wynne Webber. Winnipeg: Shillingford Publishing Inc., 2019.

Rosswurm, Steve. "An Overview and Preliminary Assessment of the CIO's Expelled Unions." In *The CIO's Left-Led Unions,* edited by Steve Rosswurm. New Jersey: Rutgers University Press, 1992.

– "The Catholic Church and the Left-Led Unions: Labor Priests, Labor Schools, and the ACTU." In *The CIO's Left-Led Unions,* edited by Steve Rosswurm. New Jersey: Rutgers University Press, 1992.

Saarinen, Oiva. *From Meteorite Impact to Constellation City: A Historical Geography of Greater Sudbury.* Waterloo: Wilfrid Laurier University Press, 2013.

Schrecker, Ellen. "McCarthyism and the Labour Movement: The Role of the State." In *The CIO's Left-Led Unions,* edited by Steve Rosswurm. New Jersey: Rutgers University Press, 1992.

Seguin, Homer. *Fighting for Justice and Dignity: The Homer Seguin Story.* Sudbury: Journal Printing, 2008.

Smith, Cameron. *The Unfinished Journey: The Lewis Family.* Toronto: Summerhill Press, 1989.

Solski, Mike. "Struggles in Sudbury." In *The Un-Canadians: True stories of the Blacklist Era,* edited by Len Scher. Toronto: Lester Publishing, 1992.

Solski, Mike and Jack Smaller. *The History of the International Union of Mine, Mill and Smelter Workers in Canada Since 1895.* Ottawa: Mutual Press, 1984.

Southern, Frank. *The Sudbury Incident.* Toronto: York Publishing & Printing Co, 1982.

Stanton, John. *My Past is Now: Further Memoirs of a Labour Lawyer.* St John's: Canadian Committee on Labour History, 1994.

Steedman, Mercedes. "Godless Communists and Faithful Wives, Gender Relations and the Cold War: Mine Mill and the 1958 Strike against the International Nickel Company." In Laurie Mercier and Jaclyn J. Gier, eds., *Mining Women: Gender in the Development of a Global Industry, 1670 to 2005.* New York: Palgrave Macmillan, 2006.

– "The Red Petticoat Brigade: Mine Mill Women's Auxiliaries and the Threat from Within, 1940s–70s." In *Whose National Security?: Canadian State Surveillance and the Creation of Enemies,* edited by Dieter K. Buse, Mercedes Steedman, and Gary Kinsman. Toronto: Between the Lines, 2000.

Stevenson, Ray. "Ballet Ruse." In *The Un-Canadians: True stories of the Blacklist Era,* edited by Len Scher. Toronto: Lester Publishing, 1992.

– "We're Still Here: A Panel Reviews the Past and Looks to the Future." In *Hard Lessons: The Mine Mill Union in the Canadian Labour*

Movement, edited by Dieter K. Buse, Peter Suschnigg, and Mercedes Steedman. Toronto: Dundurn Press, 1993.

Swift, Jamie. *The Big Nickel: Inco at Home and Abroad.* Toronto: Between the Lines, 1977.

Verzuh, Ron. "Remembering Salt: How a Blacklisted Hollywood Movie Brought the Spectre of McCarthyism to a Small Canadian Town." *Labour/LeTravail* 76, (2015): 165–98.

– *Smelter Wars: A Rebellious Red Trade Union Fights for Its Life in Wartime Western Canada.* Toronto: University of Toronto Press, 2002.

– "The raiding of L480: A Historic Cold War Struggle for Union Supremacy in a Small Canadian City." *Labour/Le Travail* 82, (2018): 81–117.

Waiser, Bill. *All Hell Can't Stop Us. The On-to-Ottawa Trek and Regina Riot.* Calgary: Fifth House, 2003.

Whitaker, Reg, Gregory Kealey, and Andrew Parnaby. *Secret Service: Political Policing in Canada from the Fenians to Fortress America.* Toronto: University of Toronto Press, 2012.

Whitaker, Reg and Gary Marcuse. *Cold War Canada: The Making of a National State, 1945–1957.* Toronto: University of Toronto Press, 1994.

Wyman, Max. *The Royal Winnipeg Ballet, the First Forty Years.* Toronto: Doubleday Canada, 1978.

Zembrzycki, Stacey. "The Sinter Plant Boys: Jean Gagnon and the Personal Costs of Fighting to Compensate Sudbury Families." *Social History* 53, no. 108 (2020): 257–78.

CONFERENCE PRESENTATIONS

Hogan, Brian. "Hard Rock and Hard Decisions: Catholics, Communists and the IUMMSW-Sudbury Confrontations." Paper presented at the Canadian Historical Association, University of Montreal, 30 May 1985.

MA THESES AND PHD DISSERTATIONS

Black, Lawrence. "An Analysis of Inco." Master's thesis, New York University at Laurentian University, Regional Collection HD, 9539 N52 I524, 1957.

Duthie, Rick. "'What's That Tutti-Frutti [Dance] Stuff': Mine Mill's Cold War Cultural Tool." Master's thesis, Laurentian University, 2015.

Lang, John B. "A Lion in a Den of Daniels: A History of the International Union of Mine, Mill and Smelter Workers in Sudbury, Ontario, 1942–1962." Master's thesis, University of Guelph, 1970.

VIDEO

Bissonnette, Sophie, Martin Duckworth, and Joyce Rock, dir. *A Wives Tale*. Film. Sudbury, Ontario, CA: Les Ateliers Audio-Visuels du Québec, 1980.

Desjardins, Richard and Robert Monderie, dir. *The Hole Story*. Film. Ottawa, CA: National Film Board, 2011.

UNPUBLISHED SOURCES

Godin, Gilbert. "The Autobiography of a Labourer." Unpublished manuscript, 1982.

Stevenson, Ray. "Globalization and Armageddon in the Workplace: A Worker's Memoir and Survey of 20th History." Unpublished manuscript, 2004.

Solski, Mike. "Review and Critique of Red Bait: Struggles of a Mine Mill Local by Al King." Unpublished manuscript, 1999.

ARCHIVAL COLLECTIONS

Archives Ontario (Toronto): Mike Solski fonds, Mine Mill & Smelter Workers Local 598 fonds, NOLIA fonds, Jim Tester fonds.

Author's archive: "Inco Smelter Reports."

Catholic Register (online): https://www.catholicregister.org.

City of Greater Sudbury Library Public Archive (Sudbury): *Sudbury Star*.

Dance Collection Danse Archive (Toronto): Nancy Lima Dent fonds.

Greater Sudbury Public Library (Sudbury).

Laurentian University Archives (Sudbury): Barbara Dunphy fonds; Dave Lehto fonds; Inco fonds; IUMMSW Local 598; Jim Tester fonds; Mercedes Steedman fonds; Mike Solski fonds; Nelson Thibault fonds; Northern Ontario Industrial Archives.

Library and Archives Canada (Ottawa): Public use files; Dave Lehto fonds; Inco fonds; Meridian Films fonds; Rick Stow fonds; Ron Mann fonds; Cecil Ross Society fonds.

L.R. Wilson Archive & Historical Museum (Port Colborne): Uncatalogued materials.

McMaster University Library Archives (Hamilton): United Steelworkers of America, District 6 collection.

Pennsylvania State University Archive (Philadelphia): United Steelworkers of America collection.

Privy Council of Canada (online): https://publications.gc.ca/site/eng/472640/publication.html.

ProQuest Historical Newspapers (online): *Globe and Mail*; *Sudbury Star*; *Toronto Daily Star [1900-1971]*; *Toronto Telegram*.

Saskatchewan Archives (Saskatoon): Newspapers collection.

Trail City Archives (Trail, BC).

University of British Columbia Rare Books & Special Collections (Vancouver): International Union of Mine, Mill and Smelter Workers (Canada) fonds.

University of Colorado Archive (Boulder): Western Federation of Miners / International Union of Mine, Mill and Smelter Workers collection.

York University, Clara Thomas Archives and Special Collections (Toronto): Ray Stevenson fonds.

Index

Algoma Steel, 101
Alien Labour Act (Canada),
155n32
American Federation of Labor
(AFL), 156n34, 184n32
anti-communism: in the Catholic
Church, 29, 131; and the film
industry, 91, 173n43; and the
Inco strike, 94–5, 106, 121,
132–3; and the labour movement, 142–3, 167n24, 169n58,
187n69; and MMSW, 38, 73–4,
104, 134–5, 136; in Sudbury, 86.
See also Cold War; communism
anti-racism, 91. *See also* ethnicity;
race
auto industry, 7, 10, 15
"automatic check-off," 24, 50–1,
159n30, 163n11, 164n24; union
demand for, 79, 125

Barbounis, Christo, 182n6
Benard, F., 45
benefits: company responsibility
for, 58; government, 163n17;
negotiation of, 27–8, 47–8, 101,
159n30, 176n6; during the

strike, 62, 88, 96, 99; union
provision of, 89; and women,
180n51. *See also* collective
agreements; health insurance;
pensions; wages
Berrick, Ray, 87
Blue Cross, 89, 173n39. *See also*
health insurance
Boudreau, Alexandre, 86–7, 131,
132–3, 174n59
Bouvier, Emil, 183n18
Bradley, R.V., 56–7
British Columbia, 11, 22, 155n31
Brotherhood of Locomotive
Firemen and Enginemen, 90
business unionism, 145, 147, 150.
See also unions

Canada: consumer culture in, 63,
99, 173n37; economy of, xiv, 6,
10, 27, 60–1, 163n13; labour
force of, 82, 92–3; labour laws
of, 40, 145, 155n32, 157n5;
labour movement in, xvii–xviii,
11–12, 117, 145; natural
resources of, 114, 116;
population of, 174n51

MacDonald, Dorothy, 179n43
Mackenzie King, William Lyon, 15,
　19, 157n5
Marcolin, Charlie, 114
Martel, Elie, 53
masculinity, 14, 121, 153n10,
　155n33, 174n50. *See also* gender
McArthur, Archie "Fritz," 68
McCullagh, George, 157n3
McKee, Con, 86
McNabb, Don, 133
McQuaid, Millie, 57, 118
media, 94, 97; anti-communism of,
　121, 137; and consumerism, 99;
　strike coverage of, 117, 120,
　130, 177n15, 178n34. See also
　Globe and Mail
mediation, 72, 74, 75, 111–13.
　See also collective bargaining;
　conciliation
Methot, Ronald, 87, 162n5
Mine, Mill and Smelter Workers
　(MMSW), ix–x, xii, xiii–xiv; audit
　of, 182n12; bargaining by, 46–8,
　59, 101, 111–13, 122–5,
　178n33; campaign against,
　119–20, 143–4; and commu-
　nism, 187n3, 187n71; demo-
　cratic structure of, 140–1,
　163n11, 186n58; departures
　from, 170n9; economic analysis
　by, 60–1, 181n56; formation of,
　39–41, 160n18, 161n21,
　162n26; inclusivity of, 121,
　179n45; leadership of, 68–71,
　130–3, 146–7, 172n31; negotia-
　tions for, 42–5, 49–51, 54–7,
　76–7, 165n42; social programs
　of, 30, 36; on strike, 78–81, 87,
　176n7; strike preparations by,

62–7, 72–4, 168n32; strike
　strategy of, 108–9, 114, 116–17;
　support for, 102–3, 104–8,
　176n11, 177n18; unity of, 94–5,
　99; USWA raids on, 134–7,
　147–50. *See also* Inco strike;
　International Union of Mine,
　Mill and Smelter Workers
　(IUMMSW); Local 598 (Sudbury,
　IUMMSW/MMSW); Local 637
　(Port Colborne, MMSW); Strike
　Coordinating Committee; union
　halls; women's auxiliaries
Mine Mill. *See* International Union
　of Mine, Mill and Smelter
　Workers (IUMMSW)
Mine Mill General Workers Local
　902, 176n11
miners, 5–7; itinerancy of, 39;
　labour activism of, 11–12, 18,
　65, 155n33, 155nn30–1; social
　lives of, 31, 33, 35–7; strikes by,
　13–16, 68–70, 168n32; wages
　of, 10, 154n29; work done by,
　29, 67. *See also* smeltermen
mining and metals industry, xiv, xv,
　3–5, 8; growth of, 10, 148,
　155n33; and labour, 12, 15,
　154n29, 155n31; recession in,
　47–8; safety in, 158n22;
　unionism in, 41, 135, 142,
　149–50; working conditions in,
　6–7. *See also* nickel
Mosher, Aaron, 104
Murphy, Harvey, 62, 73, 104,
　175n60; communism of, 94,
　132, 187n3; and the USWA, 148

National Labour Relations Board,
　169n58